Multicultural Nationalism

Multicultural Nationalism

Islamaphobia, Anglophobia, and Devolution

Asifa Hussain and William Miller
University of Glasgow

UNIVERSITY PRESS

*This book has been printed digitally and produced in a standard specification
in order to ensure its continuing availability*

OXFORD
UNIVERSITY PRESS

Great Clarendon Street, Oxford OX2 6DP
United Kingdom

Oxford University Press is a department of the University of Oxford.
It furthers the University's objective of excellence in research, scholarship,
and education by publishing worldwide.
Oxford is a registered trade mark of Oxford University Press in the UK
and in certain other countries

British Library Cataloguing in Publication Data
Data available

Library of Congress Cataloging in Publication Data
Data available

ISBN 978-0-19-928071-1

Contents

Contents

Contents

Acknowledgements

Funding for this research was provided by grants to the authors from the Economic and Social Research Council (under ESRC grant L219252118) and the Nuffield Foundation (under grant OPD/00213/G). Additional funding was provided by the University of Glasgow. We were encouraged throughout the project by the energy and enthusiasm of Charlie Jeffery, Director of the ESRC's Devolution Programme, to whom we owe particular thanks.

The project would not have been possible without the help of those who recruited focus-group participants from Scottish minorities (ethnic Pakistanis and English immigrants) and provided venues—and often hospitality—for the discussions. A multilingual team of 37, mainly student interviewers, carried out the minority surveys with efficiency and commitment.

We were encouraged to research the attitudes of the Scottish and English majorities by John Curtice and the staff of the Scottish Social Attitudes survey and its British counterpart. We also received vital help, information, and encouragement from the staff of the Scottish Executive and the Scottish Census.

We are grateful to them and, above all, to those who took the time to tell us about their experiences and opinions: 1,510 Pakistani and English immigrant survey respondents, 81 focus-group participants, and 27 political/administrative elites who gave long and revealing in-depth interviews.

AMH
WLM
August 2005

Focus Groups

PK1: younger, mixed gender, residential south-side Glasgow
PK2: older, female, residential south-side Glasgow
PK3: older, male, residential south-side Glasgow
PK4: older, male, cosmopolitan west-end Glasgow
PK5: older, female, cosmopolitan west-end Glasgow
PK6: younger, mixed gender, cosmopolitan west-end Glasgow
E1: small-town southern Scotland
E2: suburban NE Scotland
E3: small-town southern Scotland
E4: small-town southern Scotland
E5: small-town southern Scotland
E6: urban/industrial central-belt

Political/Administrative/Activist etc. Elite In-Depth Interviewees

In order to preserve anonymity, they are listed alphabetically. The IDI code numbers assigned to them in the text *do not correspond* in any way to the alphabetic listing:

Aamer Anwar (Human Rights Lawyer)
Sheila Arthur (Glasgow Campaign to Welcome Refugees)
Jackie Baillie (Labour MSP)
Anwari Din (Youth Council Services Agency)
Maureen Fraser (Director of CRE in Scotland)
Jatin Haria (Glasgow Anti-racist Alliance Group)
Tom Harrigan (Strathclyde Police, Race Equality Officer)
Patrick Harvie (Green Party MSP)
Shella Ihsan (Reach Community Multicultural Health Project)
Rosie Kane (Scottish Socialist Party, MSP)
Dr Kausar (General Secretary of Glasgow Central Mosque)
Kenneth Macintosh (Labour MSP)
Habib Malik (Islamic Relief Charity)
Bashir Mann (former councillor, spokesperson for Central Mosque, Glasgow)
Alan McCoombes (editor of *Socialist Voice*)
Jim Murphy (Labour MP)
Mick Napier (Palestinian Solidarity Campaign)
Greg Philo (Glasgow University Media Unit)

Naeem Raza (Islamic Society of Britain)
Osama Saeed (Muslim Association of Britain)
Mohammed Sarwar (Labour MP)
Elaine Smith (Labour MSP)
Yvonne Strachan (Scottish Executive, Race Equality Unit)
Fariha Thomas (Muslim Women Resource Centre)
Mike Watson (Labour Party, MSP)
Sandra White (Scottish National Party, MSP)
Margaret Woods (Glasgow Campaign to Welcome Refugees)

1

Multicultural Nationalism

By advocates and critics alike, contemporary Britain is frequently described as a multi-ethnic and multicultural state. That alone raises difficult
issues of multicultural citizenship and multicultural democracy, sufficiently serious for some to ask whether 'multicultural democracy ... can
work' (van den Berge 2002). But from a different perspective, Britain is also
described as a multinational state (Hogwood 2001).

   This book is about how multiculturalism interacts with multinationalism within Britain. Much of the debate about multiculturalism in Britain
has focused on England (e.g. Modood et al., 1997). Consequently, some of
the findings about ethnicity and multiculturalism most frequently attributed to Britain, apply to England and are not merely absent but actually
reversed or inverted in Scotland. Moreover, much of the multicultural
debate in England has focused on its 'visible' minorities: blacks and Asians
(Mason 2003).

   Conversely, much of the debate about multinationalism has focused on
the relationship between Scotland and England, or between Scots and the
English, within a multinational Union state (Miller 2005); or on the
tension between Scottish and British identities amongst Scots (Paterson
et al., 2001: 101–20). Even when the focus has shifted to minorities within
Scotland, its 'invisible' minorities—the Irish/Catholics (Devine 2000)
together with English immigrants (Hearn 2000: 65–70; Houston and
Knox 2001; Watson 2003)—have traditionally attracted more attention
than its relatively small 'visible' minorities.

   These two debates, about multiculturalism and nationalism, have been
held in parallel without sharing even a common vocabulary. McCrone
(2002: 301) complains that 'issues of ethnicity and national identity rarely
seem to connect ... whereas the vocabulary and rhetoric of ethnicity
belong to a framework of multiculturalism ... nationalism and national
identity relate to constitutional politics and the devolution of power'.

1

So to some, it still seems shocking to apply the term 'immigrants' to English-born residents in Scotland—though rather less shocking to those directly involved than overly correct outside observers.

We aim to give equal attention to the largest 'visible' and 'invisible' minorities within Scotland, ethnic Pakistanis, and English immigrants; to treat them equally; and to impose no predefined distinction between national, ethnic, or cultural minorities. If distinctions arise (as they do), they should arise naturally from the attitudes of majority Scots or from the experiences and opinions of the minorities themselves: from the answers to our questions, not from question design.

We focus not on the uneasy relationship between multiculturalism and the state or state-nationalism, but on the even more complex and potentially even less easy relationship between multiculturalism and sub-state nationalism.

Sub-state nationalists seek disintegration—but limited disintegration. They are driven to emphasize diversity within the wider state in order to justify separation from it. But at the same time they are driven to emphasize the unity, coherence, and identity of their sub-state 'nation' or territory. An existing state can rise above ethnic and cultural diversity relatively easily. It can simply deny their relevance to state citizenship and state loyalty—as dynasties and empires have done throughout history. It can accept historically imposed diversity as a given, for which the current generation is not responsible, and get on with the business of encouraging its citizens to get along with each other and make the best of it. Or it can recognize that the price of participation in a global economy is internal diversity, that ethnic diversity has some economic advantages in terms of skills and connections. While states can try to impose a uniform culture and identity on their people, they have no need to do so, and the equation of culture, identity and state looks increasingly anachronistic in a rapidly globalizing world. For the state, functional loyalty and obedience is enough.

But sub-state nationalism cannot ignore cultural diversity so easily: 'it is usually seen to have an ethnic base' (Heath and Smith 2005: 133). It is, after all, a nationalism defined by something other than inherited boundaries and institutions. Ethnic and cultural diversity is therefore a special challenge to sub-state nationalism. And conversely, sub-state nationalism must naturally be a special challenge to ethnic and cultural diversity within its 'national' homeland.

Neither a multinational nor a multi-ethnic nor a multicultural state is a contradiction in terms. Indeed the idea of a nation-state is far more of a contradiction in terms. But a 'multinational nationalist' movement is certainly an oxymoron; and a 'multicultural nationalist' movement comes very close to being one. So it is more inherently difficult—and, if successful, it is, therefore, a correspondingly greater achievement—for sub-state nationalism to rise above ethnic and cultural diversity.

1.1 Nationalism—Ethnic, Civic, Multicultural

Many circumstances prompt nationalism. And nationalism has many ambitions. Hence, the myriad distinctions between 'territorial' and 'diaspora' nationalism; 'modernization' or 'reform' nationalism and 'conservative' nationalism; 'unification' and 'separatist' nationalism; 'nation-building' or 'state' nationalism and 'sub-national', 'anti-colonial', or 'post-imperial' nationalisms; 'official' and 'insurgent' nationalism; 'majority' and 'minority' nationalism; or between 'state-framed' and 'counter-state' nationalism. One study listed thirty-nine types of nationalism (Smith 1983: 211–29).

But a recurrent distinction made by historians, theorists, and practicing politicians focuses on the *character* of nationalism rather than its origins or ambitions. They distinguish just 'two types of nationalism' variously described as 'western' versus 'eastern' (Plamenatz 1973); American or French 'territorially based' versus German 'descent-based' (Brubaker 1992); 'political' versus 'cultural' (Chatterjee 1993); 'voluntaristic' or 'civic' versus 'cultural' or 'ethnic' (Kohn 1944, 1967; Ignatieff 1993); 'inclusive' versus 'exclusive' (Kellas 1998: 35); or simply 'benign' versus 'nasty' (Gellner 1994: 99). Despite the variations in terminology, all these distinctions are in essence the same.

Confusingly, Abizadeh (2002: 497) distinguishes between three nationalisms: 'ethnic nationalists' who stress culture and descent, 'civic nationalists' who stress culture and territory but not descent, and 'civic republicans' who stress only territory, institutions and history. But Abizadeh's 'civic republicanism' is what others call 'civic nationalism' that contrasts with the other two, labelled as varieties of 'cultural nationalism'. We are back with the familiar two.

More usefully for our purposes, Sweeney (2005: 58–61) defines 'three types of nationalism: state, civic and ethnic'. He equates 'ethnic nationalism' with bottom-up 'popular nationalism'. But he distinguishes between two kinds of top-down nationalisms: 'state nationalism' which 'asserts the dominance of a particular ethnicity' while 'civic nationalism ... is more tolerant of diversity, and is marked by a recognition of different ethnicities, even *multiculturalism* [our emphasis]'. He continues: 'states may exhibit one or other of these types of nationalism [i.e. state or civic]'. But he implies that 'state nationalism', although a well-defined category and familiar enough with history, has been abandoned by modern European states, leaving only a contest between two nationalisms: popular ethnic nationalism and elite civic nationalism. At the same time he hints at the possibility of a new third nationalism, that goes beyond the merely civic and 'tolerant', when he introduces the idea of a nationalism that is 'marked by . . . *multiculturalism*'. His narrowly defined 'state nationalism' may no longer be relevant to European states (though after 9/11 and the London bombings it may be resurrected), but there may remain 'three types of nationalism': 'ethnic, civic, and multicultural'. Similarly Brown (2000: 126–7) explicitly argues that there are '*three* competing nationalist visions', not two: 'ethnocultural', 'civic', and 'multicultural'. He defines 'multicultural nationalism' as 'a vision of a community which respects and promotes the cultural autonomy and status equality of its component ethnic groups'.

In the UK in particular, Sweeney argues 'British state nationalism, dominant in the eighteenth and nineteenth centuries, has given way to a more tolerant civic nationalism . . . . Britain [now] seeks to develop its image . . . as a multicultural society . . . state funding to set up faith-specific schools [is] evidence of elite commitment to the notion of multiculturalism'. In part at least, Colley (1992*a*: 327) reinforces this interpretation of the development of British nationalism: 'Britain . . . [was] an invented nation that was not founded on the suppression of older loyalties so much as superimposed on them . . . [and it was] heavily dependent for its raison d'être on a broadly Protestant culture'. In that view, the British state formed by the Union of 1707 aimed to be multinational though monocultural in the eighteenth and nineteenth centuries. (Catholics were excluded from that state-authorized culture and discriminated against in law.)

Yet while the simple civic or ethnic dichotomy may be 'overburdened' (Brubaker 2004: 146), almost a 'cliché' (Kymlicka 2001: 243), it is nonetheless the distinction with 'the greatest resonance today, especially outside the narrow circle of researchers working primarily on nationalism' (Brubaker 2004: 133). And that alone makes the distinction and the terminology important. As Brubaker (2005: 473) argues, 'we must take vernacular categories and participants' understandings seriously'. Even when they are not ideal 'categories of social analysis', they are 'categories of ethnopolitical practice'. Crude, however, intellectually or theoretically deficient they may be, they still guide the thoughts and actions of both public and politicians.

Former Home Secretary, Blunkett (2005: 9) has argued not just for a 'civic value-led sense of Britishness' but even for a 'civic Englishness' to match the supposedly civic nationalism of Scotland. In Scotland itself, this civic or ethnic distinction escaped long ago from the seminar rooms and became part of the language of journalism, public debate, and even casual conversation. Both the devolutionists of the Scottish Constitutional Convention (which included Labour and Liberal leaders) and the more nationalist Scottish National Party, (SNP)—which stood outside the Convention—proclaimed their commitment to a non-ethnic, inclusive, 'civic' rather than 'ethnic' concept of nationalism (CSG 1998: Annex H; Henderson 1999: 138: Hearn 2000: 59–65). SNP leader Alex Salmond asserted, for example, that 'Scotland is not Quebec ... the linguistic and ethnic basis of [Quebec] nationalism is a two-edged sword ... we [in Scotland] follow the path of civic nationalism' (*The Scotsman*, 1 November 1995 quoted in Brubaker 2004: 135). Indeed, both devolutionists and nationalists agreed that a devolved or independent Scotland should aim to be *more* inclusive than in the past, not just the same as before, and most certainly not less. While ethnic nationalism is 'exclusive', stressing common descent, civic nationalism would be 'inclusive in the sense that anyone can adopt the culture and join the nation' (Kellas 1998: 65).

Even the term 'multicultural' was used approvingly (CHE 2000). Scottish nationalists certainly celebrated Scottish history and culture. But that did not make them ethnic nationalists. Civic nationalists may also promote local culture:

the critical difference between promoting local cultural identity and ethnic nationalism [is that] ethnic nationalism does not respect diversity ... the civic nationalist model, with its toleration of diversity, ought to be the most successful in curbing the excesses of ethnic nationalism ... this would appear to fit the situation in Scotland. (Sweeney 2005: 67–8)

But there are a number of problems with this comforting 'civic-v-ethnic' distinction and problems with stretching the concept of 'civic nationalism' to encompass multiculturalism.

1.1.1 *Ambiguity*

First, it may be difficult or impossible to keep nationalism entirely 'civic'. 'National identities frequently carry ethnic characteristics which is why civic and ethnic distinctions have to be handled with ... skepticism' (McCrone 2002: 310). 'Civic nationalism has a cultural component'

5

(Kymlicka 2001: 244; see also Brubaker 2004: 137). So much so that the civic/ethnic distinction is inherently 'ambiguous' (Brubaker 2004: 136–44). There is an ethnic flavour even to Blunkett's plea for 'civic Englishness'. Briefing journalists (Ashley and White 2005) on his argument, Blunkett explained that 'people from other backgrounds ... can be Pakistani and British, Indian and British, whereas I can be English and British, just as the Scots are Scottish and British'. The tone is moderate but English, Scottish, Pakistani, and Indian are treated as alternatives while dualism is reserved for 'and British': there is no 'and English' cited here for 'people from other backgrounds'. Similarly, SNP leader Samond (2005) recently argued that 'Scotland would be better off independent, but that is *not* the fundamental argument for freedom. The essential argument is that *the natural state for a nation is to be self-governing* [our emphasis]'. Again, despite its moderate tone, this makes the characteristically 'ethnic' claim that the 'nation' in some sense 'exists' irrespective of political boundaries or public attitudes towards them. It is difficult for example to see how a multi-ethnic or multicultural population could have a 'natural state ... to be self-governing'. Hearn (2000: 193–4) 'questions the common theoretical dichotomization of ethnic and civic forms of nationalism' claiming that 'the peaceful, democratic, and liberal cast of Scottish nationalism deserves credit and respect but is inseparable from the process of culture' and indeed is 'culturally determined'. He regards Scottish nationalism as being both civic and ethnic—and liberal and benign—all at the same time.

1.1.2 Degeneration

Others see a more dynamic—and darker—connection between civic and ethnic nationalism: they may be different, but the one can degenerate into the other. Gellner (1994: 1–2) sees 'nationalist sentiment' as at root a 'feeling of anger' and it may return to its roots. Citing both the course of German history after 1848 and the anti-colonial movements in Africa and India moving on from what he calls 'universalist' (liberal, human rights) claims to 'ethnic criteria'. Breuilly (1993: 5–7) argues that while nationalism can in principle be asserted in a 'universalist spirit' it has 'not often been so sweetly reasonable'. In Vincent's words (1997: 294): 'nationalism will always resist being assimilated into liberalism ... and easily collapses into ... shallow expressions of blood, soil and xenophobia'. In Pulzer's yet more brutal view (1988: 287): 'nationalism degenerates ... often inspired in its first stage by the urge to emancipate, it finds its logical conclusion in a paroxysm of destructiveness'.

These are not arguments about definitional ambiguity, but about trend. Hence the dynamic title of Brian Porter's *When Nationalism Began to Hate* (2000). Porter argues that although Jewish support for Polish resistance against the Russian empire was at first welcomed, that did not prevent nineteenth century Polish nationalism sliding from an inclusive and territorial to an exclusive and ethnic concept of nationalism. To argue that civic nationalism always has a cultural ethnic component is not to say that the significance of the ethnic component cannot vary (Smith 1986: 149) and, as Breuilly, Vincent, Pulzer, and Porter suggest, increase.

1.1.3 *Discordant Perceptions*

There is the problem of street-level perceptions. Not just the subtle ambiguities that trouble academics but sharp disagreements about whether a particular nationalism is in fact 'civic' or 'ethnic'. There is a tendency to reverse the logic of Gellner and describe 'one's *own* good, legitimate' (i.e. 'benign') nationalisms as 'civic' while castigating *their* 'illegitimate' (or 'nasty') nationalisms as 'ethnic'—a 'frankly political use of the civic–ethnic distinction to legitimize or discredit particular state policies or nationalist movements' (Brubaker 2004: 134–5). Even to many less politically motivated observers it seems more acceptable to apply the term 'ethnic nationalism' to Balkan nationalisms than to Baltic nationalisms—simply because there has been more recent bloodshed in the Balkans than the Baltics, and thus the Balkan nationalisms must surely be inherently 'nasty' while the Baltic nationalisms must be relatively 'benign'. More generally, majority nationalists may sincerely believe that they are advocating a civic conception of nationalism, while minorities may view it as ethnic. Many Czechs but very few Slovaks, for example, now respect Masaryk (Miller, White, and Heywood 1998: 90).

1.1.4 *Assimilation*

Next, minorities may decline the civic nationalists' invitation to 'adopt the culture' and/or 'join the nation' (Kellas 1998: 65). With some notable exceptions, most world religions invite outsiders to 'adopt the culture' and 'join their community'. In that respect they are inclusive, even welcoming, but definitely not multicultural.

And the same applies to a political community. The problem is particularly acute where one ethnic group is predominant and its culture is equated with 'the nation' (Miller 2000: 33). Gellner (1983: 38) has argued that modern industrial democracies require a single national culture, especially a single language, to lower the transaction costs of business and industry. But liberal nationalists argued that 'one culture shared by all members of a society [not only] lowered the transaction costs of a society ... [it was] also a moral achievement. For J. S. Mill democracy was not possible without a common shared culture' (Joppke 1998: 31). Mill claimed that 'among a people without fellow-feeling, especially if they read and speak different languages, the united public opinion, necessary to the working of representative government cannot exist' (Mill 1991: 310).

Noting Mill's enthusiasm for using 'all legitimate means' to assimilate French Canadians, Parekh argues 'there is nothing wrong with assimilation'—but only if minorities 'freely decide to assimilate' (Parekh 2000a: 46 and 197). Some degree of voluntary assimilation is natural, but in a culturally diverse society, 'the forcible and comprehensive imposition of the majority's cultural norms on minorities is only likely to aggravate the latter's sense of cultural alienation ... projects of cultural assimilation ... are bound to undermine rather than further their avowed objectives' (Laborde 2001: 730–1). 'Historically, immigrants were expected ... to assimilate into the common culture of the host society ... multiculturalism is the rejection of assimilation ... [and] after the war, western states became truly liberal [accepting that] to impose particular cultural ways ... would violate the dignity and autonomy of the individual ... [even] nationality as a cultural form is becoming separate from the state' (Joppke 1998: 31–2). And multiculturalism has become more viable as complete assimilation has become less necessary: 'modern transport and communications [sustain] old identifications in the host society' at the same time as post-war liberal states no longer require immigrants to assimilate (Joppke 1998: 32).

Worse, 'adopting the culture and joining the nation' may not be a matter of choice: it may be impossible to accept. Porter (2000: 38) argues that the concept of a 'Jewish Pole' must necessarily be 'an *oxymoron*' if both these terms are 'defined as a culturally bounded community'. In that case, Polishness might be so inseparable from Catholicism that a Jew could only become a Pole by ceasing to be a Jew. In our case, an English immigrant might feel they could only become a Scot by denying their birth: for them an 'English Scot' would be even more of an oxymoron than a 'Jewish Pole'. McCrone (2002: 312) notes that certain 'hybrid' identities, such as 'English-Scot', are 'perceived to be almost a contradiction in terms' and 'do not appear' in practice.

1.1.5 *Inclusion*

Even the most generous version of the civic nationalists' invitation, 'to join the nation' without totally assimilating culturally, may still be construed not as an act of generosity but as a threat, dangerous to refuse. Brubaker (2004: 142) suggests that 'Transylvanian Hungarians resent ... inclusive, citizenship-based rhetoric ... which construes them as members of the Romanian nation'. Conversely, Tamir (1993: 90) argues that civic nationalism can in practice be *less* inclusive than some versions of ethnic nationalism. Where inclusion is based on historical presence rather than choice then 'holding nonconformist views does not necessarily lead to excommunication'. There has been no concept of 'un-British' attitudes or activities equivalent to the concept of 'un-American' attitudes and activities (though one may now be under construction after the London bombings). French and American nationalism looks a lot less 'benign' to those who, though invited, do not want to adopt the values and lifestyles, let alone the culture, of the nation. Tamir herself cites the plight of communists in the USA. Kymlicka (2001: 273) too argues that 'the language of civic nationalism ... provides an excuse to crush' minorities within the territory of the 'civic nation'—citing post-communist Slovakia, Romania, Serbia, and Russia.

1.1.6 *Acceptance*

Even acceptance despite difference, acceptance without assimilation, can mean grudging toleration; or alternatively, a celebration of diversity. Even if civic nationalism exerts no pressure to assimilate, minorities may reject its liberal notions of toleration and equality as at least insufficient if not actually perverse: 'one might enjoy all the rights of citizenship and be a formally equal member of the community, *and yet feel an outsider* who does not belong' (Parekh 2000*a*: 237). Parekh (2000*a*: 46) distinguishes sharply between 'liberal' (Barry 2001) and 'multicultural' (Inglis 1996) alternatives to ethnic nationalism: liberalism ignores differences while multiculturalism cherishes them. Minorities are in an inherently insecure position and what they seek is positive warm reassurance—not cold, hard, grudging justice. Brown (2000: 10) goes further: from an Australian perspective he argues the need to 'correct the misconception that multiculturalism is concerned mainly with immigration and minority ethnic communities'. Instead we should 'emphasize the relevance of cultural diversity for *every* [citizen] and the importance of obtaining the greatest possible gains from our diversity'—not least in terms of economic development and growth.

1.1.7 Combining Multiculturalism with Sub-State Nationalism

There are some optimistic discussions of the viability of 'multicultural nationalism' but they tend to focus on the relatively easy case of multicultural state-nationalism—American, Spanish or Belgian, for example (Aleinikoff 1998; Maddens and Berghe 2003). The UK equivalent would be 'multicultural British-nationalism'. Even Brown (2000) discusses multicultural nationalism in Northern Ireland exclusively in terms of Catholics and Protestants, focusing on the British/non-British state-nationalism dimension—and not in terms of Blacks or Asians in Northern Ireland, though Belfast 'has been dubbed the race-hate capital of Europe' (news.bbc.co.uk 13 January 2004) for attacks on the Chinese and Pakistani minorities.

In a path-breaking cross-national analysis of forty countries, Foweraker and Landman (2002: 55) have discovered a paradox: 'unitary systems perform better than federal ones' by measures of 'minority rights'. Almost by definition, a federal system or a quasi-federal system such as devolution provides additional rights for a territorial minority when the territory of the minority becomes one of the components of the federation. But it does not automatically provide greater rights for minorities that are distributed across the different components of the federation and for whom the federal principle is irrelevant. Indeed by focusing on justice and autonomy for territorial minorities, it seems that federal systems may be distracted from the task of providing justice or autonomy for non-territorial minorities. As was so notorious throughout most of the US history, a federal system can entrench the rights of territorial minorities to persecute non-territorial minorities that are not so explicitly favoured by the constitution as the territorial minorities themselves.

Safeguarding the position of a minority-within-a-minority, or being multicultural within a sub-state, is particularly challenging. As Hearn (2000: 193–4) admits, sub-state nationalism has more ethnic overtones than state-nationalism even when it claims to be 'civic'. Thus 'multicultural Scottish-nationalism' is more problematic than 'multicultural British-nationalism'—in theory. Its viability in practice is an empirical rather than a theoretical question however. The connection between simple, clear-cut theory, and complex messy practice is loose. Brubaker (2004: 145) argues that even sub-state nationalisms 'need not be specifically ethnic' and can be based on 'territory', 'provincial privileges', or 'a distinct political history' rather than such obviously cultural factors as 'language'. But he goes on almost immediately to cite Scotland as a place where sub-state nationalism 'may partake of civic qualities' even when 'the nation is defined in cultural or ethnic terms'. There is so much stress on 'need not' and 'may' in these quotations that they simply underscore the importance of detailed empirical investigation.

1.2 Identity—'Being', 'Choosing', 'Using'

Identity is a core theme in the study—and practice—of nationalism and ethnicity. Strong, self-conscious and relevant identities are said to be an essential basis for the construction, unity, fragmentation or effectiveness of states. In particular, the UK is said to depend upon British identities, and devolution or independence for Scotland to depend upon Scottish identities. David Miller in particular has argued that 'without a common national identity there is nothing to hold citizens together' (Miller 1989*a*: 245). 'Why should taxpayers in the southern half of England pay for everyone else's needs [throughout the UK]?' (Jeffery 2005: 128). The conventional answer is: only if they 'share a common identity or common values' (Miller 1998: 48) and 'regard themselves as bound to the beneficiaries by strong ties of community' (Miller 1989*b*: 59).

If ethnic minorities are not to become disaffected and pose a potential threat to the state, perhaps they too must in some way 'share a common identity or common values' with the majority. Or to put it in a more positive way: the state and its institutions gain legitimacy and authority if the whole of society, minorities as well as majorities, can identify with them. That is particularly important for newly created and subordinate institutions like the Scottish Parliament. They have no historic legitimacy and no great coercive power. They could be suspended or even abolished within a week—as happened to the Stormont Parliament in 1972 (even though it had endured for half a century). Devolution is a situation not unlike that which produced the Round Tables to ease the transition from communism in eastern Europe: when legitimacy has to be created anew, it is important to have the widest consensus—of identification as well as mere policy approval.

But identities should not be equated with labels for fixed national or ethnic groups, or indeed with labels of any kind. They are about 'choosing' and 'using' as well as 'being'.

1.2.1 *Being*

Samond's argument (2005) that 'the natural state for a nation is to be self-governing' implies that nations or ethnic groups actually exist: that *identity is about 'being'*—an inescapable aspect of the self, determined by birth, 'passed down [by ancestors but indicated by] markers [such as] religion, language, customs' (Goldmann, Hannerz, and Westin 2000: 7–8), or ascribed and imposed by 'others'. Even when the content of culture is hollowed-out the markers remain operative: 'a drastic reduction of cultural differences ... does not correlate in any simple way with a reduction in the organizational relevance of ethnic identities, or a breakdown in boundary-maintaining processes' (Barth 1969: 32–3). But Brubaker's *Ethnicity without Groups* (2004: 79) draws attention to the fact that ethnic groups are merely analytical categories: 'not things *in* the world but perspectives *on* the world [his emphasis]'. Ethnic classification, he argues, depersonalizes individuals by transforming them 'from unique persons to exemplars of named groups' (Levine 1999: 169).

1.2.2 *Choosing*

Instead of *Ethnic Groups and Boundaries* (Barth 1969), identities are to a significant degree 'imagined' (Anderson 1991). Though partially imposed by external factors, they are nonetheless at least partially self-chosen. So *identity is also about 'choosing'* or 'constructing' an identity. And if it is a matter of choice, then the identity can be as simple or as complex, as rigid or as fluid, as we wish it to be. It is 'possible for an individual to see [themselves simultaneously as] a citizen of Edinburgh, a Lowlander, a Scot and a Briton' (Colley 1992*a*: 315). Chris Smout describes such multiple identities as 'a nest of Russian dolls' (Watson 2003: 167). But if they are freely chosen, there is no reason why multiple identities should be nested at all: 'individuals carry multiple identities ... Scottish, European, a Glasgow Rangers supporter, and a fan of [TV series] *The Simpsons*; [or] German, Roman Catholic, and a BMW driver [since there is increasing emphasis on] brand identity' (Sweeney 2005: 79). Different elements of identity may relate to different dimensions, or different contexts. They may be prioritized, but not necessarily nested.

Histories, even ancestors, can be 'chosen'. Hearn (2000: 7) claims that although 'nations are ... constantly made and remade, in some sense invented' they are 'also the outcomes of very real histories, parts of which can reach back before the modern period'. But few of those who identify with 'histories . . . before the modern period' can be sure that they are directly connected to them. The General in Gilbert and Sullivan's *The Pirates of Penzance* (Act III) was only unusual in being explicit about what is a widely understood:

Frederic. But you forget, sir, you only bought the property a year ago, and the stucco on your baronial castle is scarcely dry.
General. Frederic, in this chapel are ancestors: you cannot deny that. With the estate, I bought the chapel and its contents. I don't know whose ancestors they *were*, but I know whose ancestors they *are*, and I shudder to think that their descendant by purchase (if I may so describe myself) should have brought disgrace upon what, I have no doubt, was an unstained escutcheon.

It is equally as absurd for majority 'white' Scots as for black or Asian minorities in Scotland to identify with the foot soldiers of William Wallace in any genetic or ancestoral way. But it is equally as justified for black or Asian minorities in Scotland as for majority 'white' Scots to be inspired by, and identify with, the myth of freedom represented by the tales of Wallace. The General would have understood perfectly.

And the role of 'others' may not be to ascribe or impose an identity so much as to act as a focus for a free choice of identity. Edward Said (1978: 1–2) argues that 'the Orient . . . helped to define Europe (or the West) as its contrasting image, idea, personality, experience'; Colley (1992a: 328) emphasizes 'how much a common Protestantism contributed to an artificial British nation in the past . . . [though] the Other in the shape of [militant continental] Catholicism . . . is no longer available'. But, 'the English continue to be the central Other which defines what it means to be Scottish' (McIntosh, Smith, and Robertson 2004a: 53; see also Wright 1999). This is using the 'other' to choose or construct an identity, something quite different from letting the 'other' ascribe or impose an identity.

Since identities are multiple, and not necessarily nested, their relevance varies with the context. Sweeney's putative multiple identifier who is 'Scottish, European, a Glasgow Rangers supporter, and a fan of *The Simpsons*' will certainly see the relevance of being a Rangers supporter at a Saturday football match but may not feel it at all relevant to politics when voting in an election on a Thursday. Despite its historic Catholic roots, Celtic now has many Protestant supporters, who would see their Celtic football identity as relevant on a Saturday but not on a Sunday. Quite deeply religious people, with very strong religious identities, may feel that religion should be 'kept out of politics'. And the nationalism so evident at Scotland-England football matches seems to evaporate a day later. After his defeat at the 1992 election, the defeated SNP MP, Jim Sillars, famously complained: 'The great problem is that Scotland has too many ninety-minute patriots whose nationalist outpourings are expressed only at major sporting events' (*The Herald*, 24 April 1992: 1; see Jarvie and Walker 1994: 1). Less nationalist politicians would regard that as a great asset rather than a great problem, but they would not disagree about the prevalence of 'ninety minute patriots'. Sweeney (2005: 80) sums up the literature by claiming that identities are 'multiple ... subjective as well as ascriptive ... shadowed by opposites ... [and] shift according to context'.

Truly multiple identities however, must be distinguished from the concept of a 'hybrid' identity. It is argued that 'hybridity [such as British-Asian] is clearly not a sub-state nationality (in the way of Scottishness), it is a form of complex Britishness' (Modood et al. 1997: 10)—a single though complex identity rather than a truly multiple identity. That implies there is unlikely to be a conflict of relevance or priority between the two elements of the hybrid: they are inseparable. Consequently, there are 'limits to hybridity' (McCrone 2002: 312).

1.2.3 *Using*

The concept of fluid, multiple, and chosen identities is certainly an advance on the concept of identity as being fixed at, and by, birth. But it does not go far enough. In media studies the categorical approach of asking *what* newspaper a person reads had to be replaced by asking *why* they read it, *how* they used it, and for *what purpose*—dubbed the 'uses and gratifications' approach. It is necessary to ask the same questions about identity, to adopt an active as well as a passive perspective on identity. Even the idea of 'constructing' an identity is too static, evoking the image of a building rather than an activity or project.

There is, therefore, an 'identity versus identification debate in social theory' (Findlay, Hoy, and Stockdale 2004: 75). The verb or its derivative 'identification' may be more useful than the noun 'identity' (Brubaker 2004: 28, 41); 'identity is not to be understood as a badge or label that is pinned on us at birth or at school [but] as a complex set of cultural markers [for] a game of identification and identity construction' (McCrone 2002: 316). Or more clearly still: 'instead of talking about identities, inherited or acquired' we should speak of 'identification [as an] activity' (Bauman 2001: 152; see also McIntosh, Smith, and Robertson 2004a: 55). And moreover, an activity with a purpose: 'ethnic identities have to be treated as social and cultural accounts which participants *use* to make sense of their actions' (Brown McCrone, and Paterson 1998: 206).

But even the idea that people use identities 'to make sense' of their world or their actions does not go far enough. It is still too passive. People use identities more actively than that: 'cultural traits [and] identities ... are strategies or weapons' (Worsley 1984: 249) and 'the codification of difference is a vital part of the strategy of identity politics' (Brown, McCrone, and Paterson 1998: 208).

Underlying a lot of discussion about identities as strategies, is the scenario of the elite 'activists of identity politics' (Brubaker 2004: 59) attempting to intensify differences, divide a multinational state, and set up their own breakaway nation state. So the focus is on identity being 'used' aggressively, by ethnic elites, and for divisive purposes. It is a familiar scenario. But it is not the only scenario, and not the scenario that is most relevant to our study.

We are interested in identity primarily in relation to multiculturalism rather than nationalism—that is, as a strategy used:

- *by ordinary people* rather than elites,
- *by minorities* that have no expectation of becoming majorities through separation,
- *for inclusion* rather than exclusion—a defensive rather than aggressive strategy, aimed at stressing similarity, unity, and *cohesion rather than difference*—a tool rather than a weapon.

Psychologically as well as practically, minorities in Scotland can integrate with the majority by using identity to establish commonality. They can use the tool of identification on themselves as well as on others.

One way to do that is to focus on some element of *absolute* commonality by going to a higher level in a set of nested identities—British or European for example. It is a strategy frequently used by English immigrants— though largely unsuccessfully: 'one strategy [used by] many English-born [who] came to live in Scotland ... was to invoke being British as a shared identity with Scots as a means of inclusion—only to find that the term British was perceived by Scots as too close to English to be useful' (McCrone 2002: 309; see also Kiely, McCrone, and Bechhofer 2005: 68–9); 'many [English-born] wished to be assimilated ... and were both surprised and frustrated [by Scots' reactions] ... fluidity of identity [is] insufficient ... for achieving access to socially constructed historic tribes' (Findlay, Hoy, and Stockdale 2004: 76–7). But even if unsuccessful in altering the perspectives of Scots, such strategies might have a satisfying psychological impact on the English-born themselves: some personal sense of integration even if it were not reciprocated.

Another way to integrate through identification is to use lower levels in a set of nested identities—Scottish, or even more local identities such as Glaswegian—which provide greater opportunities for establishing *relative* commonality in contrast to the increasing numbers of 'others': non-Scots or even non-Glaswegians (there are, of course, more non-Glaswegians than non-Scots). This is a strategy used by ethnic Pakistanis in Scotland with some degree of success—mainly by identifying themselves as Scottish rather than British and joining in the routine Scottish criticism of England and the English, while emphasizing their Scottish 'birth, upbringing . . . accent . . . education . . . [and] commitment to Scotland as a place' (Hopkins 2004: 269).

Another strategy for establishing relative commonality by identification with Scotland—in contrast to England as the 'other'—is to claim a common colonial heritage under English rule. McIntosh, Smith, and Robertson (2004*b*: paras 8.2 and 8.4) argue that 'a colonial metaphor [has] a powerful resonance with many Scots' perceptions and understandings of [Anglo-Scottish] relations . . . Scots themselves . . . feel excluded [by the English] colonizing and Anglicising Scotland.' In our focus groups, ethnic Pakistanis also used this 'English colonial metaphor' with regard to Scotland:

'[before devolution] I could see people getting frustrated because everything was coming from Westminster. This is similar to the colonialism of the past.' (PK4-F[1])

And on occasion they used it explicitly as an element of Scottish-Pakistani commonality. A question about what was 'best' about Scotland elicited the reply:

'Scots understand colonialism—from their past history they understand what ethnic minorities feel.' (PK4-F)

Identifying with Scotland—especially against England—was not a strategy that English immigrants seeking inclusion felt they could use. Watson (2003: 177) claimed to detect a 'drift towards adopting a Scottish identity' amongst the rather elite sample of English immigrants that he interviewed (including four Members of Scottish Parliament (MSPs) and a Scotland Rugby player). But others report that 'the notion of describing oneself as being Scottish is seen to be a somewhat bizarre and forlorn one . . . [some] would like to be allowed to consider themselves, and to be considered by others, as Scottish—though sometimes they had in mind evading

---

[1] PK4-F indicates a quotation from person F in the fourth of six Pakistani focus groups.

continental hostility to the English when they were in Europe' (McIntosh, Smith, and Robertson 2004*a*: 55 and 54).

But English immigrants do try to lower Scots' antagonism by using their own local identities: 'one common solution was to specify a region of England ... especially if this was in the north or west of England' (Findlay, Hoy, and Stockdale 2004: 71).

What is significant is the purpose for which both these minorities (English and Pakistani) use identity strategies: for inclusion not exclusion, for integration not separation. Neither minority shows any enthusiasm for using identity to cut themselves off from the rest of Scottish society. The English-born cannot deny their birth, and the ethnic Pakistanis cannot deny their Muslim religion. But in so far as they can use identity for inclusive rather than exclusive purposes, both minorities try to do so.

1.2.4 *'Identifying with' versus 'Identifying as'*

The General in *The Pirates of Penzance* was not so much 'identifying as' a descendant of the 'ancestors' he had just bought, so much as 'identifying with' them. Abizadeh (2002: 498) accuses Miller (1995: 96) of 'trading on an ambiguity between two senses of common nationality: (*a*) sharing a common culture ... beliefs, language and (*b*) sharing a common identity ... an affective sense of belonging and commitment' arguing that 'people can affectively identify with each other despite not sharing particular norms and beliefs; the trust indispensable to social integration is not dependent upon shared national culture' (p. 507). Abizadeh even cites Mason's view (2000: 127–9) that citizens 'might in principle have a sense of belonging to their polity without thinking that there is any real sense in which they belong together ... a shared identity based on a sense of belonging to the same polity may be sufficient to buttress liberal democratic practices'. Curtice (2005: 169) suggests that the populations of England and Scotland hold 'similar values' and a 'common commitment to asymmetric devolution ... all they lack is a strong common commitment to a shared set of identities and symbols, but even here they appear to have enough in common for them to be capable of sharing the same multinational state.'

The typical identity questions, including our own, which are framed in the language of 'do you think of yourself as ... ', directly measure the extent of 'identifying as', but they may underestimate the extent of 'identifying with', though we can pick up explicit indications of 'identifying with but not as' from focus groups where participants are more able to explicitly reframe questions to fit the mould of their own mind.

1.3 Two Minorities

1.3.1 *Diverse Minorities*

We focus on *Muslim Pakistanis* and *English immigrants* in Scotland rather than on 'minorities'. The concept of undifferentiated 'minorities' has been strongly, and rightly, criticized. Mason (2003*b*: 12; 2000: 21) argues that large numbers of Cypriot, Italian, Polish, or Irish origin in Britain 'are rarely thought of as constituting ethnic minorities'. And that 'minorities' is not a term that English immigrants in Scotland would apply to themselves. Worse than that, Mason argues, 'ethnic minorities are typically seen to have more in common with one another than with the majority ... diversity among the groups so designated is thus downplayed while their purported difference from the rest of the population is exaggerated'.

That has methodological as well as social and political consequences: a study of undifferentiated 'ethnic minority' experience and attitudes would be a study of a composite 'minority' that does not exist. And if we do recognize that minorities have to be studied separately, then we need large enough samples of each minority to draw valid conclusions about it. For that reason, we chose to focus all our research resources on just two contrasting minorities.

1.3.2 *Ethnic Pakistanis*

The largest racially and culturally distinctive minority in Scotland consists of ethnic Pakistanis—almost all of whom are Muslim. They are twice as numerous as any other 'visible' minority—and particularly visible because they are concentrated in the Glasgow area of west-central Scotland where one of their numbers is a Westminster MP.

But the numbers of all 'visible' ethnic minorities in Scotland are very low. According to the 2001 Census (accessible at www.statistics.gov.uk/census2001), the first to record self-declared religion as well as self-assigned ethnicity, self-declared ethnic Pakistanis (almost all of them Muslim) constitute less than 1 per cent of the population in Scotland and Muslims as a whole just over 1 per cent.

To put these figures in context: In England, 'visible' ethnic minorities are much more numerous than in Scotland; and Carribeans, Africans, Indians, and others constitute a much larger share. The 2001 Census indicates just over 1 per cent Pakistanis though slightly over 3 per cent Muslim in England. That in turn is typical of several European countries but much less than in France where there are over three times as many Muslims as in England (see Jon Henley, 'Europe faces up to Islam and the veil', *The Guardian*, 4 February 2004: 15).

An analysis of limited data from the 1991 Census by Bailey, Bowes, and Sim (1997: 25) suggested that Scottish Pakistanis were far more likely than other Scots to live in overcrowded housing (p. 27), but also far more likely to be employers or managers and just as likely as others to have professional occupations. That contrasts with ethnic Pakistanis in England who are notably disadvantaged in terms of education, housing, health, and employment (Mason 2003).

Similar patterns emerge in the more extensive and up-to-date *Analysis of Religion in the 2001 Census* (Scottish Executive 2005) which indicates that 67 per cent of Muslims in Scotland are 'ethnic Pakistanis' (p. 13). Stereotypically, Scottish Muslims are twelve times as likely as others to live in multiple-family households (p. 25) and economic activity is particularly low amongst Muslim women (p. 44); they are over twice as likely as others to work in wholesale and retail trading, hotels or restaurants and under-represented in manufacturing and construction jobs (p. 54); and they are twice as likely as others to live in large urban areas (p. 27): 42 per cent of all Scottish Muslims (and 48 per cent of Pakistanis) live in Glasgow, 16 per cent in Edinburgh, and 7 per cent in Dundee (p. 31).

Except in very small areas, Muslims or Pakistanis never constitute a large percentage of the population anywhere in Scotland. In the 2001 Census, the greatest density was in the Glasgow Govan constituency (12 per cent Muslim, 11 per cent Pakistani), represented in parliament by Mohammed Sarwar. No other constituency contained as many as 4 per cent. There is no Scottish equivalent of constituencies like Bradford North (21 per cent Muslim in the 2002 Census) or Birmingham Ladybrook (30 per cent), still less Bradford West (38 per cent), or Birmingham Sparkbrook (49 per cent). Typically therefore, Scottish Muslims and Pakistanis live in more culturally mixed areas.

In terms of social and occupational class the position of Scottish Muslims is ambiguous. They are slightly more likely than others to own a car, just as likely as others to own a house, more likely than others to be university graduates, but also more likely than others to have no educational qualifications at all (pp. 39–40).

Muslim males are one and a half times as likely as others to be unemployed, and females three times (p. 48). (See Smith 1991 for similar findings from the earlier 1991 Census—though for a composite 'ethnic minorities'.) Compared to others, Muslims are one and a half times as likely to be self-employed with full-time employees (p. 51); twice as likely to be classified as 'managers or senior officials' (p. 53); but twice as likely to work in sales occupations (p. 53) and underrepresented in professional, technical, skilled and unskilled work, or personal services (p. 53). They are twice as likely as others to work long hours (p. 55). Our own surveys indicate that subjectively, Scottish Pakistanis feel only marginally less affluent than English immigrants.

The eight-category National Statistics Socio-Economic Classification (NS-SeC) runs from 'higher managerial and professional' to 'long-term unemployed'. If we score these occupational categories from 1 to 8 and calculate the average location of male Muslims and non-Muslims in Scotland, they come out, on average, at the same scale point. Though that is a very crude index, it is sufficient to prove that it would be misleading to describe Scottish Muslims as either more or less middle-class than other Scots. In Scotland, male Muslims are neither an occupational elite nor an occupational underclass.

Female Muslims are distinctive however: they are nine times as likely as other females to have never worked (in paid employment) or to be long-term unemployed. So on the 8-point (NS-SeC) scale, Muslim women on average come 2 points *lower* than other women. On the other hand, if we restrict comparisons only to those in gainful employment, Muslim women on average score half a point *higher* than others. Crudely stated: Muslim women in work have slightly more middle-class occupations than others— but over a third of Muslim women do not have a formal occupation.

Exactly 50 per cent of Scottish Muslims were born in the UK (p. 13), though only 40 per cent in Scotland. Though 67 per cent of Scottish Muslims are self-described 'ethnic Pakistanis', only 26 per cent were born in Pakistan. (However, 47 per cent of ethnic Pakistanis in Scotland were born in Scotland; another 11 per cent in England, and only 40 per cent in Asia.)

Muslims remain a fairly tight-knit community: 80 per cent of married Muslims have a Muslim partner (p. 18) and the remainder are predominantly Muslim males with non-Muslim female partners.

1.3.3 *English Immigrants*

By far the largest self-conscious minority in Scotland is invisible, and English. Many Scots have Irish ancestry. Most of the 16 per cent who describe themselves as Catholic in the 2001 Census could probably trace their religious heritage back to Ireland—as could a significant minority of those who describe themselves as Protestants. But very few, only 1 per cent in the 2001 Census, choose to describe themselves as 'Irish'—no more than the number who were actually born in Ireland. By contrast, over 8 per cent of those resident in Scotland were born in England and over 7 per cent describe themselves as 'white British, but neither Scottish nor Irish'— the nearest the 2001 Scottish Census comes to an 'ethnically English' category.

These English immigrants are 'invisible' but not 'inaudible': 'accent [was] one of the most critical features ... to which the English-born ... turned time and again' in interviews with Findlay, Hoy, and Stockdale (2004: 72). They seldom apply the terms 'immigrant' or 'ethnic' to themselves—at least before they make the trip across the border. But then:

'you come up here and suddenly you are the ethnic minority ... when we asked [locals about] the ethnic mix [they replied]: three Asians and you two English ... I've never felt an ethnic minority before.' (E6-F)

In our focus groups, they frequently describe themselves as 'incomers' and more occasionally as 'white settlers'. We use the term 'immigrant' as a strictly neutral term for those born in one country but resident in another. (The term 'English migrant', used by some overly correct analysts is vague and patronizing. We are not interested in all emigrants from England, but only in those who have come to Scotland.)

Proportionately, English immigrants are particularly numerous across all the rural and small-town territory south of the Edinburgh–Glasgow 'Central Belt' (17 per cent of the population on Census 2001 figures). Within the cities, they are particularly numerous in Edinburgh where they constitute 12 per cent of the capital's large population.

In complete contrast to the more tightly-knit Muslim community, there is a high rate of mixed English/Scottish households. So, in addition to the 8 per cent who were themselves born in England, another 3 or 4 per cent, who were themselves born in Scotland, have a partner who was born in England. So throughout Scotland about 12 per cent are either English immigrants themselves or are living with an English immigrant— probably rising to a fifth in Edinburgh and over a quarter throughout southern Scotland.

There are roughly twice as many Scots-born residents in England as vice versa. But since the population of England is about ten times that of Scotland, the large numbers of Scottish immigrants within England constitute a smaller percentage of the English population than do Muslims. They are relatively isolated as individuals and unlike Scots in the USA,

Canada, or Australia they do not 'proclaim an exterior identity [as Scots]' (McCarthy 2005: 182). They are not numerous enough, nor visibly different enough, nor concentrated enough to gain a significant place as a 'group' in the English imagination. They remain individuals.

1.3.4 *Relationship to Scottish Nationalism*

Scottish nationalism might threaten both ethnic Pakistanis and English immigrants, though in different ways. They might be described as 'culturally distinctive' and 'former imperial' minorities (Grodeland, Miller, and Koshechkiria 2000: 46; Miller, Grødeland, and Koshechkiria 2001: 175). 'Visibility' exposes the Pakistani minority to greater casual harassment, especially after 9/11. Yet England is '*the* significant other' with a key role in defining Scottish identity (Wright 1999) while Pakistan is not. So in an increasingly self-conscious post-devolution Scotland, English immigrants might feel as ill-at-ease as Protestants in the Irish Republic after partition (Fedorowich 1999), or as Russians in post-Soviet Central Asia or the Baltic states (Sendich and Payin 1994; Brubaker 1996: 148–78; 'Russians retreat in face of hostility', *The Guardian*, 5 August 2005: 17). During the 1990s SNG (*Siol Nan Gaidheal*—'*Seed of the Gael*') pledged to 'unstintingly campaign against English imperialism' and spawned both *Scottish Watch* and the more aptly titled *Settler Watch* to 'expose and oppose' English 'incomers' (Hearn 2000: 65–70). Such extremists were unreservedly condemned by the SNP, but most Scots remain sensitive to England and Englishness.

1.3.5 *Researching Minorities*

To see how well post-devolution Scotland has succeeded in combining multiculturalism and sub-state nationalism we use a combination of focus-group discussions and surveys with these two minorities, tightly integrated with surveys of majority attitudes towards them, and supplemented by a series of elite interviews.

1.3.6 *Focus-Groups*

While they cannot claim to be statistically representative, focus group discussions are extremely useful for providing insight and interpretation. We held 12 two-hour discussions in the winter of 2002–03, six with each minority. A total of eighty-one participants were recruited through ethnic organizations and the discussions chaired by the authors (nine by Hussain, three by Miller). Pakistani discussions used Punjabi, Urdu, and/or English according to the participants' preferences. All were video-recorded and transcribed in English—translated where necessary by Hussain.

1.3.7 Minority Surveys

These discussions were followed by 1,510 telephone survey interviews in the summer and autumn of 2003, again split equally between the two minorities. The scope of these survey samples was intentionally widened to include anyone who lived in a Pakistani or English 'household'— defined as one containing someone who was 'ethnically Pakistani' or 'born in England' (or who had such people amongst their 'very close relatives'). All findings about 'ethnic Pakistanis' are based on the 716 respondents out of 759 in the Pakistani-sample who described *themselves* as 'ethnic Pakistanis'; and all findings about 'English immigrants' are based on the 579 respondents out of 751 in the English-sample who were *themselves* 'born in England'.

The remaining 43 in the Pakistani sample and 172 in the English sample provide insight into the perceptions and attitudes of those who had very close ties—usually cohabitation—with these minorities, without themselves being part of the minorities themselves. We are particularly interested in the large numbers of Scots 'living with the English'. Broadly speaking, those 'living with' ethnic Pakistanis do not differ much from ethnic Pakistanis themselves in terms of experiences, perceptions, attitudes, or social background—except on gender: 80 per cent are female (consistent with Census findings cited earlier). But those 'living with' English immigrants do differ consistently from the English-born themselves, particularly in terms of their religion (predominantly Presbyterian) and their identification with Scotland (46 per cent 'more' or 'exclusively' Scottish rather than British, compared to just 9 per cent amongst the English-born)—though not in terms of their perceptions that Scots harass English immigrants. We shall occasionally cite findings from our sample of these Scots who are 'living with the English' where they are relevant to our argument.

Survey interviews, like focus groups, were conducted in Punjabi and Urdu as well as English according to the respondents' preferences. Half the Pakistanis were interviewed by multilingual interviewers and the remainder were offered the option of switching to a multilingual interviewer. But most Scottish Pakistanis speak English fluently and many prefer to use it to discuss matters such as devolution. So 59 per cent of the interviews with Pakistanis (and 96 per cent of interviews with those 'living with' Pakistanis) were conducted in English even though in many cases the interviewer was fluent in Punjabi or Urdu. Nonetheless, language fluency or the offer of a multilingual interviewer was valuable in establishing initial rapport even if English was functionally more effective.

To select respondents we used a mixture of random digit dialing (for the English) and ethnic name selection supplemented by limited use of snowball sampling (for the Pakistanis) in areas where the 2001 Census showed these minorities were relatively numerous. Apart from using telephones our procedure was broadly similar to that used in the 1997 British Election Survey for its ethnic minority sample (Saggar and Heath 1999). Filter-questions were used to select respondents who came within the scope of our enquiry. The samples were weighted to match interlocking age-by-gender patterns within each minority in the 2001 Scottish Census. The survey questionnaire was developed from the focus-group schedule, but taking account also of the spontaneous, unrestricted, and occasionally surprising comments of participants in those focus groups.

Our surveys indicate that 65 per cent of Pakistanis had either been born in Scotland or lived in Scotland for over twenty years. By definition, none of the English immigrants had been born in Scotland and only 38 per cent had spent over twenty years in Scotland.

Just under half the Pakistanis primarily use Punjabi or Urdu within their household, just under a quarter English, and the rest a mixture—though for the survey interviews, 59 per cent opted for English and another 24 per cent a mixture. Few chose to answer exclusively in Punjabi or Urdu. For most, subcontinent languages were therefore a resource and a pleasure, not a constraint.

There is little evidence of a ghetto mentality in either. The most frequently read papers in both minorities are described by their readers as 'Scottish': 33 per cent of Pakistanis and 38 per cent of the English (and 51 per cent of those 'living with the English') rely on a 'Scottish' paper. Rather less (18 per cent of Pakistanis, 28 per cent of the English) rely on 'British' papers. 'Ethnic' papers come far behind: only 14 per cent of Pakistanis depend upon a 'Pakistani' paper (mainly the *Jang*) and 11 per cent of the English on what they describe as an 'English' paper. In Pakistani focus groups some confessed that they read Urdu:

'very, very slowly' (PK1-B); 'an hour to read a page' (PK1-A); 'I wish I could read Urdu fluently' (PK1-C); 'I could read Asian stuff when I was six years old' (PK6-C); 'I read *Jang* but I prefer the English pages.' (PK5-G)

More personally: almost all the English have 'close' friends who are '*not* English', two thirds have 'close' relatives who are '*not* English', and almost half a partner who is (or was) *not* born in England'. Very few Pakistanis (5 per cent) in our survey have a non-Pakistani partner though many are still single. But three quarters have 'close' friends who are '*neither Pakistani nor Muslim*'. Indeed, one quarter have 'close' relatives who are 'neither Pakistani nor Muslim' (the number possibly reflects their extensive concept of family).

Over a third of Pakistanis have lived in England, three quarters visit England regularly, and 84 per cent have 'close relatives' living in England. So Scottish Pakistanis are well aware of England and have views about England—not always positive views. Only a quarter of English immigrants say that England 'feels very different from Scotland' when they visit. But almost half the Scottish Pakistanis say it feels '*very* different—and most of the rest detect some difference.

Religion sets Pakistanis apart from English immigrants. In our survey, 99 per cent of ethnic Pakistanis claim to be Muslims, and well over half (55 per cent) claim to 'attend services or meetings connected with [their] religion' at least once a week. (Those 'living with' Pakistanis are 86 per cent Muslim, but only 36 per cent attend weekly.) English immigrants are divided on religion: 46 per cent were 'brought up' as Episcopalians though only 18 per cent remain so; only 9 per cent were brought up as Presbyterians and despite many losses, offset by a surprising number of gains, 11 per cent are now Presbyterians. Only 15 per cent attend weekly. So Pakistanis are differentiated from majority Scots more by their religiosity than faith. And historic sectarian divisions mean that English immigrants are linked to Scots more by their *ir*religiosity than by their particular faith.

1.3.8 *Majorities—in Scotland and England*

To gauge Scottish majority attitudes towards these two minorities we placed a module of questions in the 2003 SSAS (Scottish Social Attitudes Survey). And to put majority attitudes towards Muslims in Scotland in context we also placed a shorter module of questions in the 2003 BSAS (British Social Attitudes Survey). Both took place in the summer of 2003, at roughly the same time as our minority surveys.

We have restricted our analysis of these SSAS/BSAS samples to strictly-defined 'majority' populations in Scotland ($N = 1160$) and England

($N = 830$), excluding Muslims and self-described ethnic minorities in both countries, and excluding the numerous English immigrants or their partners from the SSAS sample for Scotland. These exclusions are critical to avoid serious distortions in the measurement of 'majority' attitudes and identities—not least because so many of the 'exclusively British' identifiers in Scotland are in fact English immigrants, an obvious fact that is almost always overlooked in analyses of so-called 'Scottish' identities.

1.3.9 *Scottish Elites*

Finally, Hussain conducted twenty-seven free-ranging, loosely structured in-depth interviews (all except one taped and transcribed) with Scottish elites: relevant members of the Scottish or Westminster parliaments, the civil service, quangos, or the police, along with representatives of ethnic minority, Muslim and civil rights organizations. Most gave permission for us to cite them by name but in these sensitive times we have chosen to preserve the anonymity of specific quotations. Interviewees are listed alphabetically in the Appendix, but the numerical code used in references has been randomized: it does *not* correspond to their place in that alphabetic listing.

We have divided elites into two categories however—not by personal ethnicity, but by their relationship to government: by whether they are 'insiders' or 'outsiders'. None are very 'outside': the 'outsiders' include one member of the Labour Party Executive, and the editor of a left-wing paper. They are not 'outside' the NGO/political activist elite. But the 'insiders' are either full-time government officials or elected members of the Scottish or British parliaments.

At elite level personal ethnicity is no guide to attitudes towards minorities. Reflecting the Scottish elite consensus, all the elites interviewed are broadly sympathetic to minorities. And criticisms of minorities are as likely to be voiced by those who are themselves drawn from the minorities as from others. But government insiders (indicated by a G after their code), especially MSPs, are more aware of the detailed efforts and achievements of the new Parliament, while those outside government are more aware of its limitations.[2]

---

[2] In the text, (IDI-18) indicates a quotation from the in-depth interview 18; while (IDI-17G) indicates a quotation is from in-depth interview 17, and also that the interviewee is an elected MP, MSP or government official.

1.4 The Setting—A Peculiar Nationalism, a Peculiar Multiculturalism, a Peculiar Time

The setting is important. What is possible in one time and place may not be so in others. Outside observers as well as Scottish politicians often draw attention to the peculiarly civic nature of Scottish nationalism. Less frequently, but just as important, some draw attention to the difference between European and American multiculturalism and even assert the peculiarity of British pragmatic, common-law-based multiculturalism. Both the civic nationalism of Scotland and the pragmatic multiculturalism of Britain are said to be 'benign' in the sense that both are peculiarly accommodating, non-confrontational versions of nationalism and multiculturalism. Finally, these are peculiar times for the prospects of multicultural nationalism. The place may be benign, the times are not.

1.4.1 *A Peculiar Scottish Nationalism*

The claim that Scottish nationalism is a peculiarly civic and benign version of nationalism is almost as much of a cliché as the civic/ethnic distinction itself, but it has some substance. Islamophobia is:

'not as bad in Scotland as in some parts of England . . . partly because of the political balance of forces . . . partly because [of] the media [in Scotland]' (IDI-18); 'nationalism does not always have dark connotations' (IDI-20G); 'extreme nationalism can be very dangerous . . . [but] that is not the type of nationalism we have in the mainstream of Scottish politics.' (IDI-25G)

Even those sceptical about popular sentiment still suggest that Scottish nationalism at the elite level is benign—and that this in itself is important. Miles and Dunlop (1987: 119) argue that 'what distinguishes Scotland from England is the absence of a racialization of the political process in the period since 1945 rather than an absence of racism per se.' In the 1990s, the Scottish political elite—nationalist as much as devolutionist—were united and consistent in proclaiming their vision of an 'inclusive' Scotland. Some were driven by the desire to assert Scottish moral superiority over the English. Some realized that in order to achieve devolution they needed the widest possible consensus and that even small but disaffected minorities in Scotland might fatally damage their chances of persuading Westminster to devolve power. But however mixed the motives, the elite rhetoric of inclusion was reiterated so often that it must have gradually become internalized if it were not already an article of faith.

But 'nationalism and independence doesn't have it at its core: "Lets look after the minority communities"' (IDI-25G). And ethnic inclusion often had a dry ritual quality in elite rhetoric. The term 'ethnic' seldom appeared in key documents without being coupled with 'women', the 'disabled' and/or 'the churches' (SCC 1995; SNP 1997; CSG 1998; WP 1998, col.392; SP 1999, vol.1: col. 382). CRE figures showed a sharp increase in racial incidents in Scotland after the Devolution Referendum (CRE 1999) and the press printed a rash of stories about harassment of the Pakistani and, more especially, English minorities (e.g. Rafferty 1998; CRE-Scotland 2000: 8). While there may have been an element of media hype (Hardie 1998) in this there was a growing awareness of grass-roots racism in Scotland (Cant and Kelly 1995; Horne 1995; Kelly 1999: 92–3; Kelly 2000) and such coverage could itself stimulate minority insecurity. 'Being made to feel very English was a common occurrence [amongst English immigrants] ... in the aftermath of the Braveheart film' (McIntosh, Smith, and Robertson 2004b: para 4.7).

Yet when the Scottish Parliament and its Executive took power, they enthusiastically monitored and promoted equal-opportunities provisions even though equal opportunities legislation was 'reserved' to the UK Parliament and not devolved to Scotland. Equality and inclusion could be promoted as a vision, not just as a set of laws, and the Scottish Executive backed its implementation of UK equal-opportunities legislation by defining its own vision of Scotland with an expensive advertising campaign centred on an explicitly multiculturalist slogan: *One Scotland, Many Cultures*. The campaign itself betrays an awareness that many ordinary Scots might not be as multiculturalist as the Executive and Parliament themselves. But whether or not ordinary Scots were 'racist', the elite ensured that post-devolution politics was if anything even less 'racialized' than when Miles and Dunlop made that claim in the 1980s. Nationalist as well as devolutionist elites were very sensitive to the dark side of nationalism and determined, if at all possible, to define a new inclusive nationalism, whatever its internal contradictions.

1.4.2 *A Peculiar British Multiculturalism*

There is less widespread appreciation of the peculiarity of British multiculturalism. Yet 'multicultural citizenship' (Kymlicka, 1995) is 'not an abstract demand of philosopher or activist; it is a reality in liberal states' but a reality 'couched in distinct national colours: compensation for historical oppression in the United States ... [a] counter-programme to a historically incriminated nation-state in Germany ... liberal laissez-faire in Britain ... unmistakably national' (Joppke 1999: 146).

American, specifically the United States rather than Canadian, multiculturalism is burdened by guilt for enslaving blacks and murdering native Americans. By contrast West European multiculturalism is less contrite, less inclusive but at the same time less demanding. It is 'limited to the public recognition and tolerance of the ethnic differences imported by immigration' (Joppke 1998: 36).

Whether explicit as a policy of symbolic recognition or implicit as a liberal laissez-faire ... [it]dodges the crucial challenge of a civic redefinition of nationhood in Europe [and] reinforces the ethnic tilt of European nations, in pledging tolerance towards members of other ethnic nations on their soil ... religion and state are less perfectly separated in Europe ... [and] European nations do not offer their immigrants alternative identifications ... no British Dream [like] the American Dream. (Joppke 1998: 37)

Favell (1998: 326) goes further: 'multiculturalism ... should be avoided as the frame of comparison for Britain ... because it simply does not mean the same thing in different countries'. He stresses: 'distinct constitutional frameworks for minority issues, differing legal mechanisms ... differing political forums'.

Joppke (1998: 38) argues that 'Muslims [are] the nut that Europe has to crack. The multicultural recognition of difference will be indispensable for this; but so will something more mundane: jobs, education, and full membership in the national communities of the receiving states.' Citing Gerholm and Ithman (1988) and Gellner (1992), Favell (1998: 322) agrees that 'one of the hottest issues thrown up by multiculturalism in Britain has been the growing significance of political and social issues involving Muslims' but argues 'academic comparative studies have been crude and have failed to pay attention to the peculiarities of the distinct institutional framework within which British Muslims operate *politically*'.

On the one side, 'alarmist concern with the threat of Islam ... masks the fact that the behaviour of a minority of militant British Muslims is predominantly an exception to the way multiculturalism has generally functioned in Britain ... generally successful' (Favell 1998: 323). And on the other, mainstream politicians in Britain 'seek to defuse and play down the issue rather than use it for political capital'—in sharp contrast to 'the rejection of multiculturalism in France in favour of a new, revamped republicanism' (Favell 1998: 328). He is particularly critical of 'the way false interpretations of the British case are used in Schnapper (1992), Todd

29

(1994), and Kepel (1994) to bolster their high republican arguments for immigration politics in France' (Favell 1998: 343).

'In contrast to the American and German cases, British multiculturalism sprang more from political elite anticipation than the pressure of society' (Joppke 1999: 233). Echoing Miles and Dunlop's claim about the 'non-racialisation' of Scottish politics, Favell (1998: 330) asserts:

it is difficult to argue—particularly when viewed in comparative terms—that any real political capital has been made of populist racist or anti-ethnic feelings in [British] elections since 1979, or that it is even a latent issue waiting to be tapped by a government passing some even more strict immigration controls. ... The Conservative Party officially has spared no effort in portraying itself in politically correct terms on racial and ethnic issues, while feeling far less inclined to curb open outbursts of anti-European xenophobia.

That argument hints at the possibility that anti-European xenophobia might displace anti-ethnic xenophobia in the UK—much as Anglophobia in Scotland may displace Islamophobia (a theme we discuss further in Chapter 4).

The 'key components' of this peculiarly British version of multiculturalism in Favell's view (1998: 331) are:

1. keep [ethnic] issues out of mainstream politics
2. incremental symbolic recognition to publicly defined groups
3. localize ... ethnic minority interests in religious and cultural groups
4. [distinguish] new European migrants and asylum-seekers [from] existing British ethnic minorities
5. [achieve] equal opportunities and multiculturalism [through] common law, laissez-faire, localized pluralism

and, above all:

6. keep the issues well away from ... constitutional minority rights.

'Constitutionalising' (IDI-23G) is used as a natural term of abuse by some of the Scottish elites we interviewed. Thus 'ethnic-minority protections that in Germany and the United States are grounded in constitutional human-rights guarantees have been achieved in Britain by unprincipled common law and flexible state-making' (Joppke 1999: 234). 'The flexibility of the common law [approach] is visible in its treatment of foreign marriage and divorce customs [including] polygamous marriage, the marriage of minors [and] Muslim talaq divorces ... [plus] exempting some ethnic minorities from some requirements of the law', especially Sikhs, Muslims, and Jews (Joppke 1999: 234, see 234–7 for many specific examples).

At the same time:

British race-relations law [unlike American] has desisted from endowing black immigrants with privileged group status ... [and has been] guided by the unprincipled [case-oriented] pragmatism of common sense, good manners and reasonable tolerance, [and the] remarkably tolerant [decisions of a] common law judiciary. (Joppke 1999: 225, 233)

This is a peculiarly 'home-grown' and 'curiously anachronistic' (Favell 1998: 332) but large successful approach based on

traditionally conservative principles about managing public order and devolving citizenship to localized, communitarian representation ... [which was] the dominant practice of the elite English centre towards the various national peripheries of the United Kingdom ... an idea of multicultural, multinational Britain. (Favell 1998: 339)

But he ends on a pessimistic note: 'the apparent success of racial and ethnic politics in Britain may prove to be an illusion ... a set of ideas whose time is over ... British blacks and Asians might find themselves excluded from a re-emerging English nationalism' (Favell 1998: 343, 342). Significantly, however, he does not suggest these minorities are at risk from a burgeoning Scottish nationalism.

1.4.3 *A Peculiarly Scottish Multiculturalism*

Scotland is undoubtedly affected by the advancing and receding tides of British multiculturalism. But Scotland's experience of monoculturalism and multiculturalism is different from that of England. Perhaps the simplest way to make that point is to ask the question: Does multicultural ideology in Scotland date from the celebrated Jenkins speech of 1966 (see Chapter 3), from the late nineteenth century, from 1843, or from 1707? Judged by historical benchmarks, post-1966 multiculturalism is the least challenging of these various multiculturalisms which the small population of Scotland has had to face.

Colley (1992a: 327) argued that 'Britain ... [was] an invented nation ... heavily dependent for its raison d'être on a broadly Protestant culture'. But 'Protestant culture' is an unconvincing myth: the 'killing times' in Scotland refer to a conflict between different strands of Protestantism. The Union state of 1707 specifically guaranteed a multicultural Britain— usually forgotten south of the border but seldom forgotten north of it. The consequence even now is that 'cultural difference'—within the

UK—has almost unconscious overtones of liberty, nationalism and inclusion for Scots which it does not have for the English. Even though Scotland was a largely monocultural Presbyterian land, in UK terms it had since 1707 a tolerated but deviant culture. It did not acknowledge the Head of State as the Head of its National Church as the English still do. And Scots were always aware that they were a minority, by culture as well as by birth.

Presbyterianism is notoriously schismatic however. And after the great Disruption of 1843 Scotland was split in two by rival Presbyterianisms. So after 1843 multiculturalism was internal to Scotland as well as something that guaranteed Scotland a place in the Union. And by the time most (not all) Presbyterians came back together in 1928, there was a large Irish Catholic minority in Scotland. So 'post-1945 Asian migration is neither the first nor the largest migration to Scotland' (Miles and Dunlop 1987: 122).

The Irish immigration led to multicultural state institutions that remain controversial to this day: the faith-based state-funded education system was set up by the Education (Scotland) Act 1918. Five years later the General Assembly of the Church of Scotland decided to publish as a pamphlet, its report on *The menace of the Irish race to our Scottish nationality* (Miles and Dunlop 1987: 127). Militant Protestant parties contested local elections with considerable success (Miles and Dunlop 1987: 129–30). At one point they had ten councillors in Edinburgh and in 1933 they took a quarter of the vote across the whole of Glasgow (Miller 1985: 201–2). That was the high point for explicitly Protestant parties, but Finn (1994: 105) recalls 'the potency and acceptance of anti-Catholicism in the everyday thinking in Scotland of the early 1970s'.

State-funded Catholic schools remain a very controversial issue. They provoked more discussion in our elite interviews than anything else (see Chapter 7). Many integration-minded multiculturalists take the cautious view that separate faith-based schools are undesirable but nonetheless should not be merged with other state schools against the wishes of the Catholic community. Typically, SNP leader Alex Salmond (*The Herald* 21 April 2005) argues: 'It would be wrong to end an agreement which was entered into in 1918 to bring Catholic schools into the public school system, without the full consent of the Catholic community.' Other cautious integration-minded multiculturalists feel that Muslims and Catholics should be treated the same—that they should both be able to have state-funded faith schools, and that Catholic schools should remain as long as Catholics want them—but at the same time express the hope that Muslims will not choose to exercise their right to separate state-funded faith schools since that would compound a fault.

As far as the state is involved in the 'multiculturalism of separation' rather than the 'multiculturalism of recognition and respect', such institutional multiculturalism has in practice applied to Catholics not to Muslims, to the old multicultural Scotland not to the new. So far it has been a leftover from the early twentieth century rather than an innovation of the twenty-first century. Not only is state multiculturalism in Scotland *not new*, it is also, at present, far *less separatist* than in it was in the early twentieth century.

1.4.4 *A Peculiar Time*

The Scottish Parliament was inaugurated in 1999. But then three other events intervened to affect minorities in Scotland: 9/11 in 2001; the invasion of Iraq in 2003; and the delayed impact of the 'dispersal' policy introduced by the 1999 Immigration and Asylum Act which came to public attention some years later. Four more or less simultaneous causes, the very direction of whose impact is uncertain or conflicting, make any kind of purely statistical time-series approach impossible. We have to rely on very explicit survey questions and the still more meaning-rich analytic approach of focus groups and in-depth interviews.

The 9/11 destruction of the Twin Towers in New York triggered a wave of harassment of Muslims in Scotland as elsewhere throughout the world (Allen and Nielsen 2002). We might expect Scottish Muslims to feel increasingly alienated from Scottish society as a result. But the opposite happened, and we will show how these events bound Muslims ever more tightly to Scotland. Despite increasing harassment, Scottish Muslims felt that Scotland was a relatively (not absolutely) safe haven for Muslims in an increasingly dangerous world—safer than England as well as much safer than places outside Britain.

Whether the London bombing of July 2005 will ultimately have a similar impact remains to be seen. A survey by MORI for the BBC (news.bbc.co.uk, 10 August 2005) interviewed a small sample of 229 Muslims along with a much larger sample of the general public in the weeks after the bombing. On balance, Muslims felt there had been no change in Britain's racial tolerance. Both Muslims and non-Muslims remained strongly committed to an integrationist version of multiculturalism, though Muslims felt they should keep their 'own values and traditions'—attitudes that are consistent with our research. But in the three weeks after the London bombs, the London police reported a 600 per cent rise in crimes motivated by religious or racial hatred while the Scottish police reported a rise of only 20 per cent—thirty times less (*The Herald*, 4 August 2005: 1). So, in the short term at least, Muslims probably still thought Britain was still a relatively safe place in world terms and, more important for our argument, still thought Scotland was even safer than England.

The invasion of Iraq did more than 9/11: it bound Muslims not just to Scotland but to the SNP and to Scottish nationalism. The invasion took place during the run-up to the 2003 Scottish Parliament election. It was opposed more strongly by the SNP than by any other party. Four years earlier, North Atlantic Treaty Organization (NATO) bombing of Serbia, which occurred in the run-up to the 1999 Scottish Parliament election, was also opposed more strongly by the SNP than by any other. The SNP's anti-war policy was consistent. But in 1999 NATO was on the side of Muslims in Kosovo, while in 2003 the US-led Coalition was attacking a Muslim country (albeit not a Muslim regime) without even UN authorization. So Muslims who for decades had been more attracted to the Labour Party than any other—in Scotland as in England—and whose loyalty to Labour was reinforced by NATO action in Serbia, now found themselves in a totally new situation.

The self-consciously multiculturalist leadership of the SNP had been trying for years to attract ethnic minority votes. They were too few to be numerically significant, but they were of enormous moral significance for a party that wished to stress its 'civic nationalist' credentials. A long-standing invitation to ethnic minorities to support or even join the SNP already existed; Iraq suddenly provided a reason to accept. At last Scottish Muslims found common cause with Scottish Nationalists on an issue of great concern to them. Our survey shows they switched from Labour to SNP en masse (see Chapter 8).

The dispersal of asylum seekers from southern England to Scotland was not world news, but it had a direct impact on the streets of Glasgow and got considerable coverage in the Scottish press. It triggered public resentment against the mainly Muslim asylum seekers suddenly sent to Scotland:

'There was a huge increase in people coming on the phone to me and saying: I want to talk about this waiting list at the hospital and its all these asylum-seekers that are causing this problem. Or: I want to talk about the fact that my daughter can't get a house and all these asylum-seekers are sitting in houses.' (IDI-26G)

But public resentment was qualified by public remorse when one of the asylum seekers was murdered. And at the same time, a Scottish detention centre at Dungavel was used by the UK Home Office to hold asylum seekers. The 2003 SSAS survey shows a majority of ordinary Scots felt asylum seekers should be held in detention. But the Scottish political elite was infuriated by the insensitivity of the Home Office—first, towards asylum seekers and second, towards the new Scottish Parliament and Executive who found a detention centre on Scottish soil over which they had no influence, let alone control. They felt in exactly the same situation as the Cuban regime with respect to the American detention centre in Guantánamo Bay—and used that analogy.

Instead of stoking public fears about immigration, the Scottish political elite therefore refocused public resentment, as far as they could, against London rule. Once again, a Muslim minority in Scotland found common cause with strident Scottish nationalist elites, if not so much with ordinary Scots.

1.5 Plan of the Book

In Chapter 2 we look at what minorities spontaneously said was 'best and worst' about Britain in general and Scotland in particular—before their responses were conditioned by any of our politically oriented questions. English immigrants and ethnic Pakistanis share some views about what is 'best' or 'worst' about Britain and Scotland. But one minority puts more emphasis on racism and multiculturalism, the other on British institutions of freedom, the friendliness of majority Scots, the relatively low numbers of ethnic minorities in Scotland, and the iniquities of benefit scroungers.

These are familiar stereotypes—but is the *English immigrants* that complain most about Scottish bigotry and racism and praise Britain for its 'multiculturalism'; and it is the *ethnic Pakistanis* who praise British institutions of freedom most strongly, who praise Scottish friendliness most strongly (despite their greater experience of harassment), and who take a positive view about Scotland's low levels of ethnic minorities. The stereotypes are familiar but, as stereotypes, they fit the wrong minorities.

Chapter 3 uses an index of majority attitudes towards Muslims to compare Islamophobia in Scotland and England. Islamophobia is considerably lower in Scotland. Some of the most important influences on Islamophobia—age, generation and education—operate in much the same way north and south of the border. But English nationalism makes people significantly more Islamophobic while Scottish nationalism—even at street level—does not.

Chapter 4 restricts attention to Scotland alone, and looks at a variety of phobias, five in all, that afflict majority Scots. It touches on sectarianism,

Europhobia, and Asylophobia. But it pays most attention to Anglophobia and Islamophobia. Influences like age, generation, and education operate in much the same way on both these phobias. But religiosity affects only Islamophobia, not Anglophobia; and conversely, national identity affects only Anglophobia, not Islamophobia.

Our findings reinforce the argument of Virdee (2003), Bairner (1994), and others that Anglophobia 'displaces' ethnic minority phobias. Totalling up various phobias, street-level nationalism in Scotland *does* increase phobias—but it channels phobias into Angophobia. SNP voters, however, are not the most phobic. Conservative voters are the most phobic overall—not the most Anglophobic, but the most Islamophobic, Asylophobic, Europhobic, and sectarian.

Chapter 5 investigates minorities' perceptions of majority phobias. Their perceptions are broadly accurate. But they challenge one of the key analytic findings in Chapters 3 and 4: the importance of education. Minorities know that the relatively well-educated do not express Islamophobic or Anglophobic views. They would accept our statistical findings. But they believe the better-educated are just better at hiding their phobias—perhaps even hiding their phobias from themselves. In their view, the better educated are 'in denial'.

Within both minorities, perceptions of majority phobias are strongly influenced by experience rather than background, in particular their personal experience of ethnic jokes and insults.

Chapter 6 finds that both minorities are the butt of frequent ethnic jokes, but these jokes hurt Muslims more. And Muslims are subjected to far more—as well as more frightening—insults and abuse. But they have developed a number of 'coping strategies' in order to live with this abuse—the most important of which is the simple reflection that it is worse elsewhere, including England.

Personal experience of insults affects both minorities' perceptions of the level of conflict between their own ethnic group and majority Scots. It has at least as much impact on the perceptions of English immigrants as on those of ethnic Pakistanis. In addition, there is a 'spillover' effect: within both minorities, English as well as Muslim, their own personal experiences of jokes and insults combine with their perception of worldwide Muslim/ non-Muslim conflict to affect their perception of Muslim/non-Muslim conflict within Scotland.

Chapter 7 looks at minority attitudes towards Scottish history, culture, and symbols—symbols such as locating the Parliament in a Church of Scotland building for five years, the Saltire and emphasis on St Andrew as 'patron Saint' of Scotland, and the conspicuous absence of any Muslim MSPs.

Few English immigrants but over half the Pakistanis want to change Scottish culture, to add to the variety of Scottish customs and traditions rather than attempting to 'adapt and blend'. But they value diversity. They want a Scotland that is different from its past but different from their own past as well. They reject a ghetto mentality in favour of a multicultural society in which they would be a respected minority but a minority nonetheless—not assimilated but nonetheless fully integrated. Conversely, many English immigrants feel it is important for incomers to 'adapt and blend'. An analysis of religious change amongst English immigrants provides behavioural evidence that they themselves really do 'adapt and blend'.

Chapter 8 looks at identities. Both minorities actively 'use' identities as a means of integration—the Pakistanis more successfully than the English. English immigrants cannot identify with Scotland despite respecting its traditions (and focusing on their 'British' identity is no help towards integration except in their own minds). But Pakistanis can easily—and quickly—identify with Scotland despite wanting to change, or at least diversify, its culture. Pakistani identities are primarily cultural ('Muslim') rather than territorial, but in so far as they are territorial they are more Scottish than British. The two findings are connected: it is because territorial identities are not the primary identities for Pakistanis that they find it particularly easy to adopt a Scottish identity irrespective of whether they have been born in Scotland or not. (And the shocks of 9/11 and Iraq have *strengthened* rather than weakened their identification with Scotland and Scottish nationalism.) Conversely, since the identities of English immigrants are primarily territorial they find it exceedingly difficult to adopt a Scottish identity.

Culture and identity therefore provide both 'bridges and walls' between Scots and these minorities. But what is a bridge for one minority is a wall for the other.

Chapter 9 looks at minority perceptions of the impact of devolution—first, through devolved institutions; second, through street-level attitudes and behaviour. Like majority Scots they combine support for the principle of devolution with criticism of the performance of the Parliament. They have few reservations about the street-level impact however. For Pakistanis the ethos of devolution has been determinedly inclusive and multicultural. And even English immigrants are inclined to feel that devolution has made majority Scots 'more relaxed', less inclined as well as less able to blame the English for all their troubles. In their view, it has simultaneously increased national pride and reduced xenophobia.

Pakistani Muslims have experienced increasing harassment and abuse since devolution. But they consciously distinguish between the positive impact of devolution and the negative impact of concurrent factors—notably the new UK policy of dispersing asylum seekers from the south of England up to Scotland and, more importantly, 9/11 and the consequent Bush/Blair 'war on terror'.

Combined with the invasion of Iraq however, the paradoxical consequence has been that increasing harassment has bound Scottish Muslims ever more closely to Scotland. In absolute terms things have got worse. But in comparative terms, the Scottish Parliament and Executive have proved more sympathetic than the UK government; the SNP has proved more sympathetic than either of the two main parties that dominate politics in England; and even at street level they have enjoyed a wave of support and sympathy to balance against increased harassment.

Scottish Muslims regard devolution itself as a part of the solution, however ineffective, rather than part of the problem. Being Scottish, living in Scotland, and identifying with Scotland have allowed them to use Scottish nationalism itself as a 'coping strategy' in the face of increasing harassment on the street and their own increasing anger with the UK government.

***

Along the way towards these conclusions, we hope that our extensive use of verbatim quotations has helped to 'humanize' the subjects of our enquiry: to achieve Brubaker's aim of 'ethnicity without groups'. We have presented statistical findings, drawn from our minority and majority surveys. But statistics alone, lend themselves to viewing categories as groups, majorities as unanimities. We have been impressed by voices, by the individuality of attitudes and experiences, by the sometimes vigorous and thoughtful debate within minorities, by the real dilemmas, and by the reasoned and complex responses.

In order to convey that sense of discussion and debate we have avoided the temptation to illustrate our arguments with a few carefully selected, unusually interesting, long quotations. Instead, we have presented a very large number of often very brief quotations. They are more than illustrations: they represent the discussions, they represent the variety as well as the weight of opinion. They put more pixels in the picture.

2

What Is Best and Worst about Scotland

Inevitably, detailed questions direct respondents' attention towards the topics that we wish to study—devolution, nationalism, identity, harassment, and so on—rather than the topics they may want to discuss. So right at the start of each focus-group we asked five very simple, open, almost content-free questions: what was 'best' and 'worst' about Britain?; what was 'best' and 'worst' about Scotland?; and 'how would you compare Scotland with other parts of Britain?'

Such questions have a long history. In the late 1950s, Almond and Verba (1963: 64) sought insight into what they called the 'democratic culture' by asking the public in various countries: 'speaking generally, what are the things about this country that you are most proud of?' In the old established democracies of the USA and UK, the most frequent answers referred to political institutions. By contrast, Germans and Italians at that time took little pride in their system of government, citing instead the virtues of the German people and the Italian scenery.

After the first referendum on Scottish devolution in 1979, these questions were adapted to provide insight into Scottish attitudes towards state and sub-state (Brand and Miller 1979). Scots most frequently cited political institutions ('justice', 'democracy', even 'monarchy') for their pride in Britain. But like post-war Italians and Germans, Scots most frequently cited the scenery (33 per cent) and the people (31 per cent) for their pride in Scotland.

More recent but fragmentary data indicate that, just prior to devolution, Scots still remained more proud of their scenery than anything else (Curtice 1999: 127). And even after devolution majority Scots are probably still more proud of Scotland's scenery than its much criticized new political institutions. But minorities might have a different view.

2.1 What Is Best and Worst about Britain

Overwhelmingly, both minorities cite government and institutions as the best things about Britain. But they cite different institutions. English immigrants frequently cite things that are completely ignored by ethnic Pakistanis: royalty, tradition, the unity of the UK.

2.1.1 *History and Tradition*

English immigrants cite British 'history' (E1-H) and 'traditions' (E1-H, E1-A) and the diversity of traditions across the historic nations of the UK (E2-F, E2H). Royalty is part of that:

'the Queen does a very good job' (E1-B, E1-C agrees) ... 'Charlie too' (E1-H); 'I am a fanatical royalist.' (E1-A)

and so is the unity of the UK:

'a united Britain' (E1-E); 'gathered together to be so successful' (E3-F); 'a multicultural nation ... *if we ignore the minority ethnic groups that have come in* [our emphasis], if we just look at the four nations that make up Great Britain we are reasonably tolerant of each other.' (E6-D)

2.1.2 *Freedom and Good Government*

Freedom is frequently cited by both minorities; but amongst the English as a slogan, without detail, just another part of tradition, not a matter of contemporary experience:

'freedom' (E1-E, E1-H, E3-B, E5-C, E5-A, E5-B); 'freedom of speech' (E3-D, E3-F); 'say what we like without being imprisoned' (E1-A); 'express opinions without fear' (E4-C); 'not subject to police raids at two a.m.' (E6-G)

But they never get personal. And they were probably unaware that under Thatcher, BBC-Scotland *was* raided 'at two a.m.' by Metropolitan police sent up from London to seize an entire series of TV programmes (Ewing and Gearty 1990: 147–52; Miller, Timpson, and Lessnoff 1996: 368).

More remarkably, even in the aftermath of '9/11' that led to increased street-level harassment and imprisonment-without-trial, ethnic Pakistanis were at least as likely as English immigrants to cite 'freedom' as the best thing about Britain. And they did get into detail:

'freedom' (PK3-B); 'we are allowed to do things that are denied in other countries.' (PK1-C) ... 'friends from other countries, although from Muslim countries, have a lot of problems practising their religion. We don't have that kind of restriction here' (PK1-D); 'Britain might not be great but it is still better than many other countries [for] freedom of practising religion' (PK4-D); 'women have a lot more freedom here' (PK2-D); 'great for women' (PK5-A); 'as a female in Pakistan you need to be shy and more reserved' (PK6-B, PK6-D agrees); 'freedom of speech ... respect towards other cultures—we come across racism but you will find that in every society and it is openly condemned [here] ... human rights: no other country can match this.' (PK4-B)

For both minorities freedom was reinforced by orderliness and fairness. The 'best' things about Britain include:

'fair play' (E4-G); 'orderliness ... fairness' (E3-C); 'set procedures' (PK2-A); 'the country is run very legally and there is no corruption.' (PK2-B)

2.1.3 *Social Welfare*

As in Almond and Verba's study, social welfare is still cited as one of the 'best' things about Britain—though less often than freedom and good government:

'more opportunities ... free education, health service' (PK1-C); 'education' (PK5-C, PK5-D) ... 'the health service' (E6-A); '[public] services' (PK3-A); 'helpful doctors' (PK5-B); 'the distribution of things like education, health' (E3-C); 'free education ... free medicines ... opportunities .... Back in Pakistan ... you can get an education only if you have money.' (PK5-F)

2.1.4 *Crime, Vandalism, Scroungers*

By far the most frequent criticism of Britain concerns incivility—crime, vandalism, scroungers, and welfare cheats. English immigrants cited:

'abuse of public property ... bad language' (E3-B); 'racism' (E3-H); 'when we were kids we didn't damage bus shelters' (E6-A) ... 'the situation has deteriorated ' (E6-G) ... 'got out of hand' (E6-F) ... 'we could do with a better system of punishment and policing ... then people wouldn't live in fear' (E6-A) ... 'the big problem is drugs.' (E6-G)

Ethnic Pakistanis also:

'dislike the vandalism' (PK4-D); 'the yob culture' (PK1-C); 'you cannot send children alone to school' (PK2-A); 'a lot of youth are totally out of control ... vandalism and abuse ... the elderly feel threatened and intimidated.' (PK4-E)

And ethnic Pakistanis—though not English immigrants—cite welfare scrounging as the 'worst' thing about Britain:

'people abuse the system ... there should be strict rules' (PK4-B) ... 'bring [back] conscription' (PK4-A); 'I want all the benefits to be stopped.' (PK5-A)

2.2 What Is Best and Worst about Scotland

Like majority Scots, minorities cite the scenery and the people as the 'best' thing about Scotland. But the English put more emphasis on the *scenery*, and Pakistanis more emphasis on the *people*. Moreover, insofar as they cite the people, the English focus on the Scots' legendary inventiveness and sense of identity, while Pakistanis focus more on their friendliness. In addition, the English tend to assess Scotland in absolute terms, while Pakistanis insist on viewing it in comparative perspective—frequently comparing Scotland favourably with England—even before they are asked to make a comparison.

2.2.1 *The Best*

English participants, more often than city-dwelling Pakistanis, frequently say the 'best' thing about Scotland is:

'the land is beautiful' (E3-C); 'land and space' (E3-E); 'countryside' (E4-B, E4-F agrees); 'roads clear of traffic' (E1-H, all agree); 'not so many people' (E3-F); 'the scenery' (PK1-B); 'countryside and wildlife.' (E2-H)

They cite Scottish history, culture, and sense of identity while ethnic Pakistanis do not. The English admire:

'the culture ... wonderful history' (E2-H); 'identity' (E6-D, E6-A agrees); 'this great sense of their national identity' (E4-D); 'a sense of community' (E6-E); 'strong identity ... in rural areas.' (E3-B)

Even with envy:

'Scots are proud of their heritage' (E6-D) ... 'a very proud race' (E6-A) ... 'the English have difficulty in hanging on to anything' (E6-D) ... 'you don't even feel English until you come up here' (E6-A, E6-B agrees); 'a cultural identity [that] England doesn't [have]' (E4-D); 'because Scots have had to live for centuries measuring themselves up against an elephant' (E4-D); 'smallness ... is an advantage.' (E5-A)

The English occasionally cite the historical stereotype of the clever and industrious Scot:

'their inventiveness ... the value of education' (E4-D) ... 'the number of inventions ... ideas.' (E4-C)

Both cite the friendliness of Scots:

'not over-the-top friendly ... but genuinely' (E3-H, E3-E agrees); 'very friendly ... I was very surprised' (E5-A); 'friendly place' (E5-C); 'very friendly' (PK4-D, PK2-A); 'a very friendly welcoming country.' (IDI-2); 'Scottish people are friendlier.' (PK1-F, PK1-B similar)

2.2.2 *The Worst*

Ethnic Pakistanis are inclined to suppress criticisms of Scotland while English immigrants are inclined to voice them, even unasked. In several different focus groups, Pakistanis were quite explicit. There is

'nothing bad' (PK2-A); 'nothing embarrassing about Scotland' (PK5-C); 'nothing'. (PK6-E, all agree)

Conversely, English immigrants articulate a miscellany of criticisms, sometimes even when they have been asked what is 'best' about Scotland:

'Scotland's divided ... you have Irish Republicanism here' (E6-C); 'lack of public transport from London' (E1-B, all agree)

and the cost of the new Scottish Parliament building:

'the [Scottish] Parliament' (E1-E, E1-F agrees) ... 'it's good entertainment' (E1-G) ... 'expensive entertainment' (E1-H) ... 'and escalating.' (E1-E)

Criticisms of drink and crime come almost exclusively from ethnic Pakistanis—who live in inner city areas, rather than from English immigrants who generally live in rural areas, suburbs or upmarket areas. Pakistanis are embarrassed by the way the general perception of Scots' addiction to alcohol is applied to them:

'what embarrasses me is the way Glaswegians are portrayed as drunks' (PK5-F); 'people say: where are you from? Scotland? You like a drink then.' (PK1-C)

And crime affects Pakistanis more directly:

'so many burglaries ... in this area' (PK3-A); 'the big gangs—they don't live in your area but they come and break windows' (PK5-G) ... 'mothers just go and sit in the pubs for hours ... don't even know where their children are.' (PK5-E)

Pakistani participants are willing to speak at length about racism and their experience of racism when they are asked about it explicitly. But only one spontaneously cited it as the 'worst' thing about Scotland. In complete contrast, many English immigrants do cite Scots' bigotry, narrow-mindedness, Anglophobia, or racism (occasionally using that word!) as the 'worst' thing about Scotland:

'ardent nationalism ... narrow minded ... bigoted ... but then they had to put up with the arrogance and bigotry of England in the past' (E4-D); 'isolationist' (E5-B); 'amazing lack of tolerance ... incredible lack of understanding' (E6-E); 'English-referencing all the time, which looks very bad for Scotland' (E3-G,E3-E agrees) ... '[though] that in part has been imposed on Scotland.' (E3-A)

'bigotry' (E4-C) ... 'Do you mean Catholic/Protestant or Scottish/English, what sort of bigotry?' (Moderator) ... 'Whatever, even [names one small town] against [names another]' (E4-C) ... 'which are only 7 miles apart ... astonishing.' (E4-F) ... 'Catholic versus Protestant' (E4-D) ... 'north [Scotland] against south [Scotland].' (E4-B, E4-C agrees)

While they argue that Scottish bigotry seems to exist almost independent of any specific target, English immigrants are particularly sensitive to Anglophobia:

'the inability of Scottish people to recognise their racism towards the English' (E6-E); '[an] in-built dislike of the English' (E5-B); 'as long as the English lose it doesn't really matter who wins' (E5-A); 'Scots are aware of racism where it concerns people who are clearly and obviously different ... by virtue of skin-colour ... but when it comes to the English they do not consider their remarks to be in any way offensive or racist' (E6-G) ... 'yet if we said the same about the Scots it would be a different matter' (E6-F) ... 'absolutely' (E6-A) ... 'they are aware of racism ... but they don't consider their remarks about the English fall into the same category' (E6-D) ... 'don't see it as racism at all.' (E6-F)

2.3 Scotland in Comparison

Finally, we asked: 'How would you compare Scotland with other parts of Britain? Is it better or worse?' Of course, there is a positive bias in such a comparison: all the participants lived in Scotland, many through their own choice. Nonetheless, it is subjective perceptions that affect whether minorities feel truly 'at home' or 'at ease' in Scotland.

English participants cited less congestion:

'you had to queue to get into the Lake District and queue to get out. [But] here—wonderful panorama, nobody on the roads' (E2-H); 'the Lake District ... is absolutely overrun' (E3-A, E3-F agrees); 'in Dorset . . . traffic was nose to tail . . . and that was in a rural area.' (E1-E)

Pakistani participants cited the unfriendliness of people in England:

'when I was a young boy, we went down to England to stay in Middlesbrough . . . the people were toffee nosed. My mum said I don't want to stay here, let's go back to Glasgow. She told my dad he could work in the barras [Glasgow flea-market] and she would work in the factory . . . . In Glasgow, I don't think they are racist . . . . In England, places like Manchester and Birmingham are well known to have problems of racism.' (PK3-C); 'Scotland is definitely better than other parts of Britain' (PK4-D) . . . 'there is racism in Scotland but there is worse racism in England. Go to Birmingham or Manchester and then you find out that Scotland is much better' (PK4-C) . . . 'I lived in Manchester for five years and found the Scots were far more welcoming' (PK4-A); 'Scottish people are very sweet and you can become good friends. In England you say hello and they ignore you. I know the difference—I lived in England for three and a half years . . . my husband would go to work and I would sit in the garden. No one would talk to me and I was lonely.' (PK5-E)

Pakistanis—and only Pakistanis—say Scotland is better than the rest of Britain because it does *not* have high numbers, or high concentrations, of ethnic minorities like themselves:

'what I find frightening is cities like Leicester or Bradford with large populations of Asians—they are not willing to mix with whites and I think that is quite frightening. In Scotland, we don't have that many Asians so they are willing to make an effort to know other communities' (PK5-F); 'Scotland is one of the nicest parts of Britain to live in' (PK1-C) . . . 'definitely' (PK1-B, all agree) . . . 'a nice balance of different cultures—some parts of England tend to be populated with different minorities . . . Brixton in London is full of Blacks . . . I have nothing against blacks [but] Scotland has a general balance all over, especially where I stay—one minority does not overpopulate it in anyway' (PK1-C) . . . 'a good point . . . we don't have ghettos as such in Scotland, not like they have in England' (PK1-D) . . . 'one particular group can cause trouble in certain areas in England, while having a mix of people can tend to neutralise that.' (PK1-C)

2.4 Crossing the Border

Towards the end of the focus group discussions we asked participants whether England 'felt different' from Scotland, if and when they crossed the border to visit. When they went south and crossed the border, English immigrants were automatically transformed from a minority into a part of the majority; but ethnic Pakistanis remained a minority, and now found themselves in alien surroundings—irrespective of whether these were white or Asian areas of England.

The greater concentration of visible ethnic minorities in England has only a slight impact on English immigrants' perceptions of life but it affects Scottish Pakistanis' perceptions rather more—because they are more likely to visit these areas of high ethnic-minority concentration rather than just talk about them. And Scottish Pakistanis express their alienation and discomfort with these high concentrations of ethnic minorities in England. Sometimes the ethnic minority is not Asian:

'South London ... black people everywhere ... a culture shock.' (PK6-E); 'Scotland is evenly mixed and that is not a bad thing ... I was in Birmingham two weeks ago and the number of African guys was unbelievable. I am not a racist person but phew I wanted to get out! [jokingly].' (PK6-C)

But even a concentration of Pakistanis, made Scottish Pakistanis uncomfortable:

'when I go to England it feels like I am in Pakistan. Everyone speaks in his or her own language and they shout to each other across the street.' (PK1-F); 'a culture shock when you go to England. Everywhere you go it is mostly Asians. The Asians there have not even heard of Glasgow. They think you are on a different planet.' (PK1-G); 'when you visit England ... it is totally like being in Pakistan and India ... everyone is speaking their own language ... crowded ... the atmosphere is similar to Pakistan. You could feel at home, but not completely. ... My mother would find it comfortable—but I am more comfortable in the mixed culture in Scotland.' (PK6-G)

The second way in which the atmosphere in England seemed different concerned the friendliness of the people. Some English immigrants feel the Scots (and Welsh) are less friendly:

'in Lancashire it was standard joke to have a go at people from Yorkshire because of the wars of the Roses, but it was all in good humour ... never nasty [unlike here] (E6-G); 'The Welsh feel very strongly about incomers ... English people buying holiday homes in Wales and the Welsh people burning them down. There was a touch of that attitude in Scotland not so long ago ... trying to keep the English out' (E6-D) ... 'Settler Watch.' (E6-G)

But, echoing their comments about what was 'best and worst' about Scotland, Scottish Pakistanis found England is a less helpful, friendly place:

'I will give you an example of the different attitudes in Scotland and England ... my car broke down [in England] ... I asked a policeman where the nearest garage was.

He coldly said he did not know—[and it] was [just] around the corner.' (PK4-C); 'if you had asked a Scottish person, he would have said come on and I will show you the way, that is the difference.' (PK4-E, responding to PK4-C)

'Scottish people are helpful ... I was trying to find a place. I asked a young man about the directions, I was in the car and he was on foot. He said follow me and he was practically taking me there he was so helpful [she laughs].' (PK5-A) ... 'You would not get that kind of help in England.' (PK5-F, responding to PK5-A)

'If you ask someone the direction in England they completely refuse.' (PK3-C); 'if you are lost and you ask an English person for directions, they will always lie to you.' (PK2-A, others laugh)

On visits to England they had found people cold and reserved:

'English people are not open with their feelings. If you are standing at a bus stop in Glasgow the lady standing next to you will start telling you her whole life story. If you are in England sitting on the train ... they don't look you in the eye.' (PK5-F)

'Scottish people try to show their hospitality. I don't know why English people behave in that [inhospitable] manner.' (PK5-G); 'they don't have the time.' (PK5-B); 'probably scared in case they say the wrong thing.' (PK5-F)

And people in England react to Scottish Pakistanis as Scots—more than as Asians:

'other Asians living in England only notice you are different because of your accent.' (PK6-E); 'The English listen to your accent and know you're Scottish.' (PK2-A); 'the English do treat you funny when they hear your accent.' (PK2-B); 'they do not even like Scottish pound notes ... I have had problems' (PK3-E); 'Even the post office in England dislikes Scottish notes.' (PK3-B); 'when I gave them Scottish notes they were hesitating ... only treating us in that way because we were Scottish *not because we were Pakistani*.' (PK2-B); 'It is because they hear our Scottish accents that they act strange *not because we are Asians*.' (PK2-C); 'The English attitude is not just bad towards Asian people but also bad towards the Scots. They think they are superior because they ruled over us. They think the Scots are a lower class.' (PK4-C); 'English people ruled all over the world and think they're special. They think we are a lower class ... I have had bad experiences in England.' (PK5-A)

Even without adding Scottish nationalist overtones, Pakistanis accused English people of being simply unfriendly, prejudiced, racist:

'I am a pure Muslim ... born in Lahore ... I like Scotland better than England. I don't like English people, I just don't get on with them.' (PK3-C); 'Scottish people are friendlier ... more welcoming.' (PK1-E); 'in Leicester all my friends were Irish, Jamaican and Pakistani, there were no English. I found that strange.' (PK5-G)

2.5 Conclusion: The Wrong Stereotypes

Like majority Scots: both minorities cite government and institutions as the best thing about Britain but despite devolution and the new Parliament they cite the land and the people as the best thing about Scotland. They differ in detail and emphasis however. The one minority puts more emphasis on racism and multiculturalism, the other on British institutions of freedom, the friendliness of majority Scots, the relatively low numbers of ethnic minorities in Scotland, and the iniquities of benefit scroungers.

These sound like very conventional stereotypes—except that it is the *English immigrants* that complain most about Scottish bigotry and racism and praise Britain for its 'multiculturalism' (defined however to comprise the historic national cultures of the British Isles rather than Asia). And it is the *ethnic Pakistanis* who praise institutions of freedom most strongly; who praise the friendliness of the people most strongly (despite their later tales of greater harassment than the English minority have to endure); and who take a particularly positive view about Scotland's low levels of ethnic minorities and feel alienated by high concentrations of minorities in England. The stereotypes—as stereotypes—are the wrong way round!

3

Islamophobia—In England and Scotland

Across Europe, Muslim minorities are under threat of collateral damage from the 'War on Terror'. Within Scotland, the long debate over devolution, rising nationalism, and the possibility that Scottish nationalism might develop an 'ethnic' as well as a 'civic' dimension—all pose a potentially additional challenge to them. Parochial nationalism goes naturally with racist and ethnic phobias. There is an inescapable tension between nationalism and multiculturalism and a historic tendency for them to prove incompatible. The genuinely inclusive nationalism of the Scottish political elite may not apply down 'at street level'.

'Multicultural nationalism' is a natural oxymoron. If it works, it works despite its internal contradictions, not because it has any internal coherence. But like car engines, so frequently described as a 'triumph of development over design', multicultural nationalism may indeed work remarkably well in practice. We find that Islamophobia is significantly lower in Scotland than in England—despite the growth of Scottish national identity and the advent of a separate Scottish Parliament. And though Islamophobia is clearly tied to English nationalism within England, it is almost uncorrelated with Scottish nationalism within Scotland. This may imply, as Heath and Smith (2005) suggest, that English nationalism is more 'ethnic' while Scottish nationalism is more 'civic' and 'benign'.

Even in Scotland our findings show that street-level nationalists are not in fact particularly pro-Muslim. But a multiculturalist elite may have exerted sufficient influence on the street to at least control and moderate the level of street-level antipathy between Muslims and local nationalists that exists within England. Alternatively however, the tendency of Scots to define themselves negatively as 'not-English' may simply provide some shelter for other 'non-English' groups within Scotland (a theme we explore in Chapter 4). And Scottish nationalism may indirectly be part of the problem for Muslims in England. Kumar (2003) argues that Scottish nationalism has stimulated the growth of English nationalism, while Heath and Smith (2005: 151; see also Curtice and Heath 2000) argue that this growing English nationalism has 'parallels with the far right [such as] the French Front National'.

3.1 The 'Death of Multiculturalism' and the Growth of Islamophobia

British multiculturalist ideology is usually traced back to 29 May 1966 (Joppke 1999: 225) when the then Home Secretary Roy Jenkins distinguished sharply between integration and assimilation. Jenkins argued in favour of 'integration' but insisted that should not mean 'the loss, by immigrants of their own national characteristics and culture'. He defined integration 'not as a flattening process of assimilation but as equal opportunity ... cultural diversity ... mutual tolerance' (Banton 1985: 71).

That vision, or sometimes conveniently distorted misrepresentations of it, is now under attack from several different perspectives. 'The death of multiculturalism' has been declared (Kundnani 2002: 67). Well before 9/11, theorists like Greenfeld (2000: 28–9; see also Barry 2001) argued that 'plainly put, cultural validation and empowerment of ethnic identity and ethnic diversity endanger liberal democracy'. In Britain, the Chair of the CRE (Commission for Racial Equality), Trevor Phillips, opened a CRE-sponsored debate (CRE *Connections*, Winter 2004/5) by challenging what he saw as 'outdated concepts of multiculturalism—the ideology of difference—as opposed to the fact of diversity' arguing, like Jenkins a generation earlier, for 'an integrated society where we are all equal, but free to be different'. Confusingly, that phrase suggests the 'death of multiculturalism' is remarkably like the 'birth of multiculturalism' as defined by Jenkins.

Recurring questions thrown up in this CRE debate concern 'separatist multiculturalism' and 'an imposed uniform [British] identity'. It was 'a false debate' since advocates of multiculturalism 'such as Parekh, Taylor, Young and Kymlicka do not advocate separatism' (Modood 2004). But that did not stop the then Home Secretary David Blunkett attacking the 'over-emphasis on cultural difference and moral relativism' (*The Guardian*, 14 December 2001) that had allegedly characterized British multiculturalism since Jenkins. 'From the state's point of view, the multiculturalist settlement, which has dominated race relations thinking in Britain for two decades, is no longer working ... the old multiculturalist formula of *celebrating difference* ... [is] to be replaced [by a] new strategy of *community cohesion* [our emphasis]' (Kundnani 2002: 67–8). Ethnic minorities were themselves allegedly disillusioned: 'those who were born and grew up here wanted to remake society, not just be tolerated by it ... multiculturalism became an ideology of conservatism'; the old order worked through community leaders, 'ethnic fiefdoms ... a [classic] colonial arrangement' (Kundnani 2002: 68–9; see also Cantle 2001 for the Home Office report: *Community Cohesion*).

'Community cohesion [requires] a set of core values ... to put limits on multiculturalism ... greater acceptance of the principal national institutions ... an oath of allegiance to the British state ... by the logic of the multiculturalist consensus, faith schools were to be encouraged ... from the new perspective of community cohesion, Muslim schools are dangerous breeding grounds for separatism' (Kundnani 2002: 70–1). How oddly that reads in contemporary Scotland where allegiance to a British state would be widely contested if ever made explicit, where the Union Jack is for many a sectarian symbol, and where a very extensive system of state-funded minority-faith schools has been in place since 1918 and is widely regarded as politically untouchable!

The 9/11 attack brought the final 'end of multiculturalism ... the security state demands ... cultural homogenization and forced assimilation ... eschews pluralism and fears diversity' (Fekete 2004: 21). 'Following Sept 11th, British Muslims have been criminalized further, with racial profiling in policing becoming acceptable' (Kundnani 2002: 72). The 2004 Runnymede-backed *Commission On British Muslims* (Richardson 2004) found Islamophobia had grown in scope and intensity even since Runnymede's 1997 report *Islamophobia*. There had been a 302 per cent increase in the numbers of Asians stopped by the police under 'stop and search' powers in 2002–3. The numbers of British Muslims in prison had increased by 834 per cent between 1991 and 2003. Muslims now comprised 9 per cent of those in prison though only 3 per cent of the general population. Fekete (2004) argued: '[post-9/11] counter-terrorist measures are casting Muslims, whether settled or immigrant, as the enemy within' (p. 1); and that 'the intelligence services have moved on to profile Muslim communities wholesale' (p. 9) using 'that notorious catch-all of "passive" support for [terrorism]' (p. 8) and 'internment-without-trial for foreign nationals only' (p. 6). Indeed the 'current political agenda [aims] to create a culture of suspicion against Muslims' (Fekete 2004: 14).

Growing numbers of asylum seekers, often Muslims, fuelled public concern. It was no longer quite so 'difficult to argue' that popular racism was only 'a latent issue waiting to be tapped by a government passing some even more strict immigration controls' Favell (1998: 330); nor quite so easy to agree with Favell that the Conservative Party had 'spared no effort in portraying itself in politically correct terms on racial and ethnic issues' (see Favell in Chapter 1). British politicians of both major parties now play to public concerns.

Traditionally, most immigrants and asylum seekers stayed in the south of England. That changed after 1999. Immigration and asylum were matters reserved to Westminster, not devolved to the Scottish Parliament. And to ease the burden on support services in South East England, the 1999 UK *Immigration and Asylum Act* introduced a policy of UK-wide dispersal. In the event, Glasgow was the only Scottish local authority included in the scheme. But by 2001 it was by far the top location for dispersal in the whole of the UK, taking as many as Birmingham plus Manchester combined. Almost half came from Iraq, Iran, or Afghanistan and many were Muslims (Joint Council for the Welfare of Immigrants, accessible at www.jcwi.org.uk). Disused council properties in run-down areas were rapidly refurbished—and furnished—for the new arrivals, which caused local resentment. In August 2001, a Kurdish asylum seeker was murdered on the Sighthill estate in Glasgow (UNHCR at www.unhcr.org.uk). His death prompted widespread feelings of guilt and a coalition of asylum seekers and local people to articulate their common grievances. At the same time, the Dungavel detention centre located in central Scotland, but controlled exclusively by the UK Home Office in London, was used to hold asylum seekers and their children who had not yet been granted permission to stay. Despite Scottish protests, the UK Home Office insisted it would 'continue to detain the children of asylum-seekers at Dungavel' (*The Herald*, 6 September 2004: 6).

Both the new dispersal policy and Dungavel underlined the impotence of the new Scottish Parliament and irritated nationalists and even many devolutionists. Since so many of the asylum seekers were Muslims, they also irritated Muslims. So asylum issues, like the invasion of Iraq, which was so strongly opposed by the SNP, brought nationalists as well as devolutionists together with ethnic minorities. Against the tenor of debate in England, the Labour 'First Minister' in the Scottish Parliament declared that Scotland needed *more* immigrants, *more* asylum seekers and *more* ethnic minorities (McConnell 2003). The SNP leader, John Swinney, accused Labour of 'racism' in its ill-treatment of Muslim asylum seekers

(*The Herald*, 8 September 2003), repeatedly branding their treatment as a '*national* shame' (*The Herald*, 12 September 2003) or a '*national* disgrace' (*The Herald*, 10 October 2003, our emphasis)—despite the fact that a large majority of ordinary Scots favoured detaining these asylum-seekers (SSAS 2003). For high-minded liberal and inclusive elites, devolution or even independence meant responsibility rather than freedom; and anti-minority phobias were not just a threat to minorities but an affront to their perhaps overromanticized image of a virtuous Scotland, which they hoped would be at least morally if not economically superior to England.

In this context, Swinney found it easy to incorporate anti-racism into his nationalism. More surprisingly perhaps, ethnic minorities found it remarkably easy to incorporate Scottish nationalism into their anti-racism. Both elite nationalist politicians and ethnic minorities characterized racism as fundamentally anti-Scottish. Swinney's language found an echo in one of our Muslim focus groups when a participant declared that:

'ninety percent of the people here are nice but the other ten percent are racist—which is a *shame for the image of Scotland*' [our emphasis]. (PK3-D)

Although 9/11 and the rapid increase in Muslim asylum seekers did tend to increase Islamophobia in Scotland as in England, issues of asylum and ethnicity were not 'racialized' by political elites in Scotland as much as in England—and especially not by SNP leaders. The problems and ill-treatment of ethnic minorities, Muslims in particular, could be blamed by minorities on London and paradoxically, provide a basis for greater commitment to Scotland, and greater 'community cohesion' (within Scotland) rather than greater alienation.

On the other side, majority Scots could blame London simultaneously for the ill-treatment of asylum seekers in Dungavel, and for sending so many of them to Scotland; and then wrap these two less-than-consistent views together by blaming London for withholding power from the Scottish Parliament over what seemed to Scots very domestic affairs: prisons, health, schooling (of asylum seekers' children), and housing.

3.2 Measuring Street-Level Islamophobia

It would be misleading, even absurd, to include the views of the minorities themselves in any measure of anti-minority phobias. So it is wrong to measure Islamophobia using a representative sample of all residents. We have evidence that even non-Muslim minorities are significantly less

Islamophobic than average. By our calculations on BSAS/SSAS 2003 data, black and Asian minorities in England—by no means all of them Muslim—are 21 per cent less Islamophobic than the white majority. Even more strikingly, the white English immigrant minority in Scotland is 12 per cent less Islamophobic than majority Scots.

So we use a fairly tight definition of 'majorities' in England and Scotland. We define 'majority English' as:

- 'white', non-Muslim, living in England.

And we 'majority Scots' even more tightly as:

- 'white', non-Muslim, living in Scotland—but restricted to those born in Scotland and whose partners (if any) are also Scottish-born.

These are statistically adequate analytic definitions. They do not take account of statistically insignificant 'special cases'. And it is extremely important to emphasize that they are *not* ideological definitions: they are *not*, for example, definitions of 'real Scots' or 'true Scots'. They are simply required to avoid the absurd underestimates that result from basing measures of anti-minority phobias on the views, even in part, of the minorities themselves.

3.2.1 Comparable Indicators

We have five strictly comparable indicators of Islamophobia in England and Scotland that cite Muslims explicitly. Since the wording of these questions is critical, we reproduce it in detail. We began:

People from lots of different backgrounds live in Britain. I would now like to ask you some questions about one of these groups—Muslims. By Muslims I mean people who follow the Islamic faith.

Then we asked respondents to place themselves on various 5-or 7-point scales:

M1 (Economic resentment): Muslims who come to live in Britain/Scotland (1) *take jobs, housing and healthcare* from other people in Britain/Scotland or (7) *contribute a lot* in terms of hard work and much needed skills. (7-point numerical scale)

M2 (Nationalist distrust): Muslims living in Britain/Scotland (1) are *really committed* to Britain/Scotland or (7) *could never be really committed* to Britain/Scotland. (7-point numerical scale)

M3 (Nationalist distrust): How much do you agree or disagree: British Muslims/ Muslims in Scotland are *more loyal to other Muslims* around the world than they are to other people in this country. (5-point scale from Agree strongly to Disagree strongly)

M4 (Fears for national identity): How much do you agree or disagree: England/ Scotland would begin to *lose its identity* if more Muslims came to live in England/Scotland. (5-point scale from Agree strongly to Disagree strongly)

M5 (Social exclusion): How would you feel if a close relative of yours married or formed a long-term *relationship with a Muslim*? (5-point scale from Very happy to Very unhappy)

Following familiar English usage, some of these questions use the term 'Britain' instead of 'England' in England; in Scotland they use the term 'Scotland' without exception.

Islamophobia is indicated by feeling on balance that Muslims: 'take jobs, housing and health care from other people'; 'could never be really committed to Britain/Scotland'; 'are more loyal to other Muslims around the world' than they are to 'this country'; that 'England/Scotland would begin to lose its identity' if more Muslims came; and that they would 'feel unhappy if a close relative married or formed a long-term relationship with a Muslim'.

Together, these five questions provide a comparative index of Islamophobia in England and Scotland—and with minor modifications they can provide a comparative index of Scottish Anglophobia which we use in Chapter 4. But in addition, we have one indicator that applies specifically to Muslims after 9/11 and is not generalizable to Anglophobia. So we discuss it separately and exclude it from our overall index of Islamophobia. It is:

M6 (Condemnation of terrorism): How much do you agree or disagree: Muslims living in Britain *have done a great deal to condemn* Islamic terrorism (5-point scale from Agree strongly to Disagree strongly)

The Islamophobic side of the question in M6 is of course disagreement. Muslims argue:

'We have, I have . . . [but it is] just the excuse to attack Muslims. They only want [us] to condemn the terrorism which is committed by Muslims. . . . Osama Bin Laden and President Bush are working hand in hand to promote terrorism.' (IDI-6G)

We should not overstate the extent of Islamophobia in either country. Nonetheless (excluding DKs and those who give replied codes 'mixed/ neither'), around a third of majority Scots feel some economic resentment towards Muslims and express socially exclusive attitudes towards them; half feel Scotland would begin to lose its identity if more Muslims came to live in

Scotland; half doubt Muslims' commitment to Scotland; and four-fifths feel Muslims' first loyalty lies outside Scotland. But on every indicator, the majority English are more Islamophobic than majority Scots. The difference is least on the two indicators of nationalist distrust and also on condemnation of terror. It is much greater on economic resentment, on fears for their country's national identity, and above all on social exclusion. Scots seem to be much more confident—and therefore more relaxed—about their country retaining its distinctive national identity. And perhaps their attitude towards social exclusion indicates that they are more confident and relaxed about retaining more personal and family identities also.

Judged by whether they would be unhappy (rather than happy) if a close relative 'married or formed a long term relationship' with a Muslim, only a third of Scots but half the English feel socially exclusive. And any suspicion that answers to this question is affected by political correctness cannot explain why the responses are so very different in Scotland and England. Indeed the intensity of happiness and unhappiness varies between Scotland and England: 26 per cent of majority Scots but only half as many majority English go far beyond political correctness to claim they would actually be '*very* happy' to have a Muslim relative. Conversely, twice as many in England as in Scotland say they would be '*very* unhappy'.

Excluding those with no opinion or mixed opinions, an average of 63 per cent of the majority in England agree with M1-5. By contrast only an average of 49 per cent of majority Scots agree with M1-5. So, on strictly comparable indicators, Islamophobia in England runs 14 per cent ahead of Islamophobia in Scotland (Table 3.1).

Table 3.1. Comparative phobias

	Majority Islamophobia in Scotland (%)	Majority Islamophobia in England (%)
Take jobs	30	46
Not really committed to Scotland [Britain]	53	62
More loyal to own	79	86
Scotland [England] lose identity if more came	52	69
Unhappy for relative to marry	32	52
Average: strictly comparable indicators	49	63
Muslims *not* done a great deal to condemn terror	55	63

Note: [ ] indicates wording in England.
DK's and undecided excluded from calculation of percentages.
Source: SSAS/BSAS 2003.

The usual explanation of racist or ethnic phobias is simply 'small-mindedness': parochialism rather than cosmopolitanism brought on by living a physically, intellectually, or emotionally restricted, constricted, and frustrating life. Social factors, such as low education, may increase phobias against the 'other', irrespective of the particular 'other' in question. Political and cultural factors such as nationalism or religion, may have a more targeted impact however, since they themselves may define a particular 'other'.

3.3 Social Foundations of Islamophobia

Lack of education, especially lack of *higher* education, is a key variable underlying parochialism. Generation—rather than age itself—could also be significant since the development of mass media and cheap mass transport have globalized the mental world of the average person to an unprecedented degree. Indeed, globalization may have eroded critically relevant information differences between the educated and uneducated even as (higher) education itself has become more widespread. Cosmopolitan awareness can no longer be equated with formal education, which can be narrow and technical. By contrast globalization may intensify class divisions: the working class, operating in a relatively local employment market and engaged in relatively routine activities are not only likely to have restricted parochial outlooks but are more exposed to hard economic competition from immigrants and incomers—whether these come from other cultures or not.

3.3.1 *Age and Generation*

Age and generation have a significant impact on Islamophobia in both England and Scotland. Our composite measure of Islamophobia varies by 20 per cent across the age cohorts (from aged under 35 to 65 and over) on both sides of the border. By margins of 29 per cent in England and 21 per cent in Scotland, the old are more apprehensive than the young that Britain (or Scotland) would begin to lose its identity if there were an influx of Muslims. By margins of 30 per cent in England and 24 per cent in Scotland, the old are more likely to feel that to be 'truly English/Scottish' a person must be White. By smaller margins the old are more likely to feel that to be 'truly *British*' a person must be White. But age has by far its greatest impact on social inclusion: by margins of 55 per cent in England

and 48 per cent in Scotland, the old are more unhappy than the young at the thought of having a Muslim relative. There is some indication of a 'step effect' at around age 55—a generational shift rather than a purely progressive age effect.

3.3.2 *Education*

Comparing university graduates with those who have no educational qualifications education seems to have more impact than almost anything else. By margins of 49 per cent in England and 34 per cent in Scotland those without qualifications are more Islamophobic than graduates. The pattern is very consistent though not quite monotonic: those with 'higher education below degree level' are slightly more Islamophobic than those with the highest level of school qualifications (Table 3.2).

Only newspaper choice (closely linked in Britain to education) has a greater apparent impact on Islamophobia, and there the causal direction is ambiguous. English readers of the high-brow and left-leaning *The Guardian* or *The Independent* score only 13 per cent on Islamophobia, compared to readers of *The Sun* who score 80 per cent. That puts *The Sun* readers on a par with those without any educational qualifications. But it has an even more striking effect at the other end of the scale: it rates *The Guardian* or *The Independent* readers only half as Islamophobic as university graduates. *The Guardian* and *The Independent* readers are typically graduates from particular academic faculties however. And we know that British graduates in the social sciences are generally far more liberal and less parochial than

Table 3.2. Impact of education

	Degree (%)	Hi ed < deg (%)	A level equiv (%)	O level equiv (%)	CSE equiv (%)	None (%)
Take jobs	7 [17]	24 [35]	22 [44]	43 [55]	37 [61]	39 [56]
Not really committed	27 [28]	49 [55]	43 [48]	55 [70]	65 [75]	67 [78]
More loyal to own	58 [56]	80 [88]	75 [82]	82 [91]	86 [94]	83 [92]
Lose identity if more came	32 [30]	44 [62]	37 [49]	61 [74]	61 [86]	67 [90]
Unhappy marry	17 [22]	24 [46]	11 [31]	31 [49]	38 [68]	56 [83]
Islamophobia: average M1-5	*28 [31]*	*44 [57]*	*38 [51]*	*54 [68]*	*57 [77]*	*62 [80]*
Muslims not done a great deal to condemn terror	36 [41]	50 [63]	53 [64]	70 [67]	59 [73]	63 [67]

Notes: % outside [ ] are for Scotland; % inside [ ] are for England.
DK's and undecided excluded from calculation of percentages.
Source: SSAS/BSAS 2003.

58

business, engineering, or medical graduates (Miller, Timpson, and Lessnoff 1996: 255–7). *What* you learn matters as well as *how much* you learn.

3.3.3 *Contacts and Knowledge*

Compared to those who say they know at least 'quite a lot' about Muslims, those who say they 'know nothing at all' are around 25 per cent more Islamophobic. These 'know nothings' are also around 16 per cent more likely to criticize Muslims for not sufficiently condemning terrorism, and around 20 per cent more likely to cite being 'white' as a necessary condition for being 'truly' English or Scottish.

3.4 Cultural and Political Foundations of Islamophobia

The cultural and political foundations of Islamophobia are more central to the question of multicultural nationalism. Education may be the best predictor of Islamophobia but it is nonetheless irrelevant to our central question about the uneasy relationship between nationalism and multiculturalism. Religion is the only social factor with nationalist overtones and even religion is not so directly relevant as partisanship or national identity.

Both Scotland and England have 'National' Churches that are (or were) 'Established' by law—the (Presbyterian) Church of Scotland and the (Episcopalian) Church of England. Their connection with the state is now relatively weak and indeed obscure and ambiguous.[1] But to some of their adherents at least, the national churches remain an expression of the nation.

3.4.1 *Religion*

In both Scotland and England the majority divide into only three large religious groups: the National Church, Catholics, and, most numerous of

---

[1] The Church of England remains a formally 'Established' Church. It is in communion with the Scottish Episcopal Church—though that was disestablished in 1689, and for some time thereafter a persecuted minority. It remains very different from the Church of England. The Church of Scotland describes itself thus: 'independent in spiritual matters, but recognised in law as the national church ... neither established in the sense of the Church of England nor unestablished ... [which] implies responsibility rather than privilege' (Church of Scotland Evidence to the Evangelical Alliance *Faith and Nation Commission of Inquiry 2000* accessible at the Evangelical Alliance website www.eauk.org). The Queen or her High Commissioner attends the annual General Assembly of the Church of Scotland. Princess Anne remarried in the Church of Scotland when remarriage in the Church of England would not have been possible for her.

all, the irreligious. Overall, there is little consistent difference between the Islamophobia of Catholics and adherents of the National Churches—though both are somewhat more Islamophobic than the irreligious (around 13 per cent in Scotland, though only 7 per cent in England). Church of Scotland adherents are 29 per cent more likely than the irreligious to be unhappy at acquiring a Muslim relative, and 23 per cent more concerned about their country's identity.

3.4.2 *Partisanship*

We use voting at the 2001 British General Election as an indicator of political partisanship. Within each country, Islamophobia is lowest amongst Liberal-Democrats and highest amongst Conservatives—though non-voters come a close second. Labour voters fall in the middle, though nearer to the Conservatives than the Liberal-Democrats. Most significantly however, although Islamophobia amongst SNP voters is far higher than amongst SNP leaders (at least as far as we can judge from SNP leaders' public statements) it is on a par with Islamophobia amongst Scottish Labour voters.

Taking the seven partisan voter-groups separately: the level of Islamophobia is lowest of all amongst Scottish Liberal-Democrats and highest of all amongst English Conservatives (they differ by 34 per cent). And between these extremes, SNP voters are closer to the Scottish Liberal-Democrats than to the English Conservatives. Conservatives, especially in England, are also the most likely to cite race as a necessary condition for being truly English/Scottish or British—well over twice as likely as Liberal-Democrats. So judged by their levels of Islamophobia, it is not SNP voters but English Conservatives that best merit the description: 'narrow, parochial nationalists' (Table 3.3).

3.4.3 *Sub-State National Identities*

One measure of sub-state national identity is provided by answers to the 'Moreno' question:

Which, if any, of the following best describes how you see yourself?

1. English/Scottish, not British
2. More English/Scottish than British
3. Equally English/Scottish and British
4. More British than English/Scottish
5. British, not English/Scottish

Table 3.3. Impact of partisanship (Vote in 2001 General Election)

	CON (%)	LAB (%)	LibD (%)	SNP (%)	DNV (%)
Take jobs	24 [50]	29 [46]	11 [23]	29	39 [53]
Not really committed	55 [67]	53 [62]	23 [41]	46	60 [64]
More loyal to own	85 [86]	78 [88]	72 [61]	76	80 [89]
Lose identity if more came	62 [79]	50 [68]	43 [48]	55	52 [68]
Unhappy marry	47 [61]	32 [49]	24 [37]	36	25 [52]
Islamophobia: average M1-5	*55 [69]*	*48 [63]*	*35 [42]*	*48*	*51 [65]*
Muslims not done a great deal to condemn terror	60 [67]	47 [65]	45 [41]	61	64 [65]

Notes: % outside [ ] are for Scotland; % inside [ ] are for England.
DK's and undecided excluded from calculation of percentages.
Source: SSAS/BSAS 2003.

In the 1980s this scale was originally conceived as a 5-point symmetric scale (Moreno 1986; 1988). But by 2003 only a quarter of *majority* English and less than 3 per cent of *majority* Scots identified more with Britain than with England/Scotland. Nearly all majority Scots along with most majority English are spread across an effectively 3-point scale running from 'exclusively' English/Scottish through to 'equally British and English/Scottish'—that is, from 'exclusive' to 'dual' identities (Table 3.4) (Identification 'more with Britain' is much more popular amongst many minorities—including English immigrants in Scotland as well as blacks and Asians in England, though *not* Asians in Scotland: see Chapter 8.).

Table 3.4. Impact of sub-state national identity

	Excl Brit (%)	More Brit (%)	Equally E/S & Brit (%)	More Engl/Scot (%)	Excl Engl/Scot (%)
Muslims:					
Take jobs	na [38]	na [46]	26 [43]	25 [39]	40 [66]
Not really committed to S [to B]	na [48]	na [73]	54 [55]	51 [58]	56 [77]
More loyal to own	na [70]	na [90]	79 [84]	74 [87]	84 [89]
S [B] lose identity if more came	na [56]	na [72]	53 [63]	51 [68]	56 [89]
Unhappy marry	na [38]	na [46]	38 [47]	28 [51]	36 [67]
Average	*na [50]*	*na [65]*	*50 [58]*	*46 [61]*	*54 [78]*
Muslims not done a great deal to condemn terror	na [52]	na [69]	53 [58]	49 [62]	65 [72]

Notes: % outside [ ] are for Scotland; % inside [ ] are for England.
DK's and undecided excluded from calculation of percentages.
Source: SSAS/BSAS 2003.

Compared to fully dual identifiers, the exclusively English are 20 per cent more Islamophobic, but the exclusively Scottish only a mere 4 per cent more Islamophobic. Furthermore, although the spread is uneven, the majority English (unlike majority Scots) do spread themselves all the way across the full 5-point scale. So arguably the proper measure of the impact of sub-state nationalism on Islamophobia in England is 28 per cent rather than 20 per cent. But by any measure, sub-state nationalism clearly has a significant impact on Islamophobia in England—yet not in Scotland.

The contrast between the impact of sub-state nationalism in England and Scotland is perhaps even greater when we assess its impact on citing race as a necessary condition for being truly English/Scottish or British. Compared to those who identify equally with Britain and England/Scotland, the exclusively English are 27–30 per cent more likely to cite race (being 'white rather than black or Asian') as a necessary condition for being 'truly British' or 'truly English'. Yet in Scotland the exclusively Scottish are scarcely any more likely (only between 2 and 4 per cent) than those who identify equally with Britain and Scotland to cite race as a necessary condition for being 'truly British' or 'truly Scottish'.

So, exclusively Scottish identifiers, like SNP voters (and they are not the same people), are not particularly warm towards Muslims, not particularly multicultural, not particularly keen to 'celebrate diversity', not so ethnically or culturally inclusive as the SNP leadership. But unlike exclusively English identifiers, exclusively Scottish identifiers do not display high levels of Islamophobia.

3.5 A Multivariate Comparison of Islamophobia in Scotland and England

We can usefully summarize and confirm our findings with a multivariate analysis. For that we have constructed 5-point scales for each of the elements of our index of Islamophobia. Some were already 5-point agree/disagree scales. Others were 7-point semantic-differential scales running for example from 'Muslims are really committed to Scotland' to 'Muslims could never be really committed to Scotland' with the intermediate points unlabelled. In these cases we merged the most extreme points with the adjacent categories to convert them into 5-point scales. Numerical values running from −2 to +2 were assigned to each scale, with

+2 being the most phobic. Those with mixed opinions, or no opinion were placed at 0, the centre point of the scale, both to avoid excluding respondents from the analysis and in order to permit averaging (at the individual level). By averaging across the five questions we get composite Islamophobic and Anglophobic scores for each respondent.

We use regression to see which of the influences we have considered actually explain phobias best, and which are redundant once more powerful explanations are taken into account. To do this we predict levels of Islamophobia from the following:

1. *age* both as a 7-point scale from young to old; and as a dichotomous *generation* marker, contrasting those above and below age 55;

2. *education* as a 3-point scale distinguishing university-level education, lower school qualifications (or none), and those with higher school qualifications or higher education below university degree level;

3. *minority contact* measured as a 4-point scale of knowledge about Muslims;

4. *religion* measured by three separate indicators of whether the respondent is or is not an adherent of the National Church, Catholic, or irreligious;

5. *national identity* measured by the 5-point Moreno scale that runs from exclusively English/Scottish to exclusively British; and

6. *political nationalism* measured by five separate indicators of whether or not the respondent voted Conservative, Labour, Liberal-Democrat, or SNP, or abstained at the 2001 British General Election (Table 3.5).

Table 3.5. A multivariate analysis of Islamophobia in Scotland and England

	Islamophobia in Scotland	Islamophobia in England
RSQ (× 100) =	14	21
	Beta (× 100)	Beta (× 100)
Higher education	−28	−38
Stronger or exclusively Scottish/English (rather than British) identity	*	16
Religious	14	*
Knows little or nothing about Muslims	14	*
LibDem voter	*	−12

* blank entries, and all predictor variables missing from this table indicate that the beta coefficient was less than 0.10; so the independent and additional impact of such variables is small (if any at all) and relatively unimportant; all beta coefficients displayed in the table are not only large enough to be politically significant, they are also statistically significant at better than the 1 per cent error level.

The multiple regressions confirm that the most important influence on Islamophobia is education. But even taking education into account some other factors (though not, e.g. age) have their own independent and additional impact. After taking account of education: Islamophobia is greater in Scotland amongst those who know little or nothing about Islam and higher amongst those who are religious. But most politically significant is the fact that English nationalism exerts a substantial impact, while Scottish nationalism does not.

3.6 Conclusion: Islamophobia and Sub-State Nationalisms

Perceptions of conflict between Muslims and non-Muslims are lower in Scotland than England: only 42 per cent of majority Scots think Muslim/non-Muslim conflict is at least 'fairly serious' in Scotland; but 61 per cent of the majority English think Muslim/non-Muslim conflict is at least 'fairly serious' in England (see Chapter 6 for the minorities' perceptions of ethnic conflicts). It does not take two to make a conflict however: one is enough. Perhaps conflict with Muslims is greater in England because Muslims themselves are different there. The numbers are certainly different. There are more Muslims in England—though still only 3 per cent. Or perhaps Muslims in England are socially different. Scottish elites, with some poetic exaggeration, highlighted the social differences between Asians in Scotland and England:

'In Scotland [Muslims] have more people from the business community... there is a very high level of unemployment among youths in Birmingham and Oldham and Burnley.' (IDI-6G); 'In England 70–80% of the [Muslim] community are unskilled labour... in Scotland 70–80% are self employed.' (IDI-4)

One participant in a Muslim focus group claimed, more brutally, that:

'Asian people in Scotland are more productive than Asian people living in England. You get a lot of Asians in England that are uneducated, unemployed and involved in crime. In Scotland, Asian people make something of themselves. In England maybe not ... Asians there are the scum of the earth ... nothing to do but watch television all day, so they are out causing riots.' (PK6-E)

Or perhaps Muslims in England just lead more segregated lives.

'In Oldham ... one side of the town is totally White while the other side is totally Asian.' (PK6-E); 'It is better to live in a mixed area than to be segregated' (PK6-G). 'Bradford is raw... ghettos are always problematic.' (IDI-9)

But another possibility is that conflict is greater in England because the majority English are different from majority Scots:

'English people are totally different ... far more racist ... the reason being that Scots considered the minority better and were kind of more akin to them, being also under the thumb of the English.' (IDI-4)

By a whole range of measures, we have found that majority Scots are less Islamophobic than the majority English. Unlike elite-level nationalists, street-level nationalists in Scotland are not particularly inclusive or multiculturalist compared to other majority Scots. But even street-level Scottish nationalists are less Islamophobic than the majority English taken as-a-whole—and far, far less than street-level nationalists in England. On our composite measure of Islamophobia, exclusively Scottish identifiers score 54 per cent and exclusively English identifiers 78 per cent. Islamophobia is not only significantly greater in England than Scotland, it is also much more closely tied to English nationalism within England than Scottish nationalism within Scotland—with which it hardly correlates at all.

We have focused on the impact of nationalism not because it is so great but because, especially in Scotland, it is so very weak. Like Sherlock Holmes, in 'Silver Blaze' (*Strand* magazine, December 1892) we have focused on the 'curious' significance of 'the dog that did not bark'. The impacts of age, generation and education are large but not unexpected, while the impact of nationalism in Scotland is so unexpectedly small that it is, almost negligible. Whether this means that Scottish nationalism is entirely 'benign', however, we leave to Chapter 4.

4

The Auld Enemy

Our analysis of Islamophobia in Chapter 3 seems to confirm the complacent conclusion of many outside observers that Scotland in general, and Scottish nationalism in particular, are 'benign' and 'civic'—at least by comparison with England and English nationalism. But internal observers like Miles and Dunlop (1987) contest 'the claim that race relations is an English problem, absent north of the border'. These internal critics have focused on sectarianism and Anglophobia more than on Islamophobia and they paint an altogether darker picture of Scotland. Some of the political elites we interviewed agreed:

'it is just hidden . . . in Scotland . . . just there under the surface . . . the willingness to pretend these things don't happen here . . . [though] the racism that we get tends to be more sectarian than [anti-Asian] racism.' (IDI-27G)

'One of the things that drives me nuts about Scotland is [claims that] we don't have a problem here, we are not racist, we are very welcoming . . . racism isn't an issue here. . . . Racism, discrimination is endemic in Scotland . . . that doesn't mean that pride in Scotland creates racism, but equally the reverse is not true. The fact that people are proud Scots doesn't mean they are not racist.' (IDI-8G)

Perhaps even that is too complacent. We have shown that Scottish nationalism does not create or inflate Islamophobia. But there are other phobias that are more sensitive to Scottish nationalism.

Long before there were substantial numbers of Pakistani Muslims in Scotland there were large numbers of Irish Catholics. By the 1850s 'the Irish [immigrant Catholics] far outnumbered the indigenous [Catholics]' and they were at first despised and later feared (Gallagher 1987: 42–3). For a century after that, the debate about multiculturalism in Scotland focused on the Irish Catholic minority and the Protestant reaction against it, which reached its peak in the 1930s. But before the Catholic Irish there was England and the English. And as Protestant/Catholic sectarian divisions became less acute after the 1950s there still remained England and the English as Scotland's defining 'Other'. In addition, Scotland was not entirely immune to Britain-wide phobias about Europe and, especially after the new post-1999 dispersal policy, about asylum seekers.

So Scottish phobias include sectarianism, Anglophobia, Europhobia, and Asylophobia as well as Islamophobia.

4.1 Scottish Phobias: The Displacement Thesis

4.1.1 *Sectarianism*

Even though sectarianism and nationalism were once two sides of the same coin, critics of Scottish 'sectarianism' have painted a darker picture of Scotland than students of 'nationalism'—as some of their emotive titles suggest: *Glasgow: The Uneasy Peace—Religious Tension in Modern Scotland* (Gallagher 1987); *Out of the Ghetto? The Catholic Community in Modern Scotland* (Boyle and Lynch 1998); *The Old Firm: Sectarianism, Sport and Society in Scotland* (Murray 2000); *Scotland's Shame? Bigotry and Sectarianism in Scottish Society* (Devine 2000); and most recently, the Church of Scotland 'Church and Nation' Committee's 2002 report to its General Assembly: *The Demon in our Society: Sectarianism in Scotland*. It was the same Church and Nation committee that, in 1923, issued the equally strongly titled report: *The Menace of the Irish Race to our Scottish Nationality*. Perspectives had changed, the dramatic language had not.

Some of the elites we interviewed continue to claim that:

'sectarianism is the biggest problem we have got: what school did you go to? ... that is asked always and it is never a benign question.' (IDI-21G); 'Irish Catholics in this part of the world suffered pretty badly ... it was perfectly obvious that if you put what school you were at on job application forms, you were not going to get the jobs ... so I am not sure that Scotland is quite the friendly, welcoming place it's made out to be.' (IDI-26G)

But others argue:

'sectarianism ... [has] gradually diminished over the years ... it is more of a problem now in smaller communities ... that are still overwhelmingly Protestant or overwhelmingly Catholic.' (IDI-18)

And sectarianism has critically changed its nature. Through the interwar years, sectarianism was a national issue between ethnic Scots and an immigrant Irish Catholic community. But insofar as sectarianism remains an issue in post-devolution Scotland, it has become an internal issue between different groups of Scots rather than between Scots and non-Scottish 'others'. It is no longer a nationalist issue and thus unlikely to be exacerbated by devolution or by growing Scottish nationalism. Indeed for some elites we interviewed, their old Irish Republican sympathies have mutated into Scottish nationalism while remaining consistently anti-English: 'I come from an Irish Catholic background [with] a very anti-English feeling and so a lot of ... hatred [of the English] comes from there' (IDI-24G). With the notable exception of one SNP President who had to resign after opposing the 1982 Papal visit to Scotland (*The Herald*, 20 July 2005: 8), forward-looking Scottish nationalists have tried to distance themselves from backward-looking sectarian divisions. And though many majority Scots retain some identification with Catholic or Protestant religion, very few now regard religion as their primary identity. Sectarian identities remain but they have become very much secondary identities (Bond and Rosie 2002, 2004) and the intensity of sectarianism had declined (see Murray 2000: ch. 14; or Bruce et al. 2004).

In principle, sectarianism is balanced and symmetric, pitting Catholics against Protestants and vice versa. But Catholics remain a minority (albeit a more observant minority); and the Protestant majority is more prejudiced against Catholics than vice versa. Our survey shows for example, that very few majority Scots now admit that they would be 'unhappy' at the thought of a relative forming a relationship with someone from the other side of the sectarian divide—though four times as many would be unhappy about a relationship with a Catholic as with a Protestant. Protestants are not only more numerous, but also individually less happy at the prospect of what they term 'mixed' relationships.

4.1.2 *Anglophobia*

Critics that focus on Scottish Anglophobia paint a picture that is perhaps a little less dark. But Anglophobia, unlike sectarianism, clearly has a continuing relevance to Scottish identity and nationalism and that will be the main concern in this chapter.

SNP leaders are not Anglophobic. Quite the reverse. Alex Salmond, for example, regularly claims to be an 'anglophile'. To take just one of many easily accessible examples of his claim, he told the House of Commons:

'I have often pronounced myself one of the most Anglophile of all Scottish Members .... We present our case for Scotland in a positive way. We do not spend our time being antagonistic about other nations.' (*Hansard*, HC (series 5) vol. 299, col. 396, 30 July 1997)

But at street level, Kidd (2003*a*; see also Kidd 2003*b*) claims that 'antipathy towards the Auld Enemy is the one form of racism that still seems to be acceptable today in an otherwise politically correct Scotland'. There is 'generalised backcloth of anti-Englishness' (McIntosh, Smith, and Robertson 2004*b*: para. 3.3) linked to 'the rise of Scottish nationalism' (IDI-26G). It was sufficient to merit a 1999 debate in the new Scottish Parliament, following the SNP's call for 'urgent consideration of anti-English discrimination' (McIntosh, Smith, and Robertson 2004*b*: para. 3.2).

Because it is so acceptable, the press is uniquely uninhibited with regard to Anglophobia, especially in the context of sport. Bairner (1994) cites the mass-circulation *Sunday Mail*'s (21 June 1992) claim that 'every real, true Scot wants to see England defeated in every sport and [on] every occasion'. He argues that even 'the good behaviour of the Tartan Army [Scottish football fans] must be understood in the light of anti-English sentiment' (Bairner 1994: 23). It was all part of 'showing up the violent, ugly, bastard English' (*Scotland on Sunday*, 28 June 1992).

Political elites that we interviewed alleged that:

'An anglophobic tendency in Scots ... comes out all the time ... supporting Cameroon against England ... bizarre.' (IDI-27G); 'my wife who is from London ... felt like a fish out of water ... banter at work ... taking pleasure in English defeats ... all *at least of the surface*, jocular.' (IDI-21G); 'When England is playing, the amount of hatred ... ridiculous ... pathetic. ... Rangers and Celtic fans coming together to hate the English' (IDI-13); 'there are people .... I am related to some of them ... that support anybody who's playing England ... automatic hatred.' (IDI-24G)

Others have suggested that the extent and depth of Anglophobia have been exaggerated however, pointing to the 'failure of the overt anti-English organizations Settler Watch and Scottish Watch which emerged in the 1990s' (McIntosh, Smith, and Robertson 2004*a*: 44; see also Jedrej and Nuttall 1996)—despite the 'resentment' caused by the 'housing boom in England', which allowed English people to sell up and profit from a move to Scotland (IDI-26G). Arguably it was 'friendly rivalry':

'When Scotland play England, God help you if you are in a pub surrounded by Scots and you are supporting England ... [but it is] friendly rivalry ... not a huge problem.' (IDI-23G); '[though] rivalry ... sometimes taken to excess ... linked to a whole history of Scotland being a subordinate, dependent nation within ... an unequal relationship ... [causing] resentment which would be removed if Scotland had independence.' (IDI-18)

Despite finding that 'anti-Englishness did exist', Watson (2003: 143) warns against 'exaggerating anti-Englishness, often confused with anti-Englandness' since it was 'a less serious problem [than] black racism and sectarianism' (p. 139)—a view expressed also in our elite interviews:

'people from England don't live in communities where ... shops are targeted with graffiti or they are beaten up in the street .... They do not have political parties [like] the BNP... whose whole raison d'être is to get rid of the English.' (IDI-18)

McIntosh, Smith, and Robertson (2004*a*: 49), like Watson, draw a distinction between antipathy towards England or 'the English-in-general' and 'the English-as-individuals'. But they undermine its significance by describing it as 'a distinction commonly made in relation to black minority groups'. Their own title: 'We hate the English, except for you, cos you're our pal' is a familiar parody of racist attitudes towards blacks and Asians.

English immigrants in our focus groups reported that:

'Once they accept you [they] forget that you're English ... they will be slagging off the English and I can be sat there ... they've forgotten I'm there.' (E6-A, E6-F agrees) ... 'they will say: oh that so and so English. And you say: pardon. And they say: we don't mean you.' (E6-G) ... 'we don't mean you' (E6-A) ... 'we know you' (E6-F) ... 'I get that a lot.' (E6-B)

Or in a patronizing version:

'A friend of mine ... said to me one day: I don't normally like English accents, I don't feel comfortable with them—but I do with you ... I thought: that's because she knows me.' (E3-A)

People do distinguish between the *acceptable* individual and the *unacceptable* country or group. But that is typical of all phobias and in no way peculiar to Anglophobia. And minorities find the distinction patronizing and offensive.

4.1.3 *Europhobia*

In so far as people in England define themselves by contrast with some external 'other', it is not Scotland or Scots that provide the basis for their self-definition however. Scotland is small, unthreatening, insignificant, and largely invisible. Historically, as Colley (1992*a*: 328) argues, Britishness was defined by contrast with 'the Other in the shape of [militant continental] Catholicism' which she adds, 'is no longer available'. But France, Germany, and (implicitly 'continental') Europe still remain as an 'Other' that helps to define Britishness and indeed Englishness. They are still available. And casual verbal abuse of the French and Germans is as acceptable in England as casual abuse of the English in Scotland. In short, Europhobia represents another British phobia and one which extends in varying degree to Scotland as well as England.

4.1.4 Asylophobia

In the immediate aftermath of devolution, there was a new phobia that was relevant to Scottish identity and nationalism—perhaps more temporary than other phobias, but nonetheless important for a time at least. That was the rapidly growing public concern about asylum seekers. It was compounded, however irrationally, by concern about an influx of east Europeans resulting from EU enlargement. And it was a UK-wide issue. But it was given a peculiarly Scottish dimension by the 1999 Asylum Act that introduced dispersal to Scotland at the same time as devolution.

Many of the asylum seekers at this time were Muslim (see Chapter 1), but in one important respect they were more like the English minority than Scottish Muslims. Two-fifths of all Muslims, and half the ethnic Pakistanis, in Scotland are Scottish-born. But asylum seekers, like English immigrants, were born outside Scotland. And because so many stress birth-place as a criterion for recognition of 'true Scots', it is possible to be *inclusive* with regard to 'our' ethnic and cultural minorities, including Muslims, while being *exclusive* with regard to asylum seekers. Scottish Muslims themselves had mixed feelings about an influx of asylum seekers.

4.1.5 Common Causes

Taking account of the internal critics, Scotland seems more like a hotbed of phobias than the 'civic' and 'benign' land discovered by visiting sociologists. There are clearly several fairly widespread anti-minority phobias within Scotland, some historic, some of recent origin. What is less clear is how they interact with each other.

One possibility is that all these phobias flow from *common causes*. Saeed, Blane, and Forbes (1999: 824) back the view of the Scottish *Sunday Times* that 'anti-English racism may not be as obvious as anti-Asian racism, but it comes from the same narrowing of vision that has caused all forms of racism to increase in recent years in Scotland' (*Sunday Times Magazine*, 4 October 1998). There is some truth in that: factors, such as low education, appear to encourage many different phobias.

Political elites also argue that phobias 'go together'. The most generally prejudiced, they say, are:

'ignorant Scots ... not educated enough ... born, bred in sectarianism.' (IDI-4); 'the same sort of ignorant, anti-foreign, anti-anything-different sentiment ... anti-Islamic ... anti-Jewish ... when my [Catholic] family came here, they would have been anti-them.' (IDI-25G); 'I was told that I had no place in Inverness ... taking their jobs ... they just hated Glaswegians ... it was really blatant ... my boss said, if somebody was a Catholic they just wouldn't get promotion in this council ... he obviously didn't know I was Catholic [as well as a Glaswegian].' (IDI-26G)

4.1.6 Reinforcement

While true, the 'common cause' thesis may not be the whole truth however. A second possibility is that: 'multiple forms of prejudice *reinforce* one another' (IDI-17G) by encouraging people to think in terms of 'our folk' versus 'others'—others of any and all kinds. A phobia against one minority may generate or sustain a mindset that encourages other anti-minority phobias to develop. The BBC report that Belfast has been 'dubbed the race-hate capital of Europe' (news.bbc.co.uk, 13 January 2004) for the number of attacks on the Chinese and Pakistani minorities. Sectarianism, whatever its origins, might directly encourage more general racism.

4.1.7 Displacement

But there is a third possibility, implicit in much of the literature on nationalism and national identity: the displacement thesis. Virdee (2003: 94) criticizes the 'popular notion ... that there is no racism in Scotland', arguing like Miles and Dunlop (1987: 119) that 'the national political process in Scotland has not been racialised [by elites] to the extent that it has in England'. But he goes on to provide another, very different explanation of different levels of street-level racism in Scotland and England: 'during the 1960s and 1970s ... blackness and Englishness were [depicted] as mutually exclusive .... In Scotland, however, the emergence of Scottish nationalism partially *displaced* racism' [our emphasis]. More generally, Bairner (1994: 24) suggests that 'in an independent Scotland, the differences between highlands and lowlands, the central belt and the rest, the cities and the small towns, Catholics and Protestants, men and women, working class and middle class, *black Scots and white* ... would become political issues of [more] pressing importance ... *only resentment of the English provides a unified [Scottish] national consciousness* [our emphasis].'

This claim that 'the English continue to be the central "other" which defines what it means to be Scottish' (Wright 1999; McIntosh, Smith, and

Robertson 2004*a*: 53) tends to be articulated as an explanation for the strength of Anglophobia. But, following Bairner, it could equally well be put forward as an explanation for the weakness of Islamophobia in Scotland. On a different scale, and with different terminology, Colley (1992*a*, 1992*b*) implicitly advances a similar displacement model when she argues that a unified British national consciousness was forged through fear of Continental Europe.

Any focus upon an *external* 'other' should bring the internal minority and majority closer together. This 'displacement thesis' is in sharp contrast (but not at all in contradiction) to the 'reinforcement thesis', which suggests that a focus on one particular *internal* 'other' may encourage a more general antipathy towards a second or a third internal 'other'.

4.2 Measuring Five Scottish Phobias

For our calculations of all Scottish phobias we use the same tight definition of 'majority Scots' as in Chapter 3:

- 'white', non-Muslims, living in Scotland—but restricted to those born in Scotland and whose partners (if any) are also Scottish-born.

Our primary focus is on Anglophobia and Islamophobia—and their relationship to nationalism—within post-devolution Scotland. It would be particularly absurd to include the numerous English immigrants or their partners in any calculation of Scottish *Anglo*phobia.

There are some reasons to expect that Anglophobia amongst 'majority Scots' might be less extensive or less virulent than Islamophobia. Muslims are not cut off from the Scottish majority but they are somewhat less closely connected by ties of friendship and far less by ties of family. Most 'majority Scots' know someone who is English but only half know a Muslim; four times as many have an English 'friend' (60 per cent) as a Pakistani friend (15 per cent); and twenty times as many have family connections with the English.

But while friendship and family might tie majority Scots more closely to the English than to Muslims, their perceptions of what it takes to be a 'true Scot' (especially birthplace) tie them more closely to Scottish Muslims than to English immigrants. Over three times as many majority Scots feel that to be 'truly Scottish' it is essential to be born in Scotland as feel it is essential to be white. Even cultural similarity might not count in favour of the English. We asked on a 7-point scale whether it was 'better for a country if almost everyone shares the same customs, religions and traditions' or 'better for a country if there is a variety of different customs, religions and traditions'. Majority Scots come down overwhelmingly on the side of cultural variety. Indeed, the most popular choice is the most extreme point at the 'variety' end of the scale and, on balance, 81 per cent opted for variety rather than uniformity.

Majority Scots are also committed to the liberal concept of ethnic equality—for English immigrants as well as Muslims. Overwhelmingly, they support the extension of anti-discrimination laws from race and gender to both religion and sub-UK origin—specifically to cover discrimination against Muslims or against English immigrants, though they are very slightly more in favour of protecting Muslims (86 per cent of those with a view) than English immigrants (82 per cent). Similarly, majority Scots are sympathetic to having both Muslim and English immigrant MSPs in the Scottish Parliament—though while they favour Muslim MSPs by over two to one, they are fairly evenly divided about the need for English MSPs.

But we are concerned with something that goes beyond cold liberal concepts of legal or statistical equality. To measure the extent of street-level Anglophobia we use 'English-immigrant' equivalents of the 'Muslim' questions that we used to measure street-level Islamophobia in Chapter 3. Only minor adjustments to the wording are required, replacing the word 'Muslims'—not with the brief and accurate but unfamiliar phrase 'English immigrants' however, but with 'English people living in Scotland' or a variant. That is particularly important in the question about forming a relationship 'with an English person now living in Scotland' because that minimizes the risk of that respondents' answers would reflect their unhappiness at their close relatives moving far away to England rather than merely forming a relationship with a locally resident English person.

Excluding those with no opinion or mixed opinions, an average of 38 per cent of majority Scots agree with E1-5 (Anglophobia) compared to an average of 49 per cent with M1-5 (Islamophobia). So on strictly comparable indicators, Anglophobia runs just 11 per cent behind Islamophobia in Scotland: Scots may be light on Islamophobia, but they make up for that with a good dose of Anglophobia (Table 4.1).

Relatively few express economic resentment of minorities taking jobs, housing and health care; but economic resentment, though generally low, is significantly lower with respect to English immigrants than Muslims. More doubt the minorities' commitment to Scotland, and are

Table 4.1. Anglophobia and Islamophobia

	Views of majority Scots	
	About English immigrant minority (%)	About Muslim minority (%)
E1/M1: English/Muslims take Scot jobs, housing, healthcare	18	30
E2/M2: English/Muslims never really committed to Scotland	44	53
E3/M3: English/Muslims more loyal to England/other Muslims than to Scotland	81	79
E4/M4: Scotland would begin to lose its identity if more English/Muslims came	42	52
E5/M5: unhappy relative marry English/Muslim	5	32
Averages	*38*	*49*

Source: Majority Scots in SSAS 2003. DK's and undecided excluded from calculation of percentages.

apprehensive that 'Scotland would begin to lose its identity' if there were an influx of English immigrants or Muslims. And despite the huge imbalance in the numbers of English immigrants and Muslims already living in Scotland, majority Scots are rather less apprehensive about the impact on Scotland's national identity of a further influx of English immigrants than they are of an increase in the number of Muslims. However, majority Scots suspect that both minorities' loyalties lie outside Scotland—and doubts about loyalty apply at least as much, perhaps slightly more, to the English than to Muslims. However, social exclusion is not a significant part of Anglophobia; a mere 5 per cent of majority Scots say they would be 'unhappy' to have a close relative form a long-term relationship with an English immigrant that contrasts sharply with attitudes towards relationships with Muslims (32 per cent unhappy).

There are fewer available indicators of sectarianism, Europhobia, and Asylophobia in the SSAS 2003, though we did insert sectarian versions of our social exclusion indicators (E5, M5): about a relationship with a Catholic (C5) or Protestant (P5). Sectarian phobias should be measured within religious groups rather than across majority Scots as a whole, however. Six per cent of Catholics would be unhappy about a relationship with a Protestant; and 12 per cent of Presbyterians would be unhappy about a relationship with a Catholic.

The only useful indicators of Asylophobia and Europhobia (neither designed by us) in the SSAS 2003 are:

AS: (Asylophobia): How much do you agree or disagree: While their cases are being considered, asylum-seekers should be *kept in detention centres*. (5-point scale)

EU: (Europhobia): Do you think Britain's long-term policy should be ... a single European government, increase the EU's powers, leave things as they are, reduce the EU's powers, [or] leave the European Union.

Despite the sympathy expressed by political elites of all persuasions, and Liberal and Nationalist protests against the Dungavel detention centre, majority Scots at street level took a hard line on asylum seekers: 71 per cent (of those with a view) would keep them in detention 'while their cases are being considered'; and 43 per cent wished to leave the EU or at least reduce its powers. In themselves these are fairly primitive indicators of Asylophobia and Europhobia, but it is nonetheless interesting to see how they vary.

4.3 The Social Foundations of Scottish Phobias

In our analysis of Anglophobia and other Scottish phobias, we focus on the same key factors that affected Islamophobia.

4.3.1 *Age and Generation*

Age and generation have very little impact on Anglophobia. Only one of the five indicators of Anglophobia—doubts about the English minority's commitment to Scotland—varies consistently across the age cohorts. That contrasts with the much greater impact of age and especially generation on Islamophobia. The old (over 65 years) are also 20 per cent more willing than the young (under 35 years) to support detention for asylum seekers, 35 per cent more inclined to quit the EU or cut its powers, and 13 per cent more unhappy about relations with Catholics (partly because older Protestants are 7 per cent more anti-Catholic; and partly because younger people are less religious, including less Protestant) (Table 4.2).

Table 4.2. Impact of age and generation on Anglophobia and Islamophobia

	Age-34 (%)	45–44 (%)	45–54 (%)	55–64 (%)	65+ (%)
Anglophobia: average E1-5	35	39	37	39	41
Islamophobia: average M1-5	42	46	45	55	62

Source: Majority Scots in SSAS 2003. DK's and undecided excluded from calculation of percentages.

4.3.2 Education

Friendship with, and knowledge of, minorities varies very sharply with education. Compared to those with no qualifications, graduates are 37 per cent more likely to have an English friend and over five times more likely to have a Muslim friend (32 per cent compared to only 6 per cent). Conversely, those without qualifications are 25 per cent more Anglophobic than graduates as well as 34 per cent more Islamophobic. Compared to graduates, the unqualified are also 35 per cent more likely to feel 'not at all' close to Europe, 16 per cent more likely to want to quit the EU or cut its powers, and 22 per cent more willing to keep asylum seekers in detention. Amongst Protestants, the unqualified are also 20 per cent more likely to feel unhappy about a relationship with a Catholic (Table 4.3).

4.3.3 Contacts with and Knowledge of Minorities

As we might expect, having a minority friend makes a difference to the attitudes of majority Scots towards minorities. Having a Muslim friend reduces Islamophobia by 21 per cent, and having an English friend reduces Anglophobia by 11 per cent. Less obviously however, having a friend in *either* minority reduces phobias towards *both* (partly because those who have a friend in one minority are much more likely to also have a friend in the other).

Having a Muslim friend also reduces support for detaining asylum seekers by 16 per cent but having an English friend makes little difference. Knowledge is also important. Compared to those who have a Muslim friend, those who say they 'know nothing at all' about Muslims are 34 per cent more Islamophobic—and also 18 per cent more Anglophobic.

Overall, the impact of age and generation, education and, to a lesser degree, contact with minorities broadly fit the 'common causes' model of phobias.

Table 4.3. Impact of education on Anglophobia and Islamophobia

	Degree (%)	Higher education below degree (%)	A level equivalent (%)	O level equivalent (%)	CSE equivalent (%)	None (%)
Anglophobia: average E1-5	22	35	30	42	45	47
Islamophobia: average M1-5	28	44	38	54	57	62

Source: Majority Scots in SSAS 2003. DK's and undecided excluded from calculation of percentages.

4.4 The Cultural and Political Foundations of Scottish Phobias

4.4.1 *Religion*

Differences between Catholics and Protestants on either Anglophobia or Islamophobia are negligible. The irreligious are around 13 per cent less Islamophobic but only a few per cent less Anglophobic. However, there are both sectarian and religiosity differences on sectarianism, asylum seekers and the EU. By varying margins, Protestants are the most sectarian, the most Asylophobic and the most Europhobic while the irreligious are the least phobic on four of the five phobias (Table 4.4).

4.4.2 *Partisanship*

Again we use the votes at the 2001 British General Election as an indicator of political partisanship. Both Anglophobia and Islamophobia are lowest amongst Liberal-Democrat voters. But while Islamophobia is highest amongst Conservatives, Anglophobia is highest amongst SNP voters.

Anglophobia amongst SNP voters is 10 per cent higher than amongst Conservatives (and 16 per cent higher than amongst Liberal-Democrats). Conversely, Islamophobia is 7 per cent higher amongst Conservatives than amongst SNP voters (and 20 per cent higher than amongst Liberal-Democrats). Non-voters come second only to SNP voters on Anglophobia, and second only to Conservatives on Islamophobia.

Many English people in Scotland vote Conservative of course, and relatively few vote SNP. So it is very important to stress that our analysis of the link between party support and Anglophobia is based—like all our analyses of phobias—entirely on 'majority Scots' defined to exclude both English immigrants and even their partners. Our findings show that *even*

Table 4.4. Impact of religion on Anglophobia and Islamophobia

	C of S/Presbyterian (%)	Roman Catholic (%)	No religion (%)
Anglophobia: average E1-5	40	41	37
Islamophobia: average M1-5	56	54	42
Keep asylum seekers in detention	81	61	66
Leave EU or cut its powers	71	63	48
Unhappy if relative marry Cath	12	na	2
Unhappy if relative marry Prot	na	6	0

Source: Majority Scots in SSAS 2003. DK's and undecided excluded from calculation of percentages. na = not applicable.

Conservatives drawn from amongst the 'majority Scots' (born in Scotland and with Scottish-born partners) are significantly less Anglophobic than most other majority Scots.

At the same time however, these Conservatives are the most Asylophobic, the most Europhobic, and by far the most anti-Catholic as well as the most Islamophobic. Compared to Liberal-Democrat voters, majority Scots who vote Conservative are only 6 per cent more Anglophobic, but 15 per cent more sectarian, 18 per cent more Asylophobic and Europhobic, as well as 20 per cent more Islamophobic (Table 4.5).

4.4.3 Sub-State National Identities

Compared to those majority Scots who identify equally with Britain and Scotland, those who identify themselves as exclusively Scottish are 13 per cent more Anglophobic though scarcely any more Islamophobic or Asylophobic. So in contrast to the impact of education—which had significantly more impact on Islamophobia than on Anglophobia, Scottish nationalism has a greater impact on Anglophobia than on Islamophobia. Indeed, the impact of Scottish national identity—in total contrast to the impact of low education—seems to be specifically Anglophobic, focused on the historic enemy, the 'significant other' that helps define Scottish identity, rather than on any minority that differs more in terms of race, religion, or culture from majority Scots. The impact of national identity is a targeted as education is not.

The two composite scales, for Angophobia and Islamophobia, correlate at 0.65 with each other, but that is the product of a combination of 'common causes' and 'targeted impacts'.

Table 4.5. Impact of partisanship on Anglophobia and Islamophobia

	Vote at 2001 General Election				
	CON (%)	LAB (%)	LibD (%)	SNP (%)	DNV (%)
Anglophobia: average E1-5	33	38	27	43	40
Islamophobia: average M1-5	55	48	35	48	51
Keep asylum seekers in detention	84	68	66	79	66
Leave EU or cut its powers	82	56	64	59	50
Unhappy if relative marry Cath	15	5	2	3	7
Prots only: unhappy if rel marry Cath	19	8	4	10	18

Source: Majority Scots in SSAS 2003. DK's and undecided excluded from calculation of percentages.

4.5 A Multivariate Comparison of Anglophobia and Islamophobia in Scotland

Again, we can usefully summarize and confirm our findings with a multi-variate analysis similar to that in Chapter 3. As before, we predict levels of Islamophobia and Anglophobia (and the other phobias) from age and generation, education, minority contacts, religion, national identity, and political partisanship. The only difference is that we replace the indicator of minority contacts used in Chapter 3, 'knowledge of Muslims', with two comparable indicators: having a 'close friend' who is 'Muslim' or 'English' (Table 4.6).

The multiple regressions confirm that the most important influence on Anglophobia as well as Islamophobia is education. But although Scottish identity has no impact on Islamophobia, it comes close to rivalling low education as an influence towards Anglophobia. The analysis suggests however, that party political nationalism (SNP voting) does not have an impact on Anglophobia, once Scottish identity has been taken into account. Beyond that, having an English friend reduces Anglophobia by about as much as having a Muslim friend reduces Islamophobia.

Not surprisingly, a similar regression shows that sectarianism—in the sense of anti-Catholic social exclusion—is best predicted from religion: it is particularly strong amongst Presbyterians, particularly low amongst Catholics and intermediate amongst the irreligious. But beyond these obvious sectarian influences upon sectarianism, education exerts an independent and additional influence. And amongst Presbyterians themselves (where by definition, sectarian influences can have no impact since they are all from the same sect) education is the dominant influence

Table 4.6. A multivariate analysis of Islamophobia and Anglophobia in Scotland

	Islamophobia	Anglophobia
RSQ ($\times$ 100) =	14	16
	β ($\times$ 100)	β ($\times$ 100)
Higher education	−29	−28
Strong/exclusive Scottish identity	*	18
Religious	14	*
Has a Muslim friend	−13	*
Has an English friend	*	−13

* blank entries, and all variables missing from the table indicate that the β coefficient was less than 0.10; so the independent and additional impact of such variables is small (if any at all) and relatively unimportant; all β coefficients displayed in the table are not only large enough to be politically significant, they are also statistically significant at better than the 1 per cent error level.

($\beta = -0.19$) on sectarianism. Other regressions show that (low) education is also the dominant influence on Asylophobia, though age and generation have more impact on Europhobia.

But these other regressions confirm our conclusion that nationalism—either in the sense of sub-national identity, or of support for the SNP—has no significant impact on any of the phobias except Anglophobia. The only significant partisan influences towards greater phobias, of any other kind, that are evident in the regression analyses are some relatively weak connections between Conservative voting and Asylophobia, anti-Catholic sectarianism and particularly Europhobia.

4.6 How Scottish Phobias Stack Up

Scotland in general and Scottish nationalism in particular have frequently been judged to be relatively 'civic' and 'benign'—not a prey to the anti-minority phobias that afflict so many other nationalisms. They are clearly not so Islamophobic as England or English nationalism. But does displacement merely redirect their phobias? We need to know 'how phobias stack up'.

One simple way of seeing 'how phobias stack up' is to sum our composite indicators of Islamophobia and Anglophobia—with or without the addition of more primitive indicators of Asylophobia, Sectarianism, and Europhobia. Education, for example affects every phobia, always in the same direction, and always by a large amount. So stacking up the phobias highlights the impact of (low) education on phobias. But by contrast, partisanship and sub-national identity affect different phobias in different ways—and not always in the same direction. So to some extent the impacts of partisanship and sub-national identity 'cancel out' rather than 'stack up'.

Summing just Islamophobia and Anglophobia rates total phobias at 109 for those without qualifications and only 50 for graduates. Liberal-Democrat voters score very low in total (at 62) because they score low on both phobias. Conservatives score 88 and SNP voters come top at 91: their high rate of Anglophobia more than compensates for their low level of Islamophobia. Exclusively Scottish identifiers score even higher, at 100.

Taking account of all five phobias is kinder to SNP voters though not to exclusively Scottish identifiers. Once again, the impact of (low) education increases every phobia—to a total of 175 compared to only 58 for graduates. Liberal-Democrat voters again score the lowest (at 96) because they score low on every phobia. Conservatives come top at 173—almost

Table 4.7. How phobias 'stack up'

	Educational Qualifications		Partisanship (2001 vote)				Sub-state national identities	
	Degree (%)	None (%)	LibDem voter (%)	LAB voter (%)	CON voter (%)	SNP voter (%)	Equally Brit and Scot (%)	Exclusively Scot (%)
Total: 5 phobias	58	175	96	118	173	139	126	144
Anglophobia + Islamophobia	50	109	62	86	88	91	83	100
Anglophobia	22	47	27	38	33	43	33	46
Islamophobia	28	62	35	48	55	48	50	54
Sectarianism	3	23	4	8	19	10	8	14
Europhobia (-50)	1	17	14	6	32	9	13	6
Asylophobia (-50)	4	26	16	18	34	29	22	24

Sectarianism—Protestant attitudes to Catholics; Europhobia—policy version, i.e. quit EU or reduce powers.
We have subtracted 50 from both Europhobia and Asylophobia indicators; this does not affect their contribution to the gradient of phobias across education, partisanship or identities.

equalling the score of those without any educational qualifications. SNP voters score less (at 139) because their higher Anglophobia is offset by lower scores than Conservatives on every other phobia. Exclusively Scottish identifiers score 144 compared to 126 amongst dual identifiers.

These are crude calculations, but they show that Scottish nationalists (whether defined by voting or by identities) are *not* particularly 'benign'. In total they score at or above average on phobias. Depending on the reach of the calculations, SNP voters are either behind Conservatives or just ahead of them in total phobias. But by any calculation, exclusively identifiers are more phobic than dual identifiers. These findings are consistent with the 'displacement thesis': Scots in general and street-level Scottish nationalists in particular have *different* phobias rather than *lesser* phobias (Table 4.7).

4.7 Conclusion: Less Phobias or Different Phobias?

This comparison of Anglophobia and Islamophobia in Scotland suggests three broad conclusions.

4.7.1 *Less Anglophobia*

Amongst majority Scots (tightly defined to exclude both English immigrants and their partners), Anglophobia runs at a lower level than Islamophobia. The difference between Anglophobia and Islamophobia is greatest on social exclusion, moderate on economic resentment, small on fears for national identity, and disappears on nationalist distrust: the majority suspect the loyalty to Scotland of English immigrants as much as they suspect the loyalty of Muslims.

4.7.2 Social Factors Affect All Phobias

Education and friendship reduce phobias; (older) age and generation increase phobias.

4.7.3 But Cultural and Political Factors have more Targeted Impacts

Scottish national identities and SNP voting increases Anglophobia but has little impact, or even a negative impact on other phobias. Conservatives score low on Anglophobia but high on every other phobia.

So is Scottish nationalism, unlike English nationalism, 'benign' rather than 'nasty' as so many external observers suggest? From the perspective of Muslims the answer must be an unequivocal 'yes'. But from the perspective of English immigrants the answer must be 'no'. And across the board, the impact of nationalism is more to redirect phobias than to increase or reduce them.

The statistical evidence is at least consistent with the theory that Anglophobia itself displaces Islamophobia by providing another target, and that England itself helps to reduce within-Scotland phobias by providing Scots with a common, external, and very significant 'Other'. Conversely however, Scotland is too small, too peripheral, too insignificant to play a corresponding role in displacing phobias within England. Yet by stimulating English nationalism without providing a truly significant 'other', Scottish nationalism may actually increase Islamophobia—in England, though not in Scotland.

5

Eyes Wide Open

O wad some Power the giftie gie us
To see oursels as ithers see us

It is not a kindly quotation. Many of us would much prefer *not* to see ourselves 'as ithers see us'. Minorities in particular are in such an inherently weak position that they may find it difficult to cope with too accurate a perception of just how the majority sees them. It is argued that individuals could not 'get up in the morning' without some trust in people around them (Markova 2004: 2). Similarly, while they may often—and legitimately—complain about harassment or discrimination, minorities are under some psychological pressure to believe that their social environment is not altogether hostile. So although adverse experiences might lead them to overestimate the extent of antagonism towards them in the wider community, the need to cope may lead them to underestimate it. How these countervailing influences balance out is not at all obvious.

Information should not be a problem however. Minorities have a far better basis for understanding majorities than *vice versa*. That is particularly true for Muslims because there are so very few of them. When 86 per cent of majority Scots say they know little or nothing about Muslims they are probably right: in previous chapters we found only 15 per cent of majority Scots had a Muslim friend. But cross-community friendship levels are almost inevitably asymmetric for small minorities: 76 per cent of Pakistani Muslims as well as 96 per cent of English immigrants say they have 'close' friends amongst majority Scots.

Only a small minority of Pakistanis (17 per cent) describe Scots as 'generally racist'. Twice as many English immigrants (34 per cent), and even more (41 per cent) of their Scottish partners describe Scots as 'generally Anglophobic or anti-English'. Given the weight of our other findings, some of this difference may reflect the more extreme overtones of the word 'racist' as compared with the phrase 'Anglophobic or anti-English'.

But it also indicates that English immigrants are at least as sensitive to Anglophobia as Muslims to Islamophobia.

Some ethnic Pakistanis agree that:

'Scottish prejudices are more to do with the English' (PK2-A) ... 'more obvious towards the English .... There is a lot of hate there and the funny thing is they are all white.' (PK2-B)

Others felt Scots would accept as Scottish 'someone born in another European country—like Spain or Italy' more readily than they would accept people like themselves:

'Europeans would have an easier time in Scotland than Asians' (PK4-F); 'Europeans would be treated like British white people' (PK6-E); 'blend in easier.' (PK5-F)

—but so did some English immigrants:

'there is an anti-English element to society in Scotland.' (E2-B); 'so intensely anti-English that they will tolerate other people ... it would not necessarily be easy for [Europeans] but I think it would be easier than being English' (E6-G); 'hating the English is a Scottish sport' (E2-H, E2-E agrees) ... 'they enjoy doing it' (E2-H) ... 'the English bashing the French and the Scots bashing the English has a deep seated ... historical justification.' (E2-E)

5.1 How Minorities Attribute Prejudice

Survey respondents thought the 'most prejudiced' Scots were 'ordinary people' rather than 'politicians and officials': 70 per cent of English immigrants and 61 per cent of ethnic Pakistanis cited 'ordinary people' while only 8 per cent of English immigrants and 21 per cent of ethnic Pakistanis cited 'politicians and officials'. But what kind of 'ordinary people'?

Some focus-group participants cite the 'underprivileged' or uneducated:

'those who were once deprived themselves' (PK4-F); '[the] jobless.' (PK2-B); 'If you were in an under privileged group ... you might well be much more resentful of incomers.' (E3-G) ... 'scapegoat the incomer, rather than look for the real solution to your problems.' (E3-A); 'badly educated Scots' (PK1-E, PK1-D agrees); 'those with the least amount of education' (PK4-E); 'educated people are not racist.' (PK2-C)

But some Pakistanis were remarkably self-critical:

'everyone is racist, including my own mum' (PK5-F); 'we are also racist ... towards white people ... [and] as racist as whites when it comes to black people' (PK6-E) ... 'more racist than white people—we don't just have the black/white issue but also the religious issues [with] Hindus and Sikhs.' (PK6-F)

—and more generally focus group participants tended to stress the subtlety and ubiquity of prejudice:

'those with two legs' (E6-G); 'bigotry is no respecter of persons' (E5-A); 'across the board' (E6-E) ... 'mixed' (E6-F); 'there is racism everywhere.' (PK6-C)

In complete contradiction to our findings in the previous two chapters, many argued that education was irrelevant:

'I work in a school with professional people and sometimes their comments, you think, hang on a minute, that was racist [i.e. Anglophobic here]' (E6-F) 'I do *not* think ... education matters, it's the attitude ... personality ... parents, family or neighbours' (E1-G); 'what's fed to them as children' (E6-A); 'a natural part of their upbringing ... even if they don't allow those feelings towards the English to come out ... so much a part of their history ... parents ... ancestry, they hardly notice it' (E6-E); 'people are racist—it does not matter if they are professional or if they are unemployed' (PK5-D); 'everyone has prejudices' (PK2-A); 'I don't think it matters if you are educated or not ... it depends on how you are brought up' (PK6-G) ... 'it has nothing to do with education.' (PK6-E)

Only the modalities of racism varied with age:

'children swear at Asians ... older people make comments with their eyes and facial expressions' (PK3-D) ... 'adults are equally racist.' (PK3-B)

—or with education. The prejudice of the well-educated was merely expressed in different ways, better hidden from view, yet at the same time more deadly:

'racism is very subtle and you get it across the board ... in colleges and universities' (PK4-E) ... 'it gets subtler further up ... a local man will call you a Paki ... the other [higher up] will use the processes and that is dangerous' (PK4-F); 'the less educated are the ones that slag you in the streets but the professionals will be the ones that do not give you a job.' (PK1-B); 'indigenous black people in Scotland ... well-qualified [are] either unemployed or working in restaurants or whatever.' (IDI-15); 'we could become the most highly qualified [but] we cannot get a job [except] to do with ethnic minorities' (IDI-13); 'I know ... an accountant ... at one of these top accountancy firms. The day after Sept 11th ... these well-educated people were staring at her .... All her colleagues are getting promoted and she is not.' (PK1-G); 'employers are racist' (PK3-B) ... 'my son did a BSc in Engineering, he was the only Muslim in the class ... all his friends got jobs but my child suffered for years' (PK3-D) ... '[Muslims] that do find jobs need to work twice as hard to get them' (PK3-B); 'at university ... people with less qualifications and experience just pass you by ... the interviewers do it in a very subtle way' (PK4-E); 'less educated people will openly curse the person ... [but] educated people can control their tongue easier . . . [and] show racism in a subtle way that you might not realize . . . [affecting] a job, access to services, attending court and facing a racist judge.' (PK6-E)

This concept of hidden prejudice amongst the well-educated was less often raised by English immigrants, though one claimed:

'there's one or two teachers in the High School that have this really strong, deep anti-English feeling . . . [it] has to be really well concealed because of their profession, but it's there.' (E6-E)

And the concept of hidden prejudice amongst the well-educated was raised repeatedly by political elites—as often by those who were *not* themselves drawn from minorities as by those who were. Who were the most prejudiced Scots? Not just the uneducated, but:

'two groups . . . upper class . . . "we are the best people in the world" . . . [and the] disadvantaged . . . "why are these immigrants getting a better living in my country than me?".' (IDI-25G); 'Some of the most racist people I've met are well-educated . . . like domestic abuse, it crosses [all society].' (IDI-23G); 'The idea that somehow it's always the poorest people that are worst, is nonsense . . . sectarianism is right throughout society.' (IDI-21G)

Elites also alleged the well educated, including officials were better at hiding it:

'the educated [are] better at hiding it . . . better at not expressing it so openly.' (IDI-9); 'more covert . . . people who are disadvantaged are very open and vocal about their feelings. [But with] politicians and various other people, there is discrimination [though] they are very polished about how they show [or hide] their racism . . . they can say the right words, use the right language.' (IDI-12); 'officials have an official line they have to follow.' (IDI-5); 'I have not had people in officialdom say anything [racist] to me, but then they wouldn't would they, they wouldn't say anything to me in my capacity as an MSP.' (IDI-20G)

—views echoed in focus groups:

'officials also discriminate [but] are not as obvious and as blatant as those people who curse us in the streets.' (PK3-D); 'people at high levels will never show they are racist, it is hard to detect.' (PK6-E)

But sometimes they did not even hide it very well: they 'pandered':

'politicians . . . and elements of the media are the most culpable because they pander to racism. [They are] not necessarily . . . personally racist. But they pander to racism because they think it is popular among the people . . . I am sure [Home Secretary] Blunkett personally is not a racist, but he panders to it for crude electoral gain and in some ways that's even worse . . . playing with fire. It's the same with newspaper editors ... on a comfortable salary ... not personally racist. But ... they use sensationalism to try and sell newspapers.' (IDI-18)

Television journalists were almost as bad:

'they say: Muslim terrorist' (PK1-D) ... 'not Christian terrorist' (PK1-B) ... '[or] Jewish terrorist ... the public are going to start believing that all Muslim people are terrorists' (PK1-D) ... 'the IRA is never linked to Catholics' (PK1-G) ... 'there is some propaganda in these terrorist accusations.' (PK1-C)

So although:

'those who are most susceptible to it tend to be young working class guys ... relatively under-educated' (IDI-18)

—they are being manipulated by well-off and well-educated politicians and journalists for political or financial gain.

Judged by these quotations, neither English immigrants, nor ethnic Pakistanis, nor political elites would agree with the finding of our analysis of majority attitudes in earlier chapters: that education is the greatest influence upon anti-minority phobias. English immigrants might be surprised mainly by the strong statistical correlation that we found with low education. Ethnic Pakistanis and political elites (irrespective of their personal ethnicity) would not be surprised by the statistical correlation, but would hotly dispute the simple interpretation that we gave to it: they would charge the well-educated with more hidden but more 'dangerous' racism—possibly self-conscious duplicity, possibly self-deceiving denial.

5.2 Accuracy, Inaccuracy, and Denial

We can assess the accuracy of minority perceptions by asking minorities about their perceptions of majority attitudes towards them and then comparing their perceptions with what we know from directly interviewing the majority. We asked how they thought *'most ordinary Scots'* viewed 'Muslim Pakistanis' or 'English people living in Scotland', using questions corresponding closely in wording to the questions M1-5 and E1-5 used in our majority surveys (see Chapters 3 and 4).

Minorities were not asked about their perceptions of majority fears for national identity (M4, E4), but they were asked whether they thought the Scottish Parliament regarded them as a problem or an asset. And they were asked a specific question about social exclusion in the workplace, which had a rough correspondence with a similar question put to majorities.

We cannot equate the percentage of a minority who think 'most ordinary Scots' are prejudiced with the percentage of majority Scots who actually are prejudiced. The two are conceptually different. But the *patterns* or components of perceived and actual prejudice can properly be compared.

Excluding about a fifth who have no view or mixed views, about half the Pakistanis (47 per cent) and a quarter of English immigrants (27 per cent) think 'most ordinary Scots' view them as 'taking jobs, housing and heath care from ordinary Scots' rather than 'contributing a lot in terms of hard work and much-needed skills to Scotland'; 60 per cent of Muslim Pakistanis and 48 per cent of English immigrants feel most Scots think they 'could never be really committed to Scotland'. Overwhelmingly, both feel their loyalty is suspect: 81 per cent of Pakistanis and 78 per cent of the English feel 'most ordinary Scots' think they will 'always be more loyal to other Muslims' or 'to England' than to Scotland. Muslim Pakistanis, though not English immigrants, also sense—correctly in each case—a degree of social exclusion: 25 per cent of Muslim Pakistanis feel that 'most ordinary Scots would be unhappy if they had to work beside a Muslim Pakistani'; and 56 per cent that 'most ordinary Scots would be unhappy if one of their close relatives married or formed a long-term relationship with a Muslim Pakistani'; few of the English sense such social exclusion—and such as it is, it applies to suspected unhappiness about workmates (8 per cent) more than relatives (5 per cent).

In short, Muslim Pakistanis sense far more economic resentment and much more social exclusion than English immigrants. But both feel surrounded by nationalist distrust. Minorities' own perceptions of Anglophobia and Islamophobia, therefore, echo the profile of actual majority prejudice.

Yet the perception of so many Pakistanis that '*most* ordinary Scots' would be unhappy to have a Muslim Pakistani for a relative is not supported by our interviews with the majority: a third of Scots do admit such feelings, but not 'most'. Perhaps, minority perceptions are more accurate than majority introspection in this regard.

5.2.1 *Reconsidering Hidden Racism and Denial*

The most explicit conflict between minority perceptions and majority introspection does not concern *levels* of social exclusion however. Instead, it centres on the role of education in reducing prejudice. The greatest conflict of evidence is between the professed lack of prejudice amongst highly educated majority Scots and the minorities' (and political elites') scepticism about them. Are the well-educated simply better at hiding their 'politically incorrect' racism? Or even denying it to themselves, because it does not fit comfortably with their own liberal, multiculturalist self-image? It is not an easy question to answer but it is sufficiently important that it needs to be addressed.

In the two previous chapters we found that (low) education correlates strongly with all the phobias. In particular, it correlates with all five indicators of Islamophobia and with responses to the (less specific) question about 'working beside a suitably qualified person from a different racial or ethnic background'. Does this merely reflect the skill of educated people to 'say the right words, use the right language' (IDI-12)—or something more?

We can usefully look more closely at the detail of these six scales. Each has a relatively racist end and non-racist end with a neutral centre. If the well-educated simply wish to avoid any accusations of racism, they could do so by opting for 'refusal' (which might draw too much attention however), 'don't know', or the neutral centre points of the scales (which might draw less attention). In fact very few refuse to answer any of these questions. 'Don't knows' are more frequent—but on every question graduates are less likely than the public as a whole to respond with a 'don't know'. Larger numbers opt for neutral responses—but on four of the six scales, graduates are less likely than the public as a whole to opt for a neutral response. That is *not* strong evidence that they avoid neutral responses, but it *is* strong statistical evidence against the hypothesis that they take refuge in neutral responses.

Another approach to the issue of hidden racism amongst the well-educated is to focus on the numbers who take the most extreme anti-racist position on each of the 5-point or 7-point scales. It would be rather unnecessary overkill to hide their racism by adopting the most extreme position at the anti-racist end. Yet on every scale, graduates are more likely than the public as a whole to opt for the most extreme anti-racist position. The difference ranges from a negligible 1 per cent on perceptions of loyalty to 13 per cent on family relationships and a massive 29 per cent on workmates. Graduates differ from the rest of the population *not* by saying they would be just 'happy' to work with someone from a different ethnic group, but by declaring that they would be '*very* happy' rather than merely 'happy' to do so. So the attitudes of the well-educated go far beyond what would be necessary to hide latent racism. (This same pattern of the highly educated opting for the most extreme anti-racist positions on extended scales is also evident in England, though it is much less strong in England.)

We have good reasons to accept the existence of 'hidden racism', to accept that some of the highly educated may be peculiarly good at disguising it by giving what they know to be 'politically correct' answers. Correlations between high education and low racism almost certainly overstate the power of education to reduce racism. But nonetheless, our evidence suggests, despite our personal scepticism, that there is also some real connection between high education and low phobias; that this connection is strongest with regard to employment matters; that it is much weaker with regard to family matters; and that it is weakest of all with regard to distrust of minority commitment and loyalty towards Scotland.

5.3 Background or Experience: The Foundations of Phobia-Perceptions

Overall, the profile of minority perceptions of majority attitudes towards them seem broadly accurate—with the possible exception of their extreme scepticism about education. But these perceptions vary from one Muslim or English immigrant to another. What makes one Muslim (or English) person feel majority Scots are more sympathetic while another thinks majority Scots are more antagonistic? Is it primarily something about the person? Or something about what has happened to that person?

This is a version of the old 'nature versus nurture' debate. Of course particular minority individuals may be predisposed by nature to be more or less optimistic about the wider society in which they live. And different social backgrounds—more or less education, income, years living in Scotland, for example—may also encourage them to take a more or less benign view of the wider society in which they live. But there is another possibility: that their perception of the majority may have been heavily influenced by their actual dealings and specific experiences, with particular people from that majority. If they have been harassed, they may try hard (and they do—see Chapter 6) to believe that their harasser is not a 'typical' Scot. Nonetheless, their personal experience of harassment may subconsciously shape their view of what Scotland and 'typical' Scots are like.

Within both minorities, perceptions of majority attitudes appear to be largely uninfluenced by such broad social background characteristics as class, gender, or education. Muslim perceptions are only weakly related to income and English perceptions hardly at all. The large number of Scots who live with English immigrants share much the same perceptions as the English themselves about majority attitudes towards the English. By contrast, direct experience of interacting with the majority, specifically in their role as a minority, has a pervasive and significant impact on both Muslim and English perceptions of majority attitudes towards them.

And though class, gender, and education are relatively unimportant, other aspects of social background exert a detectable influence on minority perceptions of majority attitudes. But these other background factors are less pervasive and more specific in two important ways.

First, the social circumstances of English immigrants and ethnic Pakistanis are very different, and they differ in nature as well as degree. So the very nature of social differences amongst English immigrants is different from that amongst ethnic Pakistanis. The social categories as well as the number of individuals within them are different. Social factors that vary within one minority, and influence individual experience and perceptions within that community, simply do not vary within the other. Almost all the English have majority Scots as close friends, for example. All the English speak the same language at home. Most of them have, or had, a job outside the home. All of them are immigrants. Yet these universal characteristics of English immigrants are lines of division within the Pakistani minority.

Conversely, almost all the Pakistanis share the same religion while religion divides the English into believers and unbelievers, practising and non-practising, and adherents of different churches with conflicting traditions. Religion means more to Pakistanis but explains less about individual differences amongst them.

Second, the different components of Anglophobia and Islamophobia have different 'elasticities', some are more open to influence than others, and some are more open to influence with regard to Anglophobia than with regard to Islamophobia. Social exclusion is much greater with respect to Muslims than English immigrants and consequently Muslim perceptions of social exclusion can vary more than English perceptions of social exclusion which are uniformly low.

5.3.1 Nature—Personal Characteristics and Social Background

Amongst English immigrants, perceptions of majority attitudes vary strongly with age and length of time in Scotland—along with related characteristics such as being in work or retired. Older or longer-established English immigrants are very much less likely (34–39 per cent less) to feel Scots doubt their commitment to Scotland—and also much less likely

(24 per cent less) to feel Scots suspect their primary loyalty is to England. By contrast Pakistanis' perceptions scarcely vary at all with either age or years in Scotland—in part because relatively few are old. But those Pakistanis born in Scotland are 11 per cent *more* likely (not less!) to feel that Scots doubt their commitment to Scotland.

Rurality also affects English immigrants' perceptions. Those living in the capital are about 18 per cent more likely than those living in rural/small town areas to feel their commitment and loyalty are questioned by majority Scots. But at the same time they are 13 per cent less likely to feel, in booming Edinburgh, that majority Scots resent them as an economic burden.

Language affects Pakistanis' perceptions. Those who speak a mixture of languages at home are the least likely to feel majority Scots are Islamophobic—whether judged by suspicions of Muslim commitment and loyalty or by social exclusion. Conversely, those who speak Punjabi or, especially, Urdu at home are the most likely to feel majority Scots are Islamophobic. Urdu speakers are 18–20 per cent more likely to sense that Scots doubt their loyalty and would be unhappy to work alongside them.

Occupation—though *not* occupational class—also affects Pakistanis' perceptions. The aspects of occupation that have most impact are the ones that differentiate ethnic Pakistanis but fail to differentiate English immigrants. These are aspects of occupations that, just like language and friendships, connect minorities with the majority or set them apart. Most English immigrants have (or had) a job outside the home, but many ethnic Pakistanis have not. Most English immigrants work for employers, often large-scale employers including public sector employers. But many Pakistanis work for themselves, or in family businesses, or look after the home. These last three categories shelter minorities from close contact with the majority more than the first two. Working in the ethnically sheltered environment of a family business or the home greatly reduces (by up to 23 per cent) Pakistani perceptions that majority Scots regard them as an economic burden but, at the same time, increases their perceptions of social exclusion (by up to 13 per cent).

Religiosity, or more specifically, frequency of attendance at a religious gathering seems to affect the perceptions of both English immigrants and Muslims in regard to social exclusion—but in opposite directions. The most observant Muslims sense the greatest degree of social exclusion, as do the most *ir*religious English immigrants. We may speculate that the religious observance of English immigrants tends to connect them with the wider Scottish public while that of devout Muslims tends to isolate them. In both cases however the impact of religiosity is weak—only a few percentage points—and should not be overstated.

5.3.2 Nurture—Experience of Friendship and Harassment

Almost all English immigrants have 'close' Scottish friends. So do most Pakistanis, but enough do not for us to investigate the impact of 'close' cross-ethnic friendships. Those who have established close cross-ethnic friendships are about 17 per cent less likely to sense social exclusion. But cross-ethnic friendships have much less impact on perceptions that majority Scots doubt the commitment and loyalty of Muslims to Scotland.

English immigrants' perceptions are directly related to what they read in the press. Those who read 'Scottish' papers are between 10 and 20 per cent *less* likely than those who read 'English' papers (by their own definition) to the feel that majority Scots doubt their commitment and loyalty or regard them as an economic burden. To put it another way, exposure to the Scottish press seems reassuring rather than alarming. Amongst ethnic Pakistanis it makes little difference whether they rely on the Scottish press or the Pakistani press.

Those who feel the Scottish Parliament regards them (either English immigrants or Muslims) 'as a problem' rather than 'making Scotland a better place' are around 37 per cent more likely to feel that 'most ordinary Scots' are Anglophobic or Islamophobic however. It might be argued that this is a tautology, that perceiving the Parliament to be Anglophobic or Islamophobic is almost the same as perceiving 'most ordinary Scots' to be Anglophobic or Islamophobic. But on a range of questions, minorities are willing to distinguish between Parliament and people. So there may be something more than mere tautology here. If the Parliament is visibly anti-racist, multiculturalist, and inclusive then it becomes more difficult to believe that 'most Scots' are not, irrespective of other more particular evidence such as street-level harassment.

But personal experience of street-level harassment certainly does have a dramatic impact. We asked:

How often have you had to listen to comments about English/Pakistani or Muslim people which were intended as humorous but which irritated you? And how often have you been deliberately insulted or abused for being English/Pakistani or Muslim?

The frequency of such ethnic jokes and insults affects both English immigrants and ethnic Pakistanis. Indeed, English immigrants are more sensitive to the frequency of jokes and insults than Pakistanis—though they are exposed to them much less frequently. Pakistanis have become, by their own account, somewhat desensitized.

Averaging across five indicators of minority perceptions of majority phobias—two indicators of nationalist distrust, two of social exclusion, and one of economic resentment—even the frequency of exposure to ethnic jokes increases minority perceptions of majority phobias (against them) by 14 per cent amongst Pakistanis and by 26 per cent amongst English immigrants. Ethnic jokes increase minority perceptions that the majority doubt their commitment to Scotland by 26 per cent amongst Pakistanis and 43 per cent amongst English immigrants. They increase Pakistani perceptions that the majority are 'racist' by 28 per cent, and English perceptions that the majority are Anglophobic by 45 per cent (Table 5.1).

Table 5.1. Impact of frequency of ethnic jokes on minority perceptions of majority phobias

	Have had to listen to irritating ethnic jokes			
	Very often (%)	Sometimes (%)	Rarely (%)	Never (%)
English immigrants' perceptions of majority Scots feelings towards them:				
not committed to Scotland	74	54	42	31
more loyal to England	93	86	72	65
take jobs, housing and health care	39	30	24	20
unhappy to work with them	26	11	2	6
unhappy to acquire them as relative	22	4	1	5
Average:	*51*	*37*	*28*	*25*
English immigrants' perceptions that majority Scots are generally 'Anglophobic or anti-English'	74	41	27	29
Pakistanis' perceptions of majority Scots feelings towards them:				
not committed to Scotland	69	63	60	43
more loyal to other Muslims	78	82	85	75
take jobs, housing and health care	47	52	46	42
unhappy to work with a Muslim Pakistani	42	29	12	30
unhappy to acquire a Muslim relative	69	65	44	43
Average:	*61*	*58*	*49*	*47*
Pakistanis' think majority Scots are generally 'racist'	37	22	6	9

Source: Minorities Survey. DK's and undecided excluded from calculation of percentages.

5.3.3 *A Multivariate Analysis of Minority Perceptions*

We can usefully summarize and confirm our findings with a multivariate analysis. For that we have constructed 3-point scales for minority perceptions of economic resentment, nationalist distrust (with respect to both commitment and loyalty), and social exclusion (with respect to both relationships and the workplace). In each case perceptions of anti-minority attitudes are coded +1, perceptions of pro-minority attitudes are coded −1, and neutral perceptions as 0. By averaging across these five questions, we can then get composite phobia-perceptions scales—indicating each minority's perceptions of majority phobia directed against themselves in particular.

We use regression to predict levels of phobia-perceptions from fifteen potential influences. Amongst ethnic Pakistanis and English immigrants we use age; gender; education; self-assessed income (both in terms of its adequacy and also relative to perceptions of 'typical' incomes); length of residence in Scotland; working in the private sector, the public sector, or in family business, or at home; religiosity (frequency of attendance); having a majority Scot as a close friend; and the frequency of their experience of ethnic jokes and insults.

In addition, amongst ethnic Pakistanis we also use the language spoken at home, and whether their primary identity is Muslim/Pakistani or something else. And amongst English immigrants, we also distinguish those who live in Edinburgh from those who live in the rural/small-town Borders, and whether their primary identity is English or something else.

The best statistical predictor of phobia-perceptions is whether the minorities feel the Scottish Parliament regards them 'as a problem' or as 'making Scotland better'—but that is so close to being a phobia-perception itself that we exclude it from the regression analysis (Table 5.2).

The multiple regressions confirm that personal experience of ethnic jokes and insults, taken together, are the most important of the unambiguously independent influences on the phobia-perceptions of both ethnic Pakistanis and English immigrants. Although we know from focus groups and survey questions that they try hard to distinguish between these personal experiences and their image of 'typical' Scots as a whole (see Chapter 6), these personal experiences nonetheless colour their general perceptions of majority Scots' phobias.

Beyond these adverse experiences, a good income reduces the phobia-perceptions of ethnic Pakistanis and (older) age reduces the phobia-perceptions of English immigrants. In addition, language has a more considerable impact on the phobia-perceptions of ethnic Pakistanis:

Table 5.2. A multivariate analysis of minorities' phobia-perceptions

	Phobia-perceptions	
	Ethnic Pakistanis' perceptions of Islamophobia	English immigrants' perceptions of Anglophobia
RSQ ($\times$ 100) =	9	18
(High) frequency of insults	15	29
(High) frequency of jokes	11	13
Speak *only* minority languages at home	18	n.a.
(Good) income	−11	*
(Old) age	*	−13

*blank entries, and all variables missing from the table indicate that the β coefficient was less than 0.10; so the independent and additional impact of such variables is small (if any at all) and relatively unimportant; all β coefficients displayed in the table are not only large enough to be politically significant, they are also statistically significant at better than the 1 per cent error level.

speaking only Punjabi or Urdu at home increases phobia-perceptions while speaking English—or still more, speaking a mixture of languages—reduces phobia-perceptions.

Yet the most striking difference between the two minorities' phobia-perceptions is not their susceptibility to different influences. Instead it is the much greater impact of jokes and insults on English immigrants' perceptions than on ethnic Pakistanis'. The English get less, and less serious, abuse. But they are more sensitive to it. Overall the predictability of English perceptions of majority Anglophobia (RSQ = 18) is twice as high as the predictability of Pakistani perceptions of majority Islamophobia (RSQ = 9).

5.4 Conclusion: Phobias Come from within, Phobia-Perceptions from Outside

There is an asymmetry in the extent of contact, friendship, and knowledge between minorities and the majority. Because minorities are small—and the Muslim minority extremely small—majority Scots have much less contact, friendship, and therefore knowledge of the minorities than the minorities have of the majority. But the minorities have very extensive connections with the majority, and their perceptions of the nature of majority Anglophobia and Islamophobia are broadly accurate. They understand not only that Anglophobia is less than Islamophobia but in precisely what ways it is similar to Islamophobia and in what ways it is different. In particular, they are aware the majority overwhelming feels that the primary loyalty of both minorities is *not* to Scotland. And they are also aware that social exclusion is greater with respect to Muslims than English immigrants—though they possibly overestimate the extent of attitudes of social exclusion towards Muslims.

Personal characteristics such as national identity and social background variables, especially education, provide powerful explanations of variations in Anglophobia and Islamophobia amongst majority Scots. But the variation in minorities' *phobia-perceptions* depends less on their personal characteristics and social background than on their personal *experience*. Phobias come from within, they are part of the personality even if that personality has been moulded by upbringing. But phobia-perceptions are learnt—through bitter experience. Even to the extent that social background does explain phobia-perceptions, it is those aspects of social background that are linked to contact and interaction rather than to character or ideology.

As might be expected the nature, as well as the extent, of interactions has a great impact on minorities phobia-perceptions. The frequency of exposure to ethnic jokes and intentional insults has a dramatic impact—even though the victims try hard to believe that their harassers are exceptional rather than 'typical'. More surprisingly perhaps, these personal experiences have significantly more impact on English immigrants' perceptions of Anglophobia than on Muslims' perceptions of Islamophobia. English immigrants suffer less harassment but cope worse with it and react more indignantly to it.

Finally, although there is some element of tautology, those who suspect that the Scottish Parliament regards them as 'a problem' are very much more likely to suspect 'most ordinary Scots' of all aspects of Anglophobia and Islamophobia. Conversely, those who feel that the Scottish Parliament regards them as an asset are very much less likely to suspect 'most ordinary Scots' of all aspects of Anglophobia and Islamophobia. If this is more than a tautology, then signals from the Parliament to minorities are critically important in determining their perceptions of 'most ordinary Scots'; and the Parliament's inclusive, multicultural publicity campaigns probably have a greater impact on minority perceptions than on majority prejudices.

6

Harassment, Discrimination, Abuse

Studies of minority abuse and harassment in Scotland have been patchy, overdependent upon press reports, small mixed samples of disparate minorities, and insufficiently detailed questioning. They have been designed primarily to counter the common assumption that racism only exists south of the border.

Nonetheless, there is some evidence of a problem long before devolution or 9/11. Two decades ago, there were reports in the Scottish press (cited by Miles and Dunlop 1987: 138) that 'minority groups are reporting increased levels of verbal, racist abuse (*The Herald*, 2 July 1984) . . . [and] racist attacks are a common experience' (*The Scotsman*, 5 February 1986; *The Herald*, 7 February 1986). In the late 1980s a survey of 'racism and harassment of Asians in Glasgow' reported that over a third of Asian households had experienced violence, threats, or harassment; that it was especially bad on housing estates; that few victims reported it to the police or other authorities; and that the City Housing Department was unsympathetic (Bowes, McClusky, and Sim 1990: 74). A more recent qualitative study of English immigrants in Scotland (McIntosh, Smith, and Robertson 2004*b*) reported that 'disparaging comments about the English were routine' (para. 3.6) and '*every interviewee* [our emphasis] . . . was able to give their own examples of anti-Englishness . . . banter . . . verbal abuse . . . [or] physical violence' (para. 3.4).

In this chapter we take a detailed look at the experience of ethnic Pakistanis and English immigrants in post-devolution Scotland.

6.1 Claiming Rights, Accepting Duties

Almost all Pakistanis and English immigrants in our surveys agree that permanent residents in Scotland should enjoy the same rights—and bear the same responsibilities—irrespective of whether they are 'truly Scottish' or not. The question was very explicit:

Do you feel that *everyone* who lives permanently in Scotland should have the *same rights and duties?*—*rights* like being able to vote in parliamentary elections, and *duties* like serving in the armed forces? Or should 'truly Scottish' people have *special rights and duties?*

By this test, their concept of citizenship—including voting and military service—is based almost exclusively on permanent residence, not on ethnicity however defined.

6.1.1 *Rights*

Even length of residence should not matter: 'if you live here you should have the same rights however long you've been here' (E5-C). But rights required:

'a permanent dwelling' (E5-C): 'an accommodation address [to get] free tuition in Edinburgh University—is taking advantage ... wrong.' (E5-B)

Excluding a very few without a view, an average of 74 per cent of English immigrants and 83 per cent of ethnic Pakistanis back extending existing anti-discrimination laws based on 'race' to cover Catholics and Protestants, Muslims, and English immigrants. Neither minority claim special favours for themselves nor differentiate much between the four groups to be protected. Political elites are almost unanimously in favour of extending the law to cover religious discrimination. Only one raised a note of caution:

'I am a secularist ... against a society [with] too much regard for religion.' (IDI-17G)

Otherwise, they favour a law against religious discrimination:

'particularly for minority religions.' (IDI-8G); 'Christianity is protected' (IDI-13); 'Sikhism and Judaism [also] ... why not bring in a law that covers everybody?' (IDI-9); 'local authorities ... still view us as Pakistanis ... [not] as a Muslim community ... the EU directive [on religious discrimination in employment] is a positive step.' (IDI-1)

—though they are sceptical about the effectiveness of laws:

'implementation ... [is] tricky' (IDI-15); 'the most important thing is *the will* to stamp out racism, Islamophobia, and religious sectarianism, rather than simply the bureaucratic law itself.' (IDI-14)

And suspicious the law might be used against them:

'I do not trust [UK Home Secretary] Blunkett ... he is not going to use [such laws] to jail people who attack the Muslim community ... he will use it to jail people in the Muslim community who speak out about the excesses of Israel.' (IDI-13)

6.1.2 *Duties*

Although the moderator asked about 'rights and duties' many focus group participants ignored 'duties' or used the word without reflection. But Pakistanis spent a lot of time discussing the duty of military service. One of the political elites had no doubts:

'if you live in Scotland, your loyalty is with Scotland, and you enjoy the society . . . law . . . benefits of Scotland . . . according to Islamic law . . . you must be loyal to that country, even if [it] is fighting a Muslim state.' (IDI-4)

But at street level there was no such easy answer:

'if we are asking for same rights, then we . . . have the same responsibilities (PK3-B) . . . 'but would you go to war?' (PK3-C) . . . 'if war is against Muslims we should not fight . . . [unfortunately] it is always against Muslims' (PK3-B, PK3-E agrees) . . . '[but] we can't be hypocrites and say we want the same rights but we won't go to war' (PK3-D); 'there is a lot of thinking to be done . . . you would feel uncomfortable if the threat was on your own territory like Glasgow.' (PK6-C); 'It is about protecting the home—but where is our home?' (PK6-G)

For some the choice was conditional:

'it depends who they are fighting against and what the cause is' (PK1-B); 'if there was a war against the French and Germans, we would fight for the British. If there is a war against a Muslim country, one should not be involved.' (PK5-D); 'I would not go to war . . . against Pakistan' (PK1-C); 'I would not fight against any Muslim country . . . I would be very sceptical about fighting against anybody—most of the causes to fight these days are dodgy.' (PK1-D); 'It would be terrible if Muslims were forced . . . to fight their own Muslims' (PK2-A) . . . 'even if [forced] . . . inside their minds, they would be refusing the duty.' (PK2-B)

They could avoid the issue by declaring a willingness to fight:

'a non-Muslim country' (PK6-E); 'Australia' (PK3-B); 'we are not allowed to fight against Muslims but if the Scots said go to war with England, I would go [all laugh]. I am not joking . . . I would wear a uniform today for Scotland and fight against the English.' (PK3-C)

Or by reminiscing:

'I did my national service . . . the chap here sitting next to me [PK4-E] was in the Territorial Army.' (PK4-D); 'a lot of Indians and Pakistanis . . . fought for the British Army . . . conscription is good for children . . . our youngsters lack discipline.' (PK4-B)

The former Territorial, PK4-E, introduced a subtle distinction between fighting Islam-as-such and fighting states that were only coincidentally Muslim:

'I would love to go to war with Pakistan [laughs] somebody needs to sort them out ... there is one stipulation—you cannot fight ... to destroy your faith ... [But] there is no Muslim country that can be identified as being a [truly] Islamic country ... so I would not be fighting a Muslim state as such.' (PK4-E)

'a valid point ... fighting simply because the opposition is Muslim is prohibited ... fighting for the national interest ... is a different matter ... it is your Islamic duty ... and the Koran said that.' (PK4-D)

'Our Holy Koran is based on peace and love and it does not like war. .... September 11th had nothing to do with Islam or the Koran .... Even the trouble in Kashmir has nothing to do with the Koran. The Koran said if Islam is being destroyed ... then Jihad could be required [but] otherwise you are not allowed to kill innocent people.' (PK4-G)

As the discussion evolved, one appealed to the long British tradition of 'conscientious objectors':

'my opinion is no different from a person who is a pacifist .... In the [Glasgow] city centre, there are [Iraq] war protests and ... the people attending are mainly white. These are the same people who are not going to fight.' (PK6-E)

This whole discussion of rights and duties is far removed from a knee-jerk defensive reaction by a single-minded community under threat. Instead, it is characterized by open, lively, and thoughtful debate; by argument and counter argument; by much greater focus on duties than in the English discussion groups; and by the intellectual depth of the arguments put forward. Duties mean more, and are potentially a lot more burdensome, to Scottish Muslims than to English immigrants.

6.2 Perceptions of Discrimination

Though they claim equal rights neither English immigrants nor ethnic Pakistanis are convinced that people regarded by the majority as 'not truly Scottish' actually do get equal treatment in their day-to-day dealings with 'ordinary Scots'—no matter how fairly they may be treated under the law by government and its officials. Formal equality under the law does not guarantee warm acceptance on the street.

6.2.1 *Harassment and Discrimination*

In the survey, around 87 per cent (excluding a few DKs, etc.) of both minorities feel Scots on occasion treat those they do not regard as 'truly

Scottish' worse than they treat others; 40 per cent of English immigrants and 47 per cent of Pakistanis feel that happens 'more than rarely'.

Perceptions are backed up by reports of personal experience: 28 per cent of English immigrants and 51 per cent of Pakistanis report that they (or someone in their own household) have been personally 'harassed or discriminated against' for being English, Pakistani (43 per cent), or Muslim (8 per cent).

A few English participants told personal tales of job discrimination:

'I got an interview [but] the minute I opened my mouth, you could see the shutters come down' (E6-G); 'the farm owner would not [employ] me ... because I had an English accent' (E4-H); 'my husband [bought] a dental practice ... [but] the sellers changed their mind [because] his address was in England.' (E4-D)

Pakistanis had far more to tell. Echoing E6-G, one reported:

'he was fine during the phone call ... but the minute I turned up in person, he went quiet and withdrawn' (PK1-E) ... 'we have all had experiences like that' (PK1-D); 'I was the most experienced person in the organisation and I was refused the job' (PK5-A); 'I did a teaching diploma ... all the women who did the same course have found [employment but] I am not being given a chance.' (PK2-A); 'my son searched for years as a graduate.' (PK2-B)

They also had problems *in* employment:

'an Asian bus driver will get the worst shift, worst bus, worst overtime [and] worst passengers.' (PK4-D)

Though participants in English focus groups occasionally complained of being caught in the crossfire of sectarianism, religious discrimination affected Pakistanis more:

'A friend of mine went for a job interview in a law firm [in] a headscarf. The interviewer said: will you be wearing a headscarf in court? ... it is obvious why she did not get the job.' (PK6-G) ... 'you need to change ... you may feel strongly about it, but [otherwise] you will not get that job.' (PK6-C)

—and some had changed the system:

'school was not very accommodating towards Muslim girls ... we took our case to ... the *Herald* [which] published our story front page ... the school changed its policy ... allowed [the] hijab.' (PK1-G)

English immigrants did not shrink from using the term 'racist' to describe their treatment:

'I have faced racism many times [mostly] on the buses.' (PK5-D); 'ill treatment ... on buses when I've asked for a ticket in [an] English [accent]' (E2-E); 'we've all had remarks made to us.' (E3-A); 'racism does exist here ... barracked about being English ... I hate that.' (E4-C)

6.2.2 Ethnic Jokes

'Harassment' and 'discrimination' are somewhat elastic terms. So we asked survey respondents more specifically:

How often have you had to listen to comments about English/Pakistani or Muslim people which were *intended as humorous* but which *irritated* you? very often, sometimes, rarely, never?

Such a specific question all but eliminated 'don't knows' or 'mixed/depends' responses: 84 per cent of both minorities report being subjected to irritating ethnic jokes; 44 per cent of English immigrants and 51 per cent of Pakistanis have had such experiences 'more than rarely'. In Chapter 5 we found that English immigrants were more sensitive to ethnic jokes, in that the frequency of such jokes had more impact on their perceptions of majority Scots. But Pakistanis are more sensitive to ethnic jokes in the rather different sense that they find them hurtful: 46 per cent of Pakistanis but only 10 per cent of the English say they have been 'hurt and annoyed' by jokes.

For the English, ethnic jokes within a multinational state could be reciprocal and good-humoured—told by everyone about everyone. Jokes would constitute an insult only if they were 'aimed' (E2-E) to wound:

'in England I heard more jokes against the Scots than I have heard against the English here.' (E1-B); 'jokes about the Englishman, the Irishman and the Scots.' (E2-F)

But jokes could be misjudged:

'intended to be humorous but went too far ... it boiled up into quite a nasty situation' (E5-A)

and they were:

'not always intended to be humorous' (E3-A); 'I was invited to [address] a St Andrews Day dinner ... it was a bit of a joke because they had got me because I was an Englishman ... I felt humiliated.' (E6-A)

Self-confident Muslim elites could cope with jokes:

'I don't mind the jokes ... the jokes you can take' (IDI-1); 'I've never been offended by a joke.' (IDI-4); 'I know the Scottish people's humour ... they say things but they do not mean it from their heart, whereas … down south … I would be very annoyed and very upset.' (IDI-2)

Even at street level, some Pakistanis can ignore ethnic jokes:

'jokes don't bother me' (PK4-C); 'jokes are annoying but not frightening … there are so many jokes made against all communities' (PK5-F, all agree); 'racist jokes happen all the time … you don't think about it anymore.' (PK1-B)

But more often Pakistanis feel hurt:

'all [such] jokes are offensive' (PK5-A, all agree); 'racist experiences are annoying … hurtful' (PK3-D, all agree); 'they are always calling us Pakis, even as a joke' (PK3-B, all agree); 'people make small racist jokes in front of me … they perceive me as being white … I worked in a bank and there were three guys I knew very well. There was a Pakistani girl who also worked there with a headscarf [and] her wee chapatti for lunch. Those guys would laugh at her and make jokes. It did annoy me.' (PK6-C); 'when whites say: are you off the banana boat?—that really hurts me' (PK4-G, PK4-F agrees); 'it does annoy you.' (PK1-C); '[jokes] hurt my children and their friends—and when they come home crying, it hurts me … if we had a choice we would not live with it.' (PK2-A)

'comedy shows on television make fun of Asian or black people and it is annoying.' (PK3-C); the odd British Asian film [with] Asian stereotype jokes and racist images.' (PK1-G) … 'I really hated "East is East"' (PK1-E) … 'really anti-Muslim … so much negativity about Muslims and stereotypes' (PK1-D) … '[but] "Bend it like Beckham" was OK' (PK1-G) … 'quite positive … Asian girls succeeding in sport' (PK1-C) … '[though] there were some anti-Muslim jokes in [that also].' (PK1-G)

6.2.3 Insults

Two-thirds of Pakistanis (64 per cent) and 42 per cent of English immigrants report being 'deliberately insulted or abused' because they were English, Pakistani, or Muslim: 30 per cent of Pakistanis and 15 per cent of English immigrants have experienced such insults 'more than rarely'. Only 3 per cent of English immigrants but 19 per cent of all Pakistanis have been 'frightened' by ethnic insults. (Of those who have been deliberately insulted, the figures are higher: 5 per cent of English immigrants but 26 per cent of Pakistanis have been 'frightened'.) And that fear extends to elites:

'when I open my mail bag it makes quite scary reading sometimes … death threats … threats to the Mosques.' (IDI-1)

Despite their complaints about job-discrimination in focus groups, nearly all of the English and 84 per cent of Pakistanis attribute their *personal experience* of harassment and discrimination 'mainly' to 'ordinary people'. In focus groups, tales of abuse and insults usually cite 'ordinary people'— though officials sometimes 'lacked the guts' to stop it.

Many complain of verbal insults. Sometimes it was trivial, bordering on an ill-judged joke, and could be ignored:

'nothing any more serious than [being called] Paki.' (PK2-D); 'We play a lot of football. ... We have had abuse that much that we just ignore it. Sometimes we even find it funny. If there is a corner kick they shout out: you've got a corner lads— are you going to build a shop?' (PK1-C); 'you eventually start to ignore it.' (PK1-D)

Sometimes humourless:

'I have been called bin Laden's wife ... terrorist' (PK1-G); 'harassed all the time because of religion.' (PK4-D); 'white children swear at me frequently. Even when people are in their cars, they still manage to swear and this includes adults.' (PK3-B)

Both minorities report being told to 'get back to your own country'; and both report envy of their 'shops':

'[In] the cinema [a girl] sitting next to my wife ... spilt her drink [but] said ... my wife had bumped into her ... Her mum suddenly said: why don't you go back to your own country.' (PK4-B); '[in] the park, white boys usually shout: go back to your own country' (PK2-C); 'this man begging for money ... said: you Asians are all loaded with your shops.' (PK5-F); 'he started off on a political ramble and it ended up with him pointing at [my] shop and saying: get back to England with your ill-gotten gains.' (E4-D)

Mostly, English participants felt they could live with low-intensity harassment or were merely irritated or annoyed rather than frightened by it. At its mildest:

'my boss used to wind me up something terrible about my English accent' (E4-H); 'we are always getting comments: how long have you been here? They take it from your accent ... [and] it's not out of interest ... it's a critical thing.' (E4-F); 'on and on all the time about my accent.' (E6-G); 'my daughters ... had an accent for school and an accent for home ... as a protective device.' (E5-C)

But more seriously:

'my eldest girl ... never had a day's problem until now ... suddenly getting picked-on because it's [emerged] that she used to live in London.'(E4-B)

Teachers 'did not have the guts' to stop bullying:

'I thought if I sit at the front of the class, the teacher would witness the bullying. And she did, but she did not have the guts to do anything about it.' (PK4-E)

Or even encouraged it by example. A teacher reported:

'[the other teachers' attitude] was always: you can bash the English and she can't say anything ... embarrassing ... very hurtful ... not nice at all ... [and] the children [then] think that they can bash the English.' (E2-F)

And occasionally harassment got *much worse*:

'I went to pick up my children from school and I parked my car ... children from another school started to throw stones ... I picked up my children, but those white kids were waiting for me around the corner. I stopped at the traffic lights and those same youths started to throw stones again at my car ... my entire windscreen smashed ... the police did not do anything.' (PK2-A)

One woman, a Scot herself, returned with her family to a very pleasant rural part of Scotland. Her young daughter, however, was in England and was:

'bullied ... physically, verbally and emotionally abused by a group of six boys ... because she spoke with an English accent ... held her physically while they all rubbed their Scottish flags in her face and then taunted her ... reporting it to the school brought little support.'

A letter to the new Parliament's First Minister elicited the reply that:

'anti-English racism ran deep in Scotland and would take many years to eradicate ... Given that my daughter has suffered such racism in a rural school, I dread to think what happens in inner-city schools.' (letter from mother to the authors)

None of our English focus groups were in 'inner-city' areas, but one was in industrial Lanarkshire where there was equally sharp criticism of:

'the inability of Scottish people to recognise their racism towards English immigrants.' (E6-E)

And again, the inability of school authorities to recognize its seriousness:

'our boys came home from school one day and they had been spat at all down the backs of their coats ... I went to see the head master [who] said: what do you expect, you are English.' (E6-B)

Even the elderly joined in:

'when our oldest child was only 10, he went next door to ask this elderly lady if her grandson could come out to play with him and—I've got to say what she said—"F off back to England, you effing English bastard"—and slammed the door in his face.' (E6-E)

107

6.3 Experience

Ethnic Pakistanis clearly experience far higher levels of harassment and abuse than English immigrants. But within each minority experiences differ according to personal circumstances and social background. As we have noted before however, social background itself varies in different ways within the two minorities. Age varies more amongst English immigrants and has an important impact on their experience of harassment and abuse. But Pakistani experience of harassment and abuse is affected by factors that do not affect English experiences: gender, birthplace, language, and the peculiarities of Pakistani occupational structure. Class, income and occupational sector have little or no impact on either minority's experience of harassment and abuse, however.

6.3.1 *Age and Generation*

Older English immigrants report between 20 and 30 per cent less harassment, irritating jokes, or intentional insults than the young but the relationship is not linear: there is a clear break point at around age 55. There is some evidence of a similar pattern amongst ethnic Pakistanis though relatively few Pakistanis are aged over 55.

6.3.2 *New Arrivals*

Long-established English immigrants report less harassment and abuse. But amongst ethnic Pakistanis the pattern is reversed: recent arrivals report about 20 per cent less harassment, jokes, and insults compared to longer established Pakistani immigrants. And ethnic Pakistanis born in Scotland report by far the *most* harassment and abuse—around 35 per cent more than recent arrivals. These are subjective reports however and those born in Scotland may feel particularly sensitive to harassment and abuse 'in the land of their birth' (Table 6.1).

6.3.3 *Gender*

Amongst ethnic Pakistanis, women are slightly (10 per cent) less likely than men to report being harassed or insulted, but there is no evidence of a similar pattern amongst English immigrants.

Table 6.1. Impact of years in Scotland on Pakistanis' experience of harassment and abuse

	10 or less years in Scotland (%)	All born outside Scotland (%)	Born in Scotland (%)
Ethnic Pakistanis' experience:			
... not harassed for being Pakistani or Muslim	65	53	29
... never irritated by ethnic jokes	31	21	8
... never deliberately insulted	56	43	21

Source: Minorities Survey. DKs and undecided excluded from calculation of percentages.

6.3.4 *Religion and Religiosity*

Religion and religiosity affect both minorities' experiences of abuse and insults—but in opposite ways. Amongst English immigrants, Presbyterians report the least harassment and abuse while the irreligious report the most—whether religion is measured by current religion or by religion of upbringing. Episcopalians fall in between. Though there are relatively few Presbyterians amongst English immigrants they are around 20 per cent less likely than the irreligious to report harassment and abuse for 'being English'.

And ignoring sectarian divisions, the most religious (frequently attending) English immigrants are around 18 per cent less likely than the irreligious to report being harassed or abused for being English. The more religious ethnic Pakistanis report no greater level of harassment 'for being Pakistani', but they do report more harassment 'for being Muslim'. So while the most religious English immigrants are *less* likely to report ethnic harassment, the most religious Pakistanis are *more* likely to do so. And while the most religious English immigrants are 21 per cent *less* likely to report being 'deliberately insulted', the most religious Pakistanis are 18 per cent *more* likely to do so.

6.3.5 *Language*

Amongst ethnic Pakistanis, language also has an impact on reports of harassment and abuse—but in the opposite direction to that which an 'integrationist' might expect. Those who are, in language terms, the most integrated are the ones who report the most deliberate insults. Those who speak English at home are 21 per cent *more* likely to report being deliberately insulted than those who speak Urdu. Their linguistic integration seems to expose them to more harassment and abuse (or make them more sensitive to it) rather than protect them from it.

6.3.6 Occupation—but not Class

Amongst ethnic Pakistanis, occupation has a large impact on experience of harassment and abuse—but class is not the key. There is a clear spectrum of harassment and abuse that runs from a maximum amongst (i) office workers down through (ii) manual workers, (iii) managers and professionals, and (iv) those who work in family businesses, to a minimum amongst (v) those with no occupation outside the home (the largest single occupational category amongst Pakistanis). Compared to office workers, housepersons are 38 per cent less likely to report being harassed, 20 per cent less likely to report irritating ethnic jokes, and 29 per cent less likely to report intentional insults. Managers and professionals fall in the middle of the spectrum but differ from manual workers by only a few per cent.

This occupational spectrum is one that evokes concepts of contact and interaction rather than class. And there are echoes of the linguistic pattern of harassment and abuse: *greater* contact through occupation, like *greater* integration through language, *increases* complaints of harassment and abuse (Table 6.2).

Amongst English immigrants the pattern of occupations—as well as the occupational pattern of harassment and abuse—is different. There are few housepersons, and few in family businesses. And unlike ethnic Pakistanis, there are sharp differences both between skilled and unskilled workers and between managers and professionals. There is no occupational spectrum of irritating ethnic jokes: English immigrants have to put up with a stream of irritating ethnic jokes irrespective of occupation. On harassment and 'intentional insults', however, there are clear occupational differences. And it is a simple divide between a higher level of harassment and abuse amongst unskilled manual workers and managerial occupations on the one hand, and a lower level of harassment and abuse amongst

Table 6.2. Impact of occupation on Pakistanis' experience of harassment and abuse

	Office worker (%)	Manual worker (%)	Professional & Managerial (%)	Family business (%)	House-person (%)
Ethnic Pakistanis' experience					
... harassed for being Pakistani	57	51	46	39	20
... harassed for being Muslim	8	7	10	7	7
... never subjected to ethnic jokes	7	11	13	21	27
... never deliberately insulted	23	25	34	42	52

Source: Minorities Survey. DKs and undecided excluded from calculation of percentages.

Table 6.3. Impact of occupation on English immigrants' experience of harassment and abuse

	Unskilled manual (%)	Managerial (%)	Professional & Managerial (%)	Office worker (%)	Skilled manual (%)
English immigrants' experience					
... harassed for being English	43	38	25	20	20
... never irritated by ethnic jokes	17	16	13	16	17
... never deliberately insulted	45	45	64	63	64

Source: Minorities Survey. DKs and undecided excluded from calculation of percentages.

professionals, office workers, and skilled manual workers on the other. Occupational differences have less impact amongst English immigrants than amongst Pakistanis, but nonetheless skilled workers are 23 per cent less likely than unskilled to report harassment, and 19 per cent less likely to report deliberate insults.

But again this is not a simple class divide. Managers and professionals are close to opposite extremes; and skilled and unskilled workers are at the opposite extremes. Nor does it evoke concepts of contact and interaction, or integration, as did the occupational spectrum amongst Pakistanis. Perhaps it reflects the more abrasive culture of both unskilled and managerial occupations (Table 6.3).

6.4 Coping

Minorities have a number of 'coping strategies' that help them through the harassment and abuse—though they are just 'coping strategies' not 'solution strategies'.

6.4.1 *Keep Silent*

Ideological minorities are reputedly subject to a 'spiral of silence' (Neolle-Neuman 1984): they become increasingly unwilling to articulate their minority views. Ethnic minorities may not react in quite the same dynamic way. Nonetheless, they may find it necessary or desirable to suppress their grievances. It is a strategy particularly useful for English immigrants—who are an 'audible' though 'invisible' minority:

'at the bus stop once or twice ... I heard people slagging off the English and I thought to myself if I open my mouth I could be in trouble here, I'm on my own ... there was a pack of them ... they can't tell can they, until you speak ... those times stuck in my mind.' (E6-A)

Even if they do not retreat into complete silence they may moderate their criticism of Scotland and things Scottish when speaking outside the trusted circle of friends or family. In the survey, 52 per cent of the English and 56 per cent of Pakistanis say they 'have to be careful what they say' to strangers about Scotland.

Pakistanis discussed a range of other coping strategies. They could lead relatively cloistered lives:

'I have had no such harassment experiences.' (PK1-A) ... 'PK1-A has had no such experiences because she locks herself up and does not go out and about.' (PK1-E); 'I have no experience of racism because I am always at home.' (PK5-C) ... 'I am also a housewife and have had no racism experiences at all.' (PK5-B)

They could balance their experience of harassment against other more positive experiences:

'a lot of people are racist [but] a lot are not.' (PK6-C); 'all our neighbours are white and they are all nice.' (PK2-B, PK2-C agrees); '90 per cent of the people here are nice.' (PK3-D, PK3-C agrees)

They can categorize their harassers in social rather than ethnic terms:

'unemployed hooligans' (PK2-B); 'drunk whites say all sorts of bad things.' (PK3-C); 'deprived ... not getting the services they should have got.' (PK4-F)

And both minorities try very hard to believe that their abusers are unrepresentative of Scots as a whole. Only 15 per cent of English immigrants and 27 per cent of Pakistanis say that 'intentional insults' merely express 'what ordinary Scots' are feeling; the rest either say it never happens or, more often, that their abusers are 'not really typical Scots' (the view of 46 per cent of the English and 49 per cent of Pakistanis).

But for Scottish Pakistanis the most important coping strategy of all, is to console themselves with the thought that harassment and abuse is worse, perhaps much worse, elsewhere:

'the problems of racism are not as bad in Scotland as they are in England.' (PK2-A); 'Scotland is better than areas such as Birmingham.' (PK2-C)

We explored this 'comparative consolation' strategy in greater detail. Apart from their immediate and direct personal experiences of harassment and abuse, minorities have more general perceptions of conflict with

majority Scots. We asked both minorities about their perceptions of conflicts between:

1. Scots and the English—apart from football and sport
2. Protestants and Catholics in Scotland—apart from football and sport
3. Muslims and non-Muslims—in Scotland? In England? Across the
   world?

Only 15 per cent of English immigrants feel there is even 'fairly serious'
English/Scots conflict, though 33 per cent rate Catholic/Protestant con-
flict within Scotland at that level, and 30 per cent rate Muslim/non-
Muslim conflict within Scotland at that level. So English immigrants rate
Scots/English conflict as much less serious than either the sectarian divide
or Muslim/non-Muslim conflict within Scotland.

Around 39 per cent of Pakistanis think there is at least 'fairly serious'
conflict between Scots and English, Catholics and Protestants within Scotland, and Muslims and non-Muslims in Scotland—though only half as
many (6 per cent) think there is a 'very serious' Muslim/non-Muslim
conflict as 'very serious' Scots/English (13 per cent) or Catholic/Protestant
(14 per cent) conflict. So Scottish Muslims rate Muslim/non-Muslim conflict within Scotland as somewhat less serious than Scots/English conflict
or the sectarian divide.

Both minorities therefore, view their 'own' conflict with Scots as less
serious than other conflicts with Scots. Our SSAS module shows that
majority Scots take much the same view as Pakistanis about Muslim/
non-Muslim conflict in Scotland (35 per cent 'fairly serious'). They detect
less Scots/English conflict (25 per cent 'fairly serious')—though that is
rather more than English immigrants themselves perceive; but more sectarian conflict (40 per cent 'fairly serious'). Under 5 per cent see conflict
with either Muslims (3 per cent) or the English (5 per cent) as 'very serious'
however, while 10 per cent view sectarian conflict as 'very serious'. So
majority Scots, like minorities, rate sectarian conflict as somewhat worse
than conflict with either minority (Table 6.4).

Scottish Pakistanis also rate Muslim/non-Muslim conflict within Scotland as far less serious than in England or across the wider world. A mere 6
per cent of Scottish Pakistanis rate Muslim/non-Muslim conflict as 'very
serious in Scotland'; but 29 per cent as 'very serious in England'; and 65 per
cent as 'very serious across the world'. Majority Scots make similar comparative distinctions, though they always rate such conflict as less serious
than Muslims themselves: only 3 per cent as 'very serious in Scotland'; 12

Table 6.4. Comparative perceptions of conflict with Scots: the sectarian comparison

	Pakistanis' perceptions (%)	English immigrants' perceptions (%)	Majority Scots' perceptions (%)
Muslim/non-Muslim conflict *in Scotland* is . . .			
very serious	6	4	3
at least fairly serious	38	30	35
DK and mixed	3	23	15
Scots/English conflict (excl. sport) is . . .			
very serious	13	2	5
at least fairly serious	41	15	25
DK and mixed	5	3	1
Catholic/Protestant conflict in Scotland (excl. sport) is . . .			
very serious	14	6	10
at least fairly serious	39	33	40
DK and mixed	8	6	1

Sources: Minorities survey and SSAS module. Note: DKs etc. not excluded in this table. Note the high number of DKs etc. when English immigrants are asked about Muslim/non-Muslim conflict in Scotland.

per cent as 'very serious in England'; and 28 per cent as 'very serious across the world'.

There is a consensus, therefore, between majority Scots and Scottish Muslims that conflict between Muslims and non-Muslims is relatively (if only relatively) low in Scotland, much higher in England, and far higher still across the world. *Even if they were both mistaken* that would be highly significant for their relationship with each other within Scotland. Their perceptions are far more important than any objective reality for feeling 'at ease' in a more independent Scotland. And as Scottish Pakistanis look south over the border, even 'Britain' appears to them as more of a problem than a solution (Table 6.5).

6.5 Explaining Conflict Perceptions

Social background has at most an indirect impact on perceptions of conflict. Its role is to structure interactions and hence experiences. So older English immigrants and especially the relatively few older Pakistanis are more likely to assert that there is no conflict with Scots. Amongst Pakistanis, office workers are 16 per cent more likely than those who work in a family business to sense conflict between Muslims and non-Muslims; and those who do not speak English at home or who rely a 'Pakistani' papers

Table 6.5. Comparative perceptions of Muslim/non-Muslim conflict: wider perspectives

	Scottish Pakistanis' perceptions (%)	Majority Scots' perceptions (%)
Muslim/non-Muslim conflict *in Scotland* is . . .		
very serious	6	3
at least fairly serious	38	35
DK and mixed	3	15
Muslim/non-Muslim conflict *in England* is . . .		
very serious	29	12
at least fairly serious	70	56
DK and mixed	10	22
Muslim/non-Muslim conflict *across the world* is . . .		
very serious	65	28
at least fairly serious	89	72
DK and mixed	4	15

Sources: Minorities Survey and SSAS module. Note: DKs etc. not excluded in this table.

are *less* likely to sense conflict between Muslims and non-Muslims in Scotland.

Personal experience of harassment and abuse, which is itself influenced by these social locations, has a more direct and a far greater impact on general perceptions of conflict. Nothing else comes close to the impact of direct experience. Moreover, personal experience has a similar and very large impact on perceptions of conflict within both minorities. The extent and frequency of personal harassment and abuse is much less for English immigrants than for ethnic Pakistanis. And it may frighten English immigrants less. But it affects their perceptions of conflict with Scots just as much or more.

Those who have been personally harassed for being English are 24 per cent more likely to rate conflict with Scots as at least 'fairly serious'. Pakistanis who have been harassed for being *Pakistani* are 11 per cent more likely to rate conflict with non-Muslims in Scotland as at least 'fairly serious'; and those who have been harassed for being *Muslim*, 22 per cent more. The frequency of intentional insults increases Pakistani perceptions of conflict with Scots by 34 per cent; but it increases English immigrants' perceptions of conflict with Scots by 52 per cent.

Some people see conflict everywhere and others nowhere. Some distinguish with exceptional clarity between one conflict and another. But for others, direct experience or strong perceptions of one conflict may inflate their estimate of other conflicts. So perceptions of one conflict tend to correlate with perceptions of other conflicts. But the degree of correlation varies sharply. Although perceptions of the *level* of Muslim/non-Muslim conflict in Scotland and England are very different, the correlation between them is high ($r = 0.53$): the same people tend to give above or below average ratings to both these conflicts. On the other hand the correlation between perceptions of Muslim/non-Muslim conflict in Scotland and 'across the world' is very much lower ($r = 0.21$). (Correlations between perceptions of Muslim/non-Muslim conflict in Scotland with other conflicts within Scotland—Scots/English or Catholic Protestant—are at an intermediate level.)

This pattern of intercorrelations suggests that the influences upon perceptions of Muslim/non-Muslim conflict in Scotland and England may be similar, while the basis for perceptions of Muslim/non-Muslim conflict 'across the world' is quite different. We can test that hypothesis by correlating personal experience of harassment and abuse with perceptions of all five conflicts. As we should expect, personal experience has the greatest impact upon perceptions of conflict between Scots and the minority that has experienced the harassment and abuse.

There are clear spillover effects shown by correlations between personal experience and perceptions of conflicts affecting other people. But amongst English immigrants these spillover effects stop at the boundaries of Scotland: they only affect perceptions of sectarian conflict and Muslim/non-Muslim conflict within Scotland. Amongst Pakistanis, spillover effects stop at the boundaries of Britain: they mainly concern perceptions of Muslim/non-Muslim conflict in England (Table 6.6).

Significantly, however, personal experiences of harassment and abuse, ethnic jokes and insults do *not* correlate with perceptions of Muslim/non-Muslim conflict around the world. We are safe to conclude therefore, that personal experience has *no impact at all* on perceptions of Muslim/non-Muslim conflict 'around the world', either amongst English immigrants or amongst ethnic Pakistanis.

Nonetheless, within both minorities there is a statistically significant and sizeable correlation of around 0.21 between perceptions of Muslim/non-Muslim conflict in Scotland and 'across the world': the two perceptions are related in some way. It is notoriously difficult to determine the direction of impact (or 'causation') by purely statistical methods. A lot must depend upon intuition and plausibility, in combination with statistical analysis. One plausible explanation is that perceptions of Muslim/non-Muslim conflict in Scotland and 'across the world' are indeed linked by cause and not just by coincidence, but that the causal direction runs *from* perceptions of the world *to* perceptions of Scotland. We have, for

Table 6.6. Correlations between personal experience and conflict-perceptions

	Catholic/ Protestant conflict in Scotland ($r \times 100$)	Scots/ English conflict ($r \times 100$)	Muslim/ non-Muslim conflict in Scotland ($r \times 100$)	Muslim/non-Muslim conflict in England ($r \times 100$)	Muslim/non-Muslim conflict across the world ($r \times 100$)
Amongst English immigrants: personal experience of . . .					
harassment or discrimination	15	29	21	12	*
frequent ethnic jokes	16	32	20	*	*
frequent insults	21	36	32	14	*
Amongst ethnic Pakistanis: personal experience of . . .					
harassment or discrimination	*	18	21	15	*
frequent ethnic jokes	19	*	34	22	*
frequent insults	10	*	29	20	*

*indicates correlations less than 0.10. All correlations shown are significant at the 1 per cent level. Note the complete lack of correlation between personal experience and perceptions of world conflict.

example, the testimony of one Pakistani focus group participant about the destruction of the Twin Towers in New York:

'It really put a shiver down my spine. I was buying a car with my uncle. The salesman had the television switched on and then came the picture of the twin towers coming down. The salesman said something like: look what those Pakis have done now. My uncle and me just looked at the salesman and then looked at the telly and said: oh my God.' (PK1-B)

It hardly took the salesman's comment to confirm that this item of world news would have repercussions within Scotland. And the salesman's comment was clearly no more than a Scottish derivative from a wider conflict. Many of our Pakistani focus group participants assumed that the destruction of the Twin Towers would have consequences within Scotland and took precautionary action—telling their children to stay at home and, if they must go out, avoid wearing a headscarf for example. From those focus group discussions we have clear, self-conscious evidence of the direction of causal impact between perceptions of Muslim/non-Muslim conflict 'across the world' and 'within Scotland'.

So it is appropriate to calculate a multiple regression predicting perceptions of Scots/English and Muslim/non-Muslim conflict in Scotland (on 4-point scales: very serious, fairly, not very, none) from:

1. personal experience of the frequency of jokes and insults (on 4-point scales: often, sometimes, rarely, never); and
2. perceptions of Muslim/non-Muslim conflict 'across the world' (4-point scale).

(We exclude perceptions of Muslim/non-Muslim conflict in England from this analysis since, although the correlation is high, both statistics and plausibility considerations suggest a two-way causal connection between perceptions of such conflict in Scotland and England.)

Amongst Pakistanis, this regression analysis indicates that personal experience of ethnic jokes has most impact on their perceptions of Muslim/non-Muslim conflict within Scotland. But both their personal experience of insults and perceptions of conflict 'across the world' have supplementary and independent impacts. The impact of perceptions of world conflict is about half that of personal experience.

English immigrants' perceptions of Scots/English conflict depend most on their experience of anti-English insults and, to a lesser degree, jokes—but, reasonably enough, *not* on their perceptions of Muslim/non-Muslim conflict across the world. However, English immigrants perceptions of Muslim/non-Muslim conflict within Scotland do depend upon their perceptions of Muslim/non-Muslim conflict 'across the world'—and to the same degree as Scottish Muslims' perceptions.

But in addition, there is the evidence of a strong spillover effect from experience of anti-English insults to perceptions of Muslim/non-Muslim

Table 6.7. Regressions predicting perceptions of Scots/English conflict, and Muslim/non-Muslim conflict within Scotland

	Perceptions of Scots/ English conflict ...	Perceptions of Muslim/non-Muslim conflict within Scotland ...	
	... amongst English immigrants:	... amongst English immigrants:	... amongst Scottish Pakistanis:
RSQ =	18	16	16
	$\beta \times 100$	$\beta \times 100$	$\beta \times 100$
Personal experience of ...			
frequent ethnic jokes (against *own* minority)	17	ns	27
frequent insults (against *own* minority)	32	33	14
Perceptions of Muslim/non-Muslim conflict 'across the world'	ns	20	18

ns: not significant. All betas shown are significant at the 1 per cent level. Note the spillover impact from experience of anti-English insults to perceptions of Muslim/non-Muslim conflict ($\beta = 33$).

conflict in Scotland. If they have personal experience of abuse from ma-jority Scots, they can well imagine that abrasive Scots have conflicts with other minorities, including Muslims. Indeed, their experi-ence of anti-English insults has more impact on their perceptions of Muslim/non-Muslim conflict in Scotland than does their perceptions of Muslim/non-Muslim conflict 'across the world'. The spillover effect from personal experience has a stronger impact than the more obviously relevant impact of international perceptions (Table 6.7).

6.6 Conclusion: More Integration, More Harassment?

Almost all ethnic Pakistanis and English immigrants feel that everyone living in Scotland should have the same rights and duties, irrespective of whether the majority regards them as 'true Scots'. But overwhelmingly, they think the majority would treat someone differently if they did not regard them as 'truly Scottish'.

Two-thirds of the Pakistanis and two fifths of the English report being subjected to 'intentional insults', though most claim their abusers are 'not really typical Scots'.

Harassment and abuse has afflicted younger English immigrants in particular, though age has not protected the Pakistanis to the same degree. Religiosity (frequency of religious observance) has opposite effects within the two minorities—reducing the harassment and abuse of English immi-grants but increasing that of Pakistanis. Integration—by for example be-coming a practicing Presbyterian—may reduce the harassment of English immigrants as they fade into the mass of majority Scots. But various indicators of integration suggest that the more the Pakistanis integrate, the more they suffer harassment and abuse. Those who were born in Scotland, those who speak English at home, and those who work outside the home or the family business, report *more* harassment and abuse, not less. For ethnic Pakistanis, more contact means more harassment and abuse—and perhaps greater sensitivity to it.

Two-fifths of Pakistanis sense at least a 'fairly serious' conflict between Muslims and non-Muslims in Scotland. Less than half as many English immigrants detect a 'fairly serious' conflict between Scots and English. These perceptions of conflict are only weakly (and indirectly) linked to social background. But they are strongly (and directly) linked to personal experience of harassment and abuse.

That abuse does not have to be severe to create a perception of conflict. Frequency matters more than severity. Even irritating ethnic jokes create a perception of conflict if they are frequent. And the impact of personal experience on perceptions of conflict with Scots is at least a strong, or even stronger amongst English immigrants than amongst ethnic Pakistanis. English immigrants are less personally frightened than Pakistanis by ethnic insults, but these insults affect English perceptions of Scots just as much as (or more than) they affect Pakistanis' perceptions of Scots. The English are sensitive to insults—though angry rather than hurt or frightened by them. Numerically a minority, they retain some of the mindset of a majority.

Amongst both minorities, perceptions of Muslim/non-Muslim conflict within Scotland are driven by perceptions of worldwide conflict between Muslims and non-Muslims. But they are driven even more by personal experience of jokes and insults—even by the spillover effect of English experience of anti-English insults. Even vicarious experience matters.

Cross-sectionally, more integration means more harassment, and personal experience of more harassment increases perceptions of conflicts. But in another sense, overtime rather than cross-sectionally, more harassment may mean more integration. Scottish Pakistanis feel that there is less conflict between Muslims and non-Muslims in Scotland than in England, and far less than there is across the world. And if these perceptions of Scotland as a relatively safe haven in an increasingly dangerous world have increased since 9/11 then, in a perverse way, greater harassment may have contributed towards greater integration within Scotland. We explore that thesis further in Chapter 9 when we look at reactions to 9/11.

7

History, Culture, Symbols

In Kellas' formulation (1998: 65), while ethnic nationalism is 'exclusive', stressing common descent, civic nationalism is 'inclusive in the sense that anyone can adopt the culture and join the nation'. Others might define 'civic nationalism' somewhat differently, but our concern in this chapter and the next is with Kellas' concept of 'adopting the culture and joining the nation', irrespective of whether that is described as 'civic nationalism' or not.

It has quite strong assimilative overtones—inclusive, even welcoming, though not multicultural. Minorities in Scotland may seek to contribute to the development of the culture and the redefinition of the nation— rather than 'adopt' an existing culture or 'join' an existing nation. The danger for them is that the civic nationalists' offer of equality and welcome may be conditional upon 'adopting and joining' what already exists.

Our findings suggest that *neither* minority—English or Pakistani—is both willing and able to accept the invitation to 'adopt the culture and join the nation': one is unwilling to 'adopt the culture', and the other is unable to 'join the nation'. We look at culture in this chapter, national identity in the next.

7.1 History: Inherited or Manufactured

In politics, history is a manufactured product. Some raw materials are necessary of course. Historical fictions are usually based, more or less loosely, on facts. But the 'debris of history'—a source of building materials for discretionary construction by current history-making entrepreneurs— is a better metaphor for historical legacies than the more deterministic image evoked by more familiar phrases such as 'the weight of history'. Entrepreneurs can use some historical facts but discard others.

7.1.1 *Fact versus Fiction*

English immigrants are particularly incensed by distorted myths being peddled as history, notably in the film *Braveheart*:

'Hollywood Scotland, no way' (E1-E); 'legends [not] real history' (E1-G) ... 'like *Braveheart*' (E1-D, E1-B); 'distort history' (E6-G); 'a strong emphasis on history is right in any country' (E3-H, E3-G agrees) ... 'as long as it is heritage, *Braveheart* was not' (E3-A); 'Scots ... go for this myth ... *Braveheart* ... a disgrace' (E4-D) ... 'emotional' (E4-A, E4-D agrees) ... 'curse the English' (E4-C); 'a lot of trouble' (E6-A); 'it evokes this emotion of nationalism ... what the SNP is all about.' (E6-E)

Scottish history teaching focused on:

'crucial parts where the English beat the Scots.' (E6-E)

—but:

'even if you changed all that, you could not change the parents passing on their hatred towards the English ... that they themselves got from their parents.' (E6-E)

Pakistanis, however, do not complain either about factual inaccuracies or excessive emotion:

'*Braveheart*, look at the sentiment' (PK4-F); 'fantastic ... Scotland's triumph' (PK6-E) ... 'good action ... also got its point through' (PK6-G); 'I see it as part of my history too' (PK1-D) ... 'it makes you feel proud about being a Scot.' (PK1-B)

7.1.2 *Past versus Future*

Despite that enthusiasm, when asked whether it was 'good for people to pay more attention to Scottish history, or should people focus more on Scotland's future and less on Scotland's past?', three quarters of Pakistanis (73 per cent) but only half the English (54 per cent) opt unequivocally for a focus on the future at the expense of the past—though many, English immigrants especially (27 per cent), find the choice too stark.

English immigrants are sympathetic to history though serious about getting it right:

'we should not forget our history, especially Scottish history' (E1-E); '[but Scots] are too interested in ... medieval history and a bit of the Stuarts ... modern Scotland is founded in the industrial revolution and they do not take that seriously at all.' (E3-H, E3-A agrees); 'it is basically a tragedy ... everything that [Scots] put their heart in turned sour' (E4-D) ... 'they are trying to ... create a unity that never was' (E4-F) ... 'Scots against England.' (E4-B)

Conversely, although Pakistanis found *Braveheart* good light entertainment, they put more serious emphasis on the future than on accurate history:

'I have seen *Braveheart* . . . people should focus on the future' (PK5-D); 'think about the future more' (PK1-B); 'concentrate on the future' (PK4-D, PK5-F; PK3-D similar); 'you cannot change the past, but you can change the future' (PK5-G, all agree); 'forget the past.' (PK2-B, PK2-A agrees)

7.1.3 Nostalgia

Whatever their personal wish to focus more on the past or the future, English immigrants say devolution was primarily designed to improve government (53 per cent) rather than motivated by nostalgia (26 per cent), to:

'improve things' (E5-B, E5C and E5A agree); 'improve government . . . build a better Scotland' (E4-E); 'Scotland very often gets a rough deal [from Westminster]' (E6-G) . . . 'I didn't believe it until we lived in Scotland' (E6-A); 'The [uniquely Scottish] legal system . . . far better [run] by people entirely involved in the system.' (E2-D)

More sceptical Pakistanis divide almost equally over whether devolution was designed 'to improve government in today's Scotland' (46 per cent) or 'satisfy nostalgia for the past' (43 per cent) however. They are more explicit about nostalgia—and critical of it:

'Scotland has its own Scottish laws and education . . . having a Parliament . . . puts a stamp on it.' (PK5-G); 'it was set up to improve society, but also to remember their past.' (PK3-C); 'a pressure from history' (PK5-F); 'nostalgia for the past' (PK6-E); 'it would be a shame if the Parliament was made just for historical reasons. Why can't people leave the past behind?' (PK3-B); 'the Scottish people got their freedom [but] the future is more important.' (PK2-B)

But both minorities used the flexibility of group discussions to step beyond the choice we offered between 'good government' and 'historical nostalgia'. Unprompted, both raised a third motivation: a political stratagem to defuse frustration while retaining control.

'to address an agenda of frustration [caused] by the fact that Westminster was a long way away' (E3-G); 'Blair had a hidden agenda . . . to defuse nationalism which might have actually resulted in an independent Scotland . . . taking the sting out of that.' (E6-G); 'to satisfy a few fanatics' (E1-G) . . . 'to keep people happy . . . because they have gone on for so long about independence' (E1-A); 'an attempt to satisfy . . . without actually making any important concessions.' (E3-A) 'to appease the nationalists ... [and] allow the Labour Party in Scotland to ... make their own decisions' (PK4-E); 'if a devolved government was not here, we would have a bloody culture ... I could see people getting frustrated because everything was coming from Westminster ... a Scottish Parliament was to defuse that situation—and, of course, Labour would stay in power.' (PK4-F); 'before [devolution] the SNP was quite popular... local councils were complaining about resources ... but now ... Westminster places the blame and responsibility on the Scottish Parliament. In reality, Scotland is now getting less resources from London than before.' (PK6-E)

7.2 Culture: Whose Culture?

Teaching history and religion is amongst the most important ways to define, build, and transmit a national culture. For both majorities and minorities the most difficult question is not so much *whether* to focus on history and religion as to decide *whose* history and *which* religion to emphasize—particularly in schools.

7.2.1 Whose History? Which Religion?

Almost ten times as many Pakistanis (38 per cent) as the English (4 per cent) say they want 'special history lessons' in their own history for their own children 'even if this means they learn less about Scottish history'. But more Pakistanis (48 per cent) and most of the English (89 per cent) feel basic history teaching should be the same for all children. And there is remarkable cross-minority agreement about religious teaching: 83 per cent of the English along with 96 per cent of Pakistanis feel state schools should teach children about *all* the major world religions.

One Pakistani coupled Scottish history with ethnic minority history:

'Scots are quite weak in their history. I am a Scot ... the only bits we remember are either connected to religion, Catholics and Protestants, or battles in which we [Scots] have done poorly or very well ... but it is important for people to hold on to the little history they can remember. The same goes for the immigrant community, they hold on to their important bits of history and that is nice to have.' (PK4-E)

The related issue of faith schools is a practical matter which requires legislative or administrative decisions—either to maintain a system of sectarian schooling in Scotland based on the 1918 and 1929 Acts, to extend it by adding Muslim schools, or to move towards a more fully integrated system. (Technically, Scottish state schools are mainly Catholic or 'non-denominational'—but the latter are widely regarded as Protestant, except in areas where there are no Catholic schools.)

As a practical legislative, administrative and, above all, highly sensitive political issue, state-funded faith schools provoked far more elite discussion than at street level and more comment from active political elites than any other issue they discussed. Some defend, even advocate sectarian or faith schools:

'very good religious, moral values running through the whole ethos of the school.' (IDI-26G); 'people should not have to surrender their Catholicism, Judaism, the Islamic faith.' (IDI-25G); 'why should [Muslim] people have to go to a Catholic school ... [to get] single sex schooling?' (IDI-5); '[Muslim schools] create a stronger identity ... [though children] are not in a fully stimulating environment where they can encourage and influence ... and be influenced by other children.' (IDI-19)

'in an ideal world ... I would not ... want to encourage separate schools. But ... Catholic schools in Scotland ... are not just good schools, they actually offer something extra.' (IDI-27G); 'in an ideal world ... we would not [want Muslim schools, but] we have extreme religious needs ... fasting, learning how to pray ... read the Quoran ... memorise it.' (IDI-9)

Even if faith schools were undesirable, equal treatment implied a right to new faith schools:

'Catholic ... Jewish ... Episcopalian schools, but still no Muslim school.' (IDI-1); 'if we accept schools for one faith, it is discrimination not to have it for others.' (IDI-25G); 'They have Catholic schools ... so Muslim schools, I would be comfortable with that.' (IDI-2); 'I would prefer no religious schools ... [but] if you are going to have [any] religious schools ... then you should have religious schools for all religious groups.' (IDI-8G); 'I am not a fan of Catholic and Jewish and Muslim schools ... [but] either abolish all of them or [learn] to live with it.' (IDI-6G); 'take Catholic [and] Jewish schools away as well and then you really make a multi-cultural environment ... [But] if you are going to give [some] state-funded schools, then I don't see why you cannot [have] others.' (IDI-9)

But opposition to faith schools could outweigh arguments for equal treatment. Some would accept existing faith schools in order to preserve public tranquility yet nonetheless argue against any more—a bit like an NHS doctor reluctantly prescribing drugs for an addict but only for an addict:

'I can't say this publicly [but] I am not in favour of any kind of faith schools ... [But] we cannot unpick the 1918 Education Act.' (MSP—code withheld); 'Catholic schools are not something I agree with in principle ... I would like to see everyone agreeing to secular education [but] I would not like to see that forced on Catholics.' (IDI-14); 'I would rather we did not [have faith schools] ... but the problem is ...

the Catholic community [might] feel ... under attack ... it has to be done by persuasion rather than coercion.' (IDI-18); 'there are more mixed [Catholic/Protestant] marriages ... maybe over time things will change.' (IDI-26G)

'you cannot pull the rug on Catholic schools because of the history ... but we should not be introducing [more] separate schools ... we should try to be multicultural.' (IDI-26G); '[Catholic schools do] not mean we should have more Jewish ... Muslim ... Hindu ... Sikh schools. That is not the answer. If we have got something that is not right, you do not make it better by compounding it.' (IDI-21G)

Religious teaching within non-separate schools might be a compromise solution:

'secular schools ... [but] freedom ... to wear what they wished ... hijab or a cross' (IDI-14); 'you won't need Muslim schools [if you] give them their religion in their [existing] school ... growing up as separate, segregated ... is not good for a multicultural society.' (IDI-4); 'why should my child have to go to the Mosque for two hours afterwards ... why can't he come home from school and play in the street like everybody else?' (IDI-9); 'I am very much against separate religious schools ... once a week ... they should be taught about different religions and cultures ... Islam, Sikh, Jewish, Hindu, Protestant, Catholic ... To pretend that there's nothing wrong with separate schools ... is just burying your head in the sand.' (IDI-20G); 'its very useful for young children to know about different religions ... to have a wider view of other faiths so that they can then put their own faith into perspective.' (IDI-12); 'I offered a model ... all children should have two papers in religious education. One compulsory introduction to all religions ... Paper B should be [for their own] religion ... [but] some Jewish people said it is introducing Islam into schools through the back door and Catholics started getting angry ... I started getting threatening letters.' (IDI-7)

But there was also unqualified opposition:

'young people eventually come out into the wider world where they are working with non-Muslims so they need to learn how to interact' (IDI-12); 'we should not have separate schools. I went to a Catholic school ... my best friend ... grew up in the ... orange tradition ... she was brought up to hate me, I was brought up to hate her.' (IDI-24G); 'I instinctively recoil from ... any religious schools ... [they] do very badly ... not in terms of academic output [but in] preparing people to live in the society ... with each other.' (IDI-17G)

'I wouldn't have Catholic schools either ... having a friend who has got a different religious belief is far more effective ... [than a] text book [on] what it is to be a Muslim.' (IDI-15); 'my dad had to use a different name because to use his own name made it obvious he was Roman Catholic ... at that time I would have gone out there and set up Irish schools [but] its moved on, its no longer necessary, let's mix these kids now … I want Muslim kids to go to school with my kids and I want my kids to fully understand the background, the culture and the religion of Islam.' (IDI-24G)

7.2.2 Adapt and Blend

The two minorities take very different views about assimilation. In the survey, respondents were reminded that:

There are different views about those who come from outside Scotland, often bringing their own customs, religion and traditions with them.

and asked:

Do you think it is best if such incomers try to *adapt and blend* into the locality? Or is it best if they *stay different and add to the variety* of customs and traditions in the locality?

By a ratio of well over 2:1 Pakistanis favour 'adding to the local variety' (53 per cent add variety: 21 per cent adapt). But by a similar ratio of 2:1 English immigrants take exactly the opposite view (46 per cent adapt: 23 per cent add variety). English immigrants favour assimilation almost as strongly as Pakistanis oppose it.

Political elites have no taste for a monocultural Scotland. Some, drawn both from minorities and majority Scots, argue it is natural for incomers to bring some of their cultural baggage with them while adjusting to local circumstances:

'They have a right to carry their baggage with them. They have a right to culture. Yet … abide by the law of the country … speak the language.' (IDI-9); 'it is sad if people lose their own identity.' (IDI-12); 'we can all bring to the table our different identities, our different beliefs and our different cultures but that table is our country.' (IDI-1); 'you can be a good British citizen and at the same time a good British Muslim.' (IDI-6G)

'notions that Muslims should blend in and be like everybody else are fundamentally racist … [let them] live as they wish … their own religious customs … dress … ideas … [though] obviously people want to be part of the community and everyone should be welcomed.' (IDI-14); 'people should be able to keep their own distinctive identities, beliefs whatever … and that can add to the multiculturalism of Scottish society … I really don't like Citizenship Ceremonies … just appalling. Somebody asked me to [officiate at] one … but I am not doing a Citizenship Ceremony … totally ridiculous.' (IDI-26G)

Others emphasized the need to adapt, even 'assimilate', while retaining their culture:

'I believe in keeping my culture, keeping my religion and even then being part of the society. Nobody should stay different.' (IDI-4); 'Muslims . . . need to do more to assimilate. They are not doing enough . . . I should be doing a lot more . . . [but after 9/11] Muslims have gone into a shell.' (IDI-9)

But there was something phoney about making an issue out of adaptation—adaptation was natural:

'sometimes in the name of multiculturalism we are going too far . . . the Scottish Executive . . . used to write Happy Christmas and this time they decided that might offend some people [so they changed it to] Seasons Greetings . . . madness, it doesn't offend . . . A lot of Muslim people phone me saying Happy Christmas . . . everyone of my constituents [gets] a Christmas card coming from a Muslim . . . peoples' perception will be that the Scottish Executive has made this decision under the pressure from the Muslim community.' (IDI-code withheld)

'how do you feel about Blunkett saying that to be more British you should be able to speak proper English?' (interviewer) . . . 'they are all learning, it is in their own interests. They have to go to hospital . . . buy things . . . why would they not learn? . . . it is not an issue, they are only making it an issue because they don't have anything else to say.' (IDI-7)

Amongst Scottish Pakistanis, linguistic integration is not an issue—despite the concern of UK ministers like Blunkett that in order to 'tackle segregation and overcome mutual hostility and ignorance . . . one factor . . . is the ability of new migrants to speak English' ('What does citizenship mean today?' by David Blunkett, *The Observer*, Sunday, September 15 2002). Blunkett was pushing at an open door:

'People who come here should learn the English language' (PK2-A) . . . 'cannot survive without the English language.' (PK2-B)

'my gran has been here for 50 years and can't speak a word of English—maybe my gran did not need to learn English and was at home with her family . . . ethnic minorities must be *made to attend* English classes' (PK6-C) . . . 'if PK6-C's gran had been *made* to go out and learn the language, it would have helped the economy and helped ethic minorities to integrate more into society [while] keeping their own identity' (PK6-E); 'immigrants that are marrying Asians from this country and gain entry should also be *made to learn* English' (PK6-E); 'There should be some sort of *immigration rule* where learning English is an requirement.' (PK6-G)

Language is not an issue in Scotland—not for anyone except perhaps the small number of indigenous Gaelic-speakers.

Ethnic Pakistanis also stress integration through work rather than welfare:

'asylum-seekers should be given jobs ... otherwise our money is basically being given to them.' (PK6-C); 'most asylum-seekers are quite educated ... prefer to earn their money rather than having it on a plate—it does hurt their pride. Is the government allowing them to earn this money? The answer is no. So other members of the public think they are misusing the system but they're not.' (PK6-G)

In respects other than language, Scottish Pakistanis want to contribute, not assimilate. They want to keep their dress codes, keep their culture, and above all keep their religion. But at the same time they want to mix with the multicultural Scottish society—and to change, expand, and enrich that culture through diversity:

'people should be encouraged to be educated and learn about the culture of the local people' (PK4-B); '[but] it is good to give to the other community.' (PK1-F)

They are strongly opposed to segregation or ghettoization:

'asylum-seekers are making the same mistakes the early Asians made, getting together in their own communities and making ghettoes ... they are isolating themselves because they feel safe in numbers.' (PK4-E)

—a somewhat inaccurate remark because asylum seekers often had no option about where they lived. But the more important point is the speaker's opposition to 'ghettoes' however caused.

'without losing your identity, you should mix as much as you can' (PK1-D, PK1-B and PK1-F agree); 'mix more' (PK5-A); 'mix with people and keep your culture' (PK5-D); 'know your neighbours' (PK4-E) ... 'offer them a pakora now and then.' (PK4-D)

Mixing does not imply abandoning culture or cultural identity:

'keep their customs' (PK6-A, PK6-G); 'adapt to your new country without losing your identity' (PK6-C); 'keep their culture, why not?' (PK4-E) ... 'as long as they keep within the law of the land.' (PK4-F)

After all:

'the British ruled over India for 200 years and they did not change their culture ... yet they are asking us to change ourselves.' (PK3-D)

Dress codes are important cultural markers:

'if they want to keep their dress they should' (PK2-B); 'we cannot change our culture and our clothes, we are what we are' (PK2-A); 'look in the mirror and you are what you are' (PK5-F); 'Shalwar kemeeze is not a necessity but it is part of Pakistani culture.' (PK2-A)

Though some stress modesty rather style:

'it is fine for young Asian people who are born in this country to wear British dress to college, university or work—as long as it covers the body.' (PK2-B)

And others draw a sharp distinction between dress codes and religion:

'immigrants and asylum-seekers should change their clothes to some extent to adapt [but] if they are Muslim let them be Muslims.' (PK3-C)

And others draw a still more subtle but explicit distinction between even 'culture' and religion:

'immigrants should keep their religion rather than their culture ... culture is more restrictive than religion' (PK1-D) ... 'gender segregation is more to do with culture than religion' (PK1-C); 'Pakistani people call themselves Muslims, yet they will want to marry within their caste rather than outside their caste. How can we [then] say we are Muslims? No we are not!' (PK5-F) ... 'in Islam such prejudices are not correct.' (PK5-A)

At street level, focus-group discussions reveal a persistent tendency for English immigrants to interpret questions about 'adapting and blending' as applying to 'others', not themselves. That might explain some of their enthusiasm for 'adapting and blending'. Without a specific and repeated request to consider *English* incomers, they spontaneously talk about Jews (E1-H), Sikhs (E1-H, E1-A), Muslims (E1-H), Pakistanis (E1-E, E2-D, E2-E), and Indians (E2-D). Even with a specific request to consider *English* incomers, they spontaneously discuss Muslims (E6-G) and Sikhs (E6-G, E6-A). They assume the perspective of a majority.

But their tendency to interpret incomers as 'others' does not explain away all of their enthusiasm for 'adapting and blending'. They also spontaneously argue that English immigrants in Saudi Arabia (E5-A), France (E3-G), Wales, or the Gaidhealtachd (E5-C) should adjust to local customs and languages. And when they do consider English incomers to Scotland, they reveal their *own* serious efforts to 'adapt and blend' by taking considerable interest in Scottish history, Scottish poetry and literature, and Scottish events. A music teacher had:

'enjoyed doing lots of Scottish songs and particularly Burns songs that I would never have done down in England.' (E2-F); 'You've got to respect their traditions ... in Wales I went to a class to learn Welsh ... in Scotland ... Scottish dancing ... it's nice to be able to join in some of their culture as well as keeping some of our own tradition ... if I was up in the Isles ... I would try and learn Gaelic.' (E5-C)

Indeed some English participants claim more awareness of traditional Scottish culture than the locals. One recalled:

'the day they wanted a piper and X was the only piper in the village and he was English.' (E2-A); 'I am surprised how little interest indigenous north-east Scots have taken [in local traditions of church music]' (E2-D); 'we like local history . . . we did a questionnaire, just a fun one, for a group of [local] people . . . and they hadn't got a clue.' (E5-C)

Others claimed to be more active than local Scots in their local communities though they were:

'not sure whether its English dynamism as whether it's just somebody new coming into a community and trying to make friends as much as anything else.' (E4-G)

Short and Stockdale (1999: 190) also report rather higher than average participation in local cultural and community activities including school boards by 'English migrants in the Scottish countryside'.

7.2.3 Behavioural Evidence of English Adaptation

Amongst English immigrants there are great differences between the religion of their upbringing and their current religion. They show a sharp decline in faith. But changes in religion also provide remarkably hard behavioural evidence of English immigrants' actual willingness to 'adapt and blend'. Of those brought up as Presbyterians, 62 per cent remain Presbyterian and only 2 per cent have switched to Episcopalianism (Table 7.1). Of those brought up as Episcopalians, only 37 per cent remain Episcopalian and 10 per cent have switched to Presbyterianism. So the ratio of Episcopalians to Presbyterians has declined from over 5:1 when they were brought up in the land of the Episcopalian Church of England,

Table 7.1. Changing religion amongst English immigrants in Scotland

	Religion in which the respondent was brought up	
	Episcopalian (%)	Presbyterian (%)
Current religion:		
Episcopalian	37	2
Presbyterian	10	62
Other Protestant	3	4
Catholic	2	0
None	47	31

Source: Minorities Survey.

to less than 5:3 now that they live in the land of the Presbyterian Church of Scotland.

Only those with no feeling for Scottish history could argue that it is only a short step between Presbyterian and Episcopalian. The hills and villages of southern Scotland, where so many English immigrants live, are littered with monuments to the 'Killing Times' of the 1680s when the state attempted to suppress Presbyterianism. And within living memory, the best-selling *Scottish Daily Express* ran a ferocious campaign in the 1960s against 'Bishops in the Kirk' after a plan to merge the Presbyterian Church of Scotland with the Scottish Episcopal Church was uncovered. It was editor Ian McColl's 'greatest campaign' ('Obituary: Ian McColl', *The Times*, 21 June 2005) and coincided with a rise in his paper's circulation to the 'astonishing figure' of 658,000 in a country with only three and a half million adults. For Epscopalians to become Presbyterians represents a remarkable willingness to adapt.

Even these numbers may understate the degree of adaptation:

'Going back to England and ... going back to the Church of England I found it completely alien compared with the Scottish Episcopal Church ... completely different going back—and I have been to village churches as well.' (E4-E)

Even those who would still class themselves as Episcopalians, had nonetheless adapted to something that they regarded as distinctively Scottish and no longer felt quite at home in the Church of their upbringing.

A comparison with changes in religion amongst the 'majority English' in England (Chapter 3) based on BSAS 2003 data underlines the impact of migration to Scotland. Of the English-born who were brought up as Episcopalians *and remain in England*, 58 per cent instead of 37 per cent remain Episcopalian; and zero per cent instead of 10 per cent have switched to Presbyterianism (Table 7.2). Conversely, of the English-born who were brought up as Presbyterians and remain in England, only 35 per cent (39 per cent if we include the URC) instead of 62 per cent remain Presbyterian and 6 per cent instead of only 2 per cent have switched to Episcopalianism.

When put to majorities, the question of whether incomers should 'adapt and blend' is about 'them' rather than 'us'. The English majority in England would interpret it as a question about immigrants, asylum seekers, blacks, and Asians. And there is some ambiguity in the way the question is interpreted (however carefully worded) when put to English immigrants in Scotland. Its wording applies to themselves as incomers, but there is a risk that some may obstinately misinterpret it in Britain-wide

Table 7.2. Changing religion amongst 'majority English' in England

	Religion in which the respondent was brought up	
	Episcopalian (%)	Presbyterian (%)
Current religion:		
Episcopalian	58	6
Presbyterian + URC	0	35 + 4
Other Christian	4	12
Catholic	1	0
None	37	43

Source: Authors' analysis of BSAS 2003. 'Majority English' in England defined as in Chapter 3.
URC: the United Reformed Church was formed in 1972 by the union of the Congregational and Presbyterian Churches in England.

'racist' terms. Yet these changes of religion provide unambiguous *behavioural* corroboration of their own expressed willingness to adapt.

7.2.4 *Valuing Diversity*

Some of the political elites, mainly *not* drawn from the minorities themselves, took a positive pleasure in diversity:

'I would like to see Scottish culture flourish, but my idea of Scottish culture ... is celebrating the people that live in Scotland currently ... it would be a shame to come here and ... pretend that you had no other history or background ... so many aspects of everyone's culture in the world that we should be proud of ... At the same time there's no point in coming here and living in a ghetto ... putting up a wall round you and not learning the language.' (IDI-27G)

'I am in favour of multiculturalism ... globalisation is culturally regressive ... I am in favour of diversity ... within Scotland ... breaking barriers between people but at the same time recognising that people are different ... I am totally opposed to the idea that everybody should learn English.' (IDI-18)

'richness comes from diversity ... we benefit from being a multicultural society... other people's cultures are absolutely fascinating ... it should never, ever be about people conforming or adapting ... more about us all learning from each other.' (IDI-23G)

'everybody has to adapt when they move to a new place ... [but] you shouldn't have to change things that are fundamental to you, to your faith, to your way of life ... it is very important [that there] should be the choice [in] personal services ... for instance women-only swimming and gym. Its not just minorities that want that ... I like living in an area where you've got lots of people from different backgrounds because I think it's much more interesting ... it works.' (IDI-5)

At street level, we asked focus groups how they would feel if there was 'more ethnic and cultural variety in the areas where you live'. Though in response to other questions they suggest that their own presence has enriched the cultural life of the locality, English immigrants sometimes interpret that as a question about more non-British, especially Asian incomers, not themselves:

'go through Leicester ... you just thought you were in Calcutta' (E1-F) ... 'our children were the only white children in the playground ... it was quite a shock because we realised how many people had come into the country' (E1-A) ... 'it's the way they carry on as well' (E1-B); 'resentment is going to come ... if they arrive here homeless, jobless ... illiterate and unable to speak the language ... because they'll be given money in their hand ... given homes' (E1-E); 'people feel defensive ... invaded.' (E1-G)

—all this in a small Scottish borders town where English immigrants comprised around a quarter of local residents.

Other English discussion groups took a more favourable view of diversity, though they all interpreted it as being provided by others, not themselves. More diversity would be:

'possibly better' (E6-A); 'you don't see enough [here] ... that coloured family ... came out with trays of drinks for these [road] workers because it was pouring with rain and none of us did anything' (E6-B); 'where we came from it was ethnically diverse and it was brilliant ... the kids had friends from all over the world.' (E6-F)

In contrast to the English however, ethnic Pakistanis always interpret the question about incomers as applying to themselves as well as to others—though close to half of them were born in Scotland, not incomers. And they also viewed it from the perspective of the overconcentration of ethnic minorities *like themselves* in particular localities: so for Pakistanis, 'more diversity' sometimes meant *less* ethnic minorities rather than more.

A few prefer the amenities of an ethnic area:

'I would like more ethnic minorities.' (PK4-E); 'more ethnic minorities ... if Pakistani or Muslim people live very far away, there will be no access to Mosques, food shops.' (PK3-D, all agree)

But a remarkably large number express a preference for living in more 'mixed' areas—in genuinely diverse or even predominantly majority areas, rather than in predominantly minority areas:

'I like the way the area is at the moment . . . mainly non-ethnic.' (PK1-C); 'although I am Asian, I prefer a mixed community.' (PK4-C, PK4-F agrees); 'when people first came here, they wanted to stay within the community and in areas near their food shops [but] now Asians have become a lot more independent.' (PK6-E)

Some go further, reacting against living in relatively ethnic areas:

'there are too many ethnic minorities [here] . . . worse if there were more . . . bad enough as it is.' (PK1-E) . . . 'There should be a balance of different ethnic groups.' (PK1-D, PK1-A agrees) . . . 'we need more people [here] who are not from ethnic minority backgrounds.' (PK1-B); 'too many ethnic minorities in this area' (PK2-B, all agree) . . . 'far too many . . . enough is enough.' (PK2-C); 'there should not be too many ethnic minorities . . . living in an area.' (PK6-G); 'I would mind if there were more Pakistanis [here], sometimes Pakistanis are more nosey.' (PK5-F)

Although many recent asylum seekers have been Muslims, ethnic Pakistanis in Scotland have only a guarded welcome for them and particularly dislike them being concentrated in large numbers:

'I would try to get on with them.' (PK6-D); 'as long as they behave themselves.' (PK5-G); 'any refugee can live next door to me as long as they do not play music at two in the morning.' (PK4-D); '[but] there should be pockets of asylum-seekers living everywhere so that they are not just integrated into the one place.' (PK6-C)

Moreover, they sympathized as much with the local non-Muslim poor as with asylum-seekers:

'problems . . . were caused because the Council dumped a mass of people into flats that nobody else would take . . . a ship load of people turned up, [were] given brand new furniture. The white people . . . see these old flats being painted and furnished . . . Central Government paid for all the improvements . . . but the local people don't see that . . . . Many of the locals felt they had more of a right to services in this country than asylum-seekers. It was simply unfair treatment—no matter what colour you are and what ethnicity.' (PK6-E)

7.3 Symbols: Flag, Venue, Presence

The inherent tensions in a 'multicultural nationalist' vision are compounded by the significance of 'political symbols, images, ceremonies, collective self-understanding and views of national identity' (Parekh 2000*a*: 203; Modood and Werbner 1997: 263). Minorities might welcome both the commitment to equal opportunities and multiculturalism—yet still feel excluded by thoughtless mono-cultural symbolism.

The nostalgic if inaccurate claim (to the applause of MSPs, however) that 'the Scottish Parliament, which adjourned on 25 March 1707, is hereby reconvened' (Scottish Parliament, Debate 1999, vol.1:col.5), or SNP leader John Swinney's more recent call to use the 'Patron Saint' (St Andrew) to promote the new Scotland (*The Scotsman*, 19 November 2002: 8), could well be exclusionist to those whose ethnic identity makes it difficult for them to identify with historic Scotland or with Patron Saints.

The enthusiasm publicly expressed by senior politicians for the film 'Braveheart' (Edensor 1997: 147; see also Edensor 2002) might have been intended as a celebration of freedom in the abstract or as a 'positive' celebration of Scottish freedom. But most neutral film-goers would detect some antagonism in it. English film-goers certainly do. But English immigrants are surprisingly sympathetic to other historical symbols—notably the Saltire, and the Parliament's location for several years in a Presbyterian building.

Muslim Pakistanis were remarkably relaxed about the Christian Saint's flag and the Presbyterian venue. But at the same time, Donald Dewar's widely reported promise (Brown et al. 1999: 13) that 'no minority would fail to get representation' in the Scottish Parliament proved empty, and they were clearly alienated by the symbolism of an all-white Parliament.

7.3.1 *The Flag*

Our survey question about the Saltire left no doubt about either its Christian or historic associations:

Should Scotland have a new flag to help the new Parliament identify with all the people of today's Scotland? Or should it keep the historic white X-shape on the blue background—often called the Saltire or the St Andrews Cross?

As a Christian symbol, with a Christian Saint's name, we might expect that Muslims would prefer a different flag; and as a community of recent origin we might expect them to take an unromantic view of any historic symbol. And so to a degree they do: 61 per cent of ethnic Pakistanis would keep the Saltire, but that contrasts with 92 percent of English immigrants. Conversely, 25 per cent of ethnic Pakistanis (and only 4 per cent of the English) would replace the Saltire with a new flag for a new Scotland.

Indeed English support for the Saltire is puzzlingly high. While the English might have few problems with a Christian symbol, they could hardly be expected to enthuse over a symbol associated with the annual nationalist festivities on the field of Bannockburn—or with the more contemporary battlefield of Wembley. So their near unanimous support for the Saltire is distinctly odd. But participants in several different English focus groups spontaneously cite the Saltire as an integral part of the Union Jack and therefore, to them, as much a British as a Scottish symbol:

'it's fine, the Saltire' (E4-C); 'the Saltire makes up the Union Jack along with all the rest' (E2-F); 'part of the Union flag ... it's their bit of the Union flag [and] reflects that Scotland is part of the UK' (E3-C); 'St Andrews Cross is part of the Union Jack ... hijacked by the independence lobby [but] so has the Union Jack ... by the fascists and the bother boys and the national party [BNP]' (E4-G) ... 'That's true in England.' (E4-E)

So what is a Scottish nationalist symbol to those at the annual Bannock-burn rally is a treasured symbol of British unity for English immigrants.

English immigrants had other, less positive reasons for holding onto the Saltire however. One was cost:

'too much spinning and too many logos—and a new flag [would be] a waste of resources' (E2-D); 'they couldn't afford to design another one.' (E1-E)

This theme was echoed by political elites:

'[the Saltire is] not a very modern symbol [but not] exclusive.' (IDI-27G); 'it would be bizarre if we had a new flag.' (IDI-17G); 'a new flag with many colours on it [is] the sort of thing the Executive would jump onto ... a tokenistic exercise [that] doesn't actually resolve the core issues, institutional racism ... the injustices, the inequalities ... get some company in, give them £500,000 to do some focus groups and discussions and to print up a new flag .... They could do much better by putting the money into the communities.' (IDI-13)

In focus groups there was some suspicion of flag-waving as such:

'I would hate any of us to become ... like the Americans, saluting the flag every morning in school ... hand on the heart ... these kinds of symbols need to be kept in their place ... I don't like flags at all.' (E4-G);

And that too was echoed by elites:

'[we could] turn it into a symbol of multiculturalism ... [though] I don't go in for flag-waving.' (IDI-18); 'nationalism ... is inward looking, parochial ... very de-structive ... we had a huge hoo-ha about flying the Saltire ... somebody wants to invent a new national anthem.' (IDI-27G); 'I don't like nationalism and I don't like flags.' (IDI-14)

Some welcomed a more multicultural flag, however:

'you could certainly incorporate something ... that would welcome all cultures.' (IDI-20G); 'great if they had a new flag ... my young nieces ... won't see themselves as ethnic minorities, they are Scots.' (IDI-12)

But despite the numbers of Pakistani survey respondents who opted for a new flag when asked, none of the participants in Pakistani focus groups raised a voice against the Saltire. Few had views about it at all and those who did could see no reason for change: Using its Christian title, one asserted:

'St Andrew's flag is Scotland's identity ... I really like this flag' (PK3-C); 'why change?' (PK1-B, PK1-D; PK5-E, PK6-C similar)

There is little evidence of Pakistanis echoing English immigrants' positive emotional commitment to the flag, but it is not an emotive issue for them either way. The idea of new, more inclusive symbols was good in principle:

'to show that it is a multicultural country.' (PK1-B)

But too difficult in practice.

'there is no symbol to represent different cultures.' (PK2-B, PK1-C similar); 'how can we keep them all happy ... with one symbol' (PK2-B); 'impossible' (PK2-A); 'Hindu, Pakistani, Italian and Chinese ... no person must feel left out ... [too] difficult ... leave things as they are.' (PK5-G)

Unnecessary:

'we don't need any more symbols.' (PK5-D, PK4-D similar); 'the St Andrew's Cross is fine ... not like the English flag which is [narrowly] patriotic' (PK6-C); 'we are Scottish and multicultural—not just multicultural.' (PK4-E)

And possibly dangerous:

'that flag was here before the ethnic minorities' (PK6-G); 'with only three per cent of Scotland's population ... you could not ask to get a name on a flag or have a symbol.' (PK6-E); 'it would be insulting.' (PK5-D)

7.3.2 *The Venue*

From 1999 to 2004, the Scottish Parliament met mainly in a Church of Scotland building—not exclusively, for it occasionally toured Scotland. (In an electronic age there is even less need to have a fixed venue for a parliament than there was to have a fixed venue for a medieval monarch's court.)

'Most of the time', we asked: 'the Scottish Parliament meets in the Church of Scotland's building in Edinburgh. Do you feel that is a good choice or a bad choice?'

Just under half of both minorities (English 47 per cent, Pakistanis 43 per cent) thought it a good choice; but over twice as many Pakistanis (33 per cent) as English immigrants (16 per cent) criticized it. We might expect Muslims to be sensitive to the religious overtones of the venue. But most of the English are not even Presbyterian, let alone Church of Scotland. Amongst the English, the venue is criticized by only 10 per cent of those who were brought up as Presbyterians, by 20 per cent of Catholics, and between 13 per cent and 16 per cent of 'other Protestants', Episcopalians, and the irreligious. So English immigrants' sensitivities to the religious symbolism of the venue are detectable but nonetheless weak.

For English immigrants the choice of venue:

'[did] not amount to a hill of beans really' (E4-E); 'not a matter of policy' (E2-E); 'temporary' (E2-B, E4-F); 'a roof' (E4-D); 'a building.' (E4-G)

But 'if it was going to be allied to the Church of Scotland on a long-term basis' (E2-B) they would have had reservations. And they 'would have wondered' when it went to meet briefly in Aberdeen if it had 'taken over a Church of Scotland place—then we would have thought there's something going on here, but it went to the University.' (E2-F)

Although asked about feelings of exclusion, English immigrants preferred to raise the issue of cost—and cost made the Church of Scotland building preferable to the new purpose-built Holyrood building. The Church of Scotland building was:

'excellent ... a lovely looking building' (E3-E) ... 'marvellous' (E5-B), 'fit for the purpose' (E5-A); 'why didn't we buy it?' (E3-E, E3-D) ... '[only because] the Church of Scotland wants to ... use it.' (E3-D) ... 'Bet they would let it go for over £300 million' (E3-G) ... 'They would probably let it go for £40 million [the original estimate of the cost of the new permanent building—the final cost was about £500 million].' (E3-E)

Indeed:

'I don't see the need for really flash premises ... it's more important what goes on inside.' (E4-G); 'They didn't have to build another one.' (E1-D); 'They could have used the old Post Office building ... the old [Royal High] School [as originally intended].' (E1-H)

The symbolism of the Parliament building *did* offend English immigrants, but *not* because the temporary building symbolized religious exclusion. It was because the new building was a symbol of extravagance and waste, perversity and incompetence.

Pakistanis were somewhat more concerned about the religious symbolism:

'Why is it in a church? It should be in a neutral place ... [locating] it in a church [suggests] it is not a mixed society.' (PK1-C); 'promoting one religion over the other' (PK1-G); 'promoting Christianity' (PK1-D); 'This gives the impression that preference is given to Christians ... [The Parliament] should be for everyone.' (PK3-D)

But the religious symbolism of the building was neither a high-profile nor an emotive issue even amongst Muslim Pakistanis. Some only became aware of it during the discussion (PK4-C, PK5-D) or only developed a negative view during the discussion (PK3-C). They frequently said it did not matter:

'as long as the Scottish Parliament gets its job done.' (PK4-B); 'people ... are not that narrow-minded about using the Church building.' (PK4-D); 'for the time being' (PK5-A) ... 'as a substitute' (PK5-G) ... 'only temporary' (PK5-G) ... 'nothing wrong with that.' (PK5-D)

—though sometimes there was a half-serious sting in the tail:

'I don't think anyone has objected to the building [but] personally I would have preferred the Gorbals Islamic Centre' (PK4-D, all laugh) ... 'I wonder what rent the Church of Scotland receives?' (PK4-E)

7.3.3 Presence—and Absence

The greatest difference between the Pakistani and English minorities over symbols concerns 'presence'. English immigrants, at over 8 per cent of the population, could expect at least ten English-born MSPs on a strictly proportionate basis—and actually had more (Spicer 2002). Proportionately, Muslims could expect only two MSPs at most, and they already had the ear of a self-consciously multicultural parliament. They were visibly represented at Westminster and in local government, including one Provost. So their conspicuous absence from the first two Scottish Parliaments was primarily a symbolic issue.

Political elites were very conscious of this failure. It did not matter in practical terms:

'It makes no difference whether there are 20 Muslims in the Parliament or not ... [though] I picked up the Scottish Parliament guide last year and every other religious festival is mentioned, except the Muslim festivals.' (IDI-9)

But it did matter in symbolic terms:

'no representation at all' (IDI-1); '[the] one minority ethnic community represented is English people ... why should people of English ethnicity be able to get
into the Parliament but not any other ethnic grouping?' (IDI-21G)

In the survey, only 41 per cent of English immigrants (and a mere 26 per
cent of their Scots partners) say there should be some English-born MSPs;
51 per cent do not care:

'what special needs do we have?' (E2-B); 'we don't want to start a sort of Aryan
discussion ... it could be very nasty indeed.' (E4-D)

Seven per cent even go so far as to say there should *not* be any English-born
MSPs in a Scottish Parliament—conceding an ethnically 'Scottish Parliament for a Scottish people':

'as an incomer I would expect there to be a Scots [MSP].' (E5-A)

English immigrants are more aware of Scottish-born MPs and Cabinet
Ministers:

'in the big house' (E4-B); 'running Westminster' (E3-E) ... 'disproportionately.' (E3-H)

But in principle, English immigrants accept that parliaments should be
visibly representative—especially of minorities other than themselves:

'technically, yes I think they should cover everybody who lives in Scotland.' (E3-B)

Though it is not an important issue for them:

'presumably it's because [other ethnic minorities] don't feel the need—as I don't
feel the need.' (E3-E)

Muslims do 'feel the need' for presence however: 88 per cent of Pakistanis
say there should be some Muslim MSPs and only 10 per cent do not care.
(Though in debriefing sessions, interviewers pointed out that Pakistani
respondents sometimes spontaneously added that there should also be
MSPs from other visible minorities.) Even Pakistani discussions of the
Parliament's venue naturally led on to its composition:

'whites are a majority, which is why they probably meet in the Church of
Scotland's building' (PK2-B) ... 'If there were more Muslims in the assembly then
it is probable that the Muslims would not like meeting in that building.' (PK2-A,
PK2-B agrees)

They care deeply:

'what annoys me is ... no black MSPs' (PK4-B); 'this is one of the biggest things' (PK1-D); 'there will never be that many.' (PK6-C); '[but] there are none because they don't have a place for us in their hearts.' (PK3-D)

Parties—more than the Parliament or people—are the problem:

'Asian candidates are trying to get into the system.' (PK2-B); '[the problem is] how the political parties select candidates' (PK4-F); 'politicians ... don't really want to change anything' (PK1-D); 'there was an Asian candidate that put his name forward but they argued they needed a woman' (PK4-C) ... 'who also happens to be white.' (PK4-D); '[and] they keep giving Asians seats ... in areas that they cannot win.' (PK3-B, PK4-D)

Perhaps it was nepotism rather than racism:

'there are so many sons and daughters in any political party.' (IDI-23G); 'you have to be on the inside track to be selected ... a culture of who's in and who's out ... your face has to fit or you're not going to be selected ... it isn't enough to be competent and highly qualified.' (IDI-8G); 'just jobs-for-the-boys ... you need to know somebody or be friends with somebody ... the Labour Party [in Scotland is] ... a jobs-for-the-boys club.' (PK6-E); 'institutional [not personal] racism.' (PK4-B)

Or just a temporary problem:

'The first opening after 300 years was a very historic moment. People in politics were too concerned about getting in themselves. The next time round will tell us how serious politicians are to reflect society.' (PK5-G) ... 'they have learnt from their mistake.' (PK5-A)

—but 'the next time round' no Muslims were elected either.

7.4 Cultural Divisions

There are sharp differences of attitude towards history, culture, and symbols within each minority. But the key symbolic issues on which Muslim Pakistanis divide are not the same as the symbolic issues on which English immigrants divide. Pakistanis are overwhelmingly in favour of a Muslim presence in the Scottish Parliament. It is important, but it unites Muslims rather than divides them. On the other hand, the issue of whether their 'children should have special lessons about their own history' systematically divides Pakistanis. Conversely, English immigrants are overwhelmingly opposed to 'special lessons about their own history'. That unites English immigrants rather than divides them. But English immigrants are systematically divided on whether incomers should 'try to adapt and blend into the locality'.

7.4.1 Ethnic History Teaching

Amongst Pakistanis, support for special ethnic history teaching for minorities varies by over 15 per cent according to cross-ethnic friendship, language, or birthplace; by 24 per cent according to occupation; and by 35 per cent according to the paper that they find 'most interesting'. It is particularly high (58 per cent) amongst those who rely on Pakistani papers (mostly the *Daily Jang*); amongst the old (44 per cent); amongst immigrants of less than ten years standing (47 per cent); and amongst those with no close friends outside their ethnic community (49 per cent), no occupation outside the home (54 per cent), or a low income (45 per cent).

Conversely, support for special ethnic history teaching is relatively low amongst Pakistanis who rely on 'British' papers (23 per cent); speak English at home (26 per cent); have a good income (30 per cent); work in the public sector (30 per cent); were born in Scotland (30 per cent); or have close friends outside their community (34 per cent).

7.4.2 Adapting and Blending

Amongst English immigrants the key factors that influence support for 'adapting and blending' are age, education, time in Scotland, location, and religiosity. It varies by around 20 per cent according to whether they are religious or not, how long they have lived in Scotland, their level of education, and whether they live in Edinburgh or small-town rural Scotland—and by 41 per cent according to age.

Support for 'adapting' is relatively high in rural Scotland (55 per cent), amongst long-established immigrants (57 per cent), Episcopalians and Presbyterians (60 per cent), those with lower educational qualifications (60 per cent) and those of pensionable age (73 per cent). And it is relatively low amongst the irreligious (42 per cent), the higher educated (41 per cent), recent immigrants (38 per cent), those who live in cosmopolitan Edinburgh (35 per cent), and the young (32 per cent). But we should remember the ambiguity of 'incomers adapting and blending' in the minds of English immigrants, however unambiguous the question.

7.5 Conclusions: Adapting to Scotland or Adapting Scotland

Of those with a clear view, one third of English immigrants and half the Pakistanis feel the Scottish Parliament was set up to satisfy nostalgia for a past they *cannot* share. Symbols such as locating the Parliament in a Church of Scotland building for five years, the increasing emphasis on St Andrew, and especially the conspicuous absence of any 'visible minority' MSPs, evoke criticism.

Only one third of English immigrants but two thirds of Pakistanis want to change Scottish culture, to add to the variety of Scottish customs and traditions rather than attempting to 'adapt and blend'. But Scottish Pakistanis value diversity. They want a Scotland that is different from its past but different from their own past also. They reject a ghetto mentality in favour of a multicultural society in which they would be a respected minority but a minority nonetheless—not assimilated, but integrated. There is little or no enthusiasm for the relatively monocultural society of Pakistan or even that of some areas in England where minorities form a local majority.

Scotland's state-funded faith-based school system, established in 1918 poses difficult questions for the future. Faith-based schooling has many critics, but they are at once reluctant to dismantle the existing system of Catholic schools yet reluctant to set up a system of Muslim schools. Almost all Scottish Muslims support the teaching of 'all major religions' in state schools; but two-fifths also think ethnic minority children should have special lessons about their own history, even if this means they learn less about Scottish history. Although we did not address the issue explicitly, a range of findings suggest most Scottish Muslims are more concerned about broadening the syllabus rather than establishing separate schools. Some elites, however, do regard separate schools as a priority, and others would at least be 'comfortable' with that, primarily on grounds of equity.

In addition to the differences between these two minorities, there are large and systematic differences within them. But the content and nature of these internal differences inevitably differ between ethnic Pakistanis and English immigrants. There is particular concern about special teaching for their children amongst Pakistanis who lack friends outside their community, speak Asian languages at home, read Asian papers, or do not have occupations outside the home or the family business. English immigrants neither care about this issue nor vary on these sociocultural dimensions.

Conversely, amongst those with a clear view, two-thirds of English immigrants feel it is important for incomers to 'adapt and blend'. Those who are older have spent longer in Scotland and generally have greater links to Scotland (through the press or religion for example) and weaker continuing links to England are more inclined to advocate 'adapting and blending'. They do, insistently, mean that other incomers should adapt and blend. But there is behavioural evidence on religious change that shows English immigrants themselves are willing to adapt.

8

Identity and Identifying

In Chapter 7 we saw that Pakistanis were willing to integrate but not assimilate: willing, even eager to contribute to the culture of the new Scotland but not to adopt the culture of the old Scotland. English immigrants, on the other hand, were remarkably willing to adopt the culture and assimilate.

In this chapter we focus on the other half of Kellas' definition (1998: 65) of civic nationalism: whether the minorities are willing to 'join the nation'. Identities are partially imposed by external factors, partially self-chosen. To a considerable, yet ultimately limited, extent they are self-consciously multiple, self-consciously fluid, and self-consciously context-dependent. And within limits, they can be used instrumentally to build bridges to the majority.

We find that English identities are primarily territorial. In consequence, their own criteria for national identity prevent English immigrants from adopting a Scottish identity—even if they are willing to adopt elements of Scottish majority culture and religion. But Pakistani identities encourage them to identify with Scotland—not because their identities are any more flexible than those of the English (indeed they are less flexible) but because they are less territorial.

These sharp differences of identity carry through—quite dramatically—into constitutional preferences and voting behaviour. Events, as much as the ethnic entrepreneurs that Brubaker (2004: 59) demonizes, have an impact on sympathy, belonging and self-image—though not necessarily in the simplistic ways implied by some (not all) of the literature cited by Brubaker (e.g. Tajfel and Turner 1986). In particular, increased harassment of Muslims in Scotland after 9/11 has not eroded their identification with Scotland. Quite the reverse: it has increased their identification with Scotland.

8.1 Multiple Identities: Nested, Hyphenated, Flexible and Instrumental

8.1.1 *Nested Identities*

Most people in Britain have multiple identities—'hyphenated' (Miller 2000: ch. 8) or 'nested'. They identify simultaneously with lots of different things. Mere hyphenation can link different dimensions of identity such as culture and space, while nested identities link two or more levels or spans of the same concept. These could be religions: 'Church of Scotland & Presbyterian & Christian & Deist'. Or they could be territories: 'Scottish & British' or 'Glaswegian & Scottish & British & European'.

We used 'Moreno scale' two-level nested identities in our analysis of majority phobias in Chapters 3 and 4: 'Scottish & British' and 'English & British' (Table 8.1). The same scales can be used to measure one aspect—though not always the most important aspect—of *minority* identities in Britain.

In England, 'English has been treated by the new Britons as a closed ethnicity rather than an open nationality' (Modood et al. 1997: 77). So ethnic minorities within England are notably reluctant to describe themselves as 'English' rather than 'British':

'only six percent of people self-styling themselves as black and seven percent of Asians say that they are 'English not British' or 'more English than British' compared with 32 per cent of the English population as a whole ... [Conversely] fully 36 per cent of blacks and 38 per cent of Asians say that they are "British not

Table 8.1. 'Moreno scale' identities

	Amongst Ethnic Pakistanis (%)	Amongst English immigrants (%)	Amongst Scots 'living with' English immigrants (%)	Amongst Majority Scots* (%)
Exclusively British	4	42	7	1
More British than Scottish	6	20	7	2
Equally British and Scottish	36	24	37	21
More Scottish than British	36	8	35	38
Exclusively Scottish	13	1	11	36
None of these	5	5	3	1

Sources: Minorities Survey; except last column, SSAS 2003. Don't Knows etc. excluded from calculation of percentages.

* 'Majority Scots': excluding those born outside Scotland or with partners born outside Scotland or who are Muslim.

English" compared with 14 per cent of the English population as a whole.' (McCrone 2002: 305; see also GHS 2002; and Curtice and Heath 2000)

Ironically, this 'Britishness thesis' does not apply to minorities throughout Britain. Previous Scottish evidence on minority identities has been fragmentary, but one study (of only sixty-three schoolchildren however) seemed to indicate that Pakistanis in Scotland might not be so reluctant to describe themselves as 'Scottish' (Saeed, Blane, and Forbes 1999). They had less need to reach for the supposedly more ethnically inclusive term 'British'. Conversely however, as Scotland's 'significant other', the English minority in Scotland are reluctant to accept the label 'Scottish' even in hyphenated form.

When asked to place themselves on the 5-point scale that runs from exclusively Scottish to exclusively British, few English immigrants or Pakistanis refuse—which is significant in itself: the scale is easily understood. But English immigrants crowd the 'British' end of the scale and Pakistanis the 'Scottish' end (even if not quite so much as 'majority Scots' do). Faced with a forced choice between British and local territorial identities, Pakistanis in Scotland—unlike their counterparts in England—reject British identity. And they do so as firmly as English immigrants reject Scottish identity: only 9 per cent of English immigrants feel more Scottish than British; and only 10 per cent of ethnic Pakistanis feel more British than Scottish. (For comparison: only 3 per cent of majority Scots feel more British than Scottish—though that rises to 14 per cent amongst Scots 'living with' English immigrants.)

In focus groups Pakistanis adopt not just a positive Scottish identity but a sense of being ill-treated (albeit mildly) as Scots:

'I was in Canterbury and when I gave them Scottish notes they said "No, we can't accept, we want British money" . . . They were only treating us in that way because we were Scottish not because we were Pakistani' (PK2-B) . . . 'it is because they hear our Scottish accents that they act strange not because we are Asians.' (PK2-C)

Conversely, participants in English focus groups frequently describe themselves as British. Some admit explicitly that it is a 'defensive' strategy (E3-G). Others temporize: 'we live in Scotland' (E3-E); 'an English person living in Scotland' (E1-G). Or use English regional identities as a defensive strategy: 'Geordie before anything else' (E1-G).

But one MSP declared: 'an emotional attachment to the rest of the UK' (IDI-25G). And in English focus groups there also seemed a genuine sense of British identity. Although some opted for 'English', an 'English' identity was frequently *reactive*, a mark of irritation at the lack of local Scottish enthusiasm for Britain:

'British as a matter of principle to symbolise that [the UK] is a United Nation.' (E2-E, all agree) ... 'but ... if it was somebody round here asking nationality, I'm English ... just to rile them a bit' (E2-H); 'I've lived in Scotland longer than I have lived in England and I used to get so upset about the anti-English feeling ... it used to make you say you were English because you had Scotland thrust at you. People were always Scottish, Scottish, so you felt that you had to say: No, I'm English.' (E1-A)

Patronizing Scottish attempts to smooth ruffled feathers only made it more irritating:

'they would say to you: Where are you from?—and I would say Newcastle, and then it would be: Oh well, you're alright, you're just like us. And I said: No I'm not like you! I am English! It used to really get me.' (E1-A)

So, while English immigrants might sometimes adopt a British identity instrumentally to build bridges with Scots, they could also stress their English identity—equally instrumentally—as part of a dispute with Scots.

But others claimed an English identity was being *imposed* on them, against their wish to be 'British':

'It always used to be British until I came here and now it's English ... I don't feel any different but I'm not accepted as British.' (E6-F); '[I feel] British ... but a lot of Scots do not recognise the idea—you are English or Scottish.' (E6-G); 'I've always said British. But in the last ten years in Scotland I have to say I'm English because the question is asked.' (E3-B); 'we said we were British but now people identify me as English.' (E3-C); 'people say to me you go to the English Church and I [now] say yes [though it was actually Scottish Episcopalian].' (E6-A)

8.1.2 *Hyphenated Identities*

Hyphenated identities link two quite different elements of identity—often two unrelated nationalities, or culture and nationality. In Britain—or more accurately, in England—the modal preference of blacks and Asians is 'equally British and ethnic-group' (Modood et al. 1997: 329; GHS 2002, Table 3.20; our own data from the BSAS 2003 corroborate this)—implying, it is claimed, that 'Britishness' is 'inclusive' (Colley 1999: 8–9; Parekh 2000b: 38). But in their earlier study of sixty-three schoolchildren Saeed, Blane, and Forbes (1999: 836) found 'Scottish Pakistani' the most popular of a set of hyphenated choices.

We asked Pakistanis to choose between four such 'hyphenated' identities. But in this larger and more representative survey the most popular choice is not 'Scottish Pakistani' but 'Scottish Muslim' (44 per cent)—followed a long way behind by 'British Muslim' (23 per cent), 'British Pakistani' (15 per cent), and 'Scottish Pakistani' (12 per cent). That suggests Pakistanis in Scotland now see themselves much more as Muslim than Pakistani as well as more Scottish than British.

In focus groups some volunteered 'hyphenated identities', a few involving Britain:

'British-Muslim' (PK2-B, all agree) ... 'because we stay here' (PK2-A) ... 'although we are proud of our Pakistani background' (PK2-C) ... 'we do use all the services in this country so we are also proud to be British' (PK2-D, all agree); 'you always see yourself as British until a certain thing happens and then you feel partly British and partly Pakistani.' (PK6-G)

But hyphenated 'British' identities were also contested on Scottish nationalist grounds:

'Why British-Muslim and not Scottish-Muslim? Were you born here or down South?' (PK1-B) ... 'I was born here but I am overall British—we don't differentiate between England and Scotland' (PK1-E) ... 'Do you think the English say British or do they say English?' (PK1-B)

And hyphenated 'Scottish' identities were expressed more often than 'British':

'[my children] are Scottish-Muslims not British-Muslims.' (PK2-A); 'I am a Pathan [but] if someone stopped me in the street I would say Scottish-Asian.' (PK4-D); 'Scottish-Asian' (PK4-D, PK6-E); 'Pakistani-Scot' (PK1-B); 'Scottish but you can add Pakistani at the end ... mainly Scottish.' (PK6-C); 'Scottish Muslim ... even though I was born in England.' (IDI-5); '100% Muslim, but ... since we are living in Scotland, I prefer Scottish.' (PK3-C); 'Scottish-Muslim because we now live in Scotland and here we will die.' (PK5-E); 'all the children ... like to be both Muslim and Scottish and there is nothing wrong with that.' (PK5-A); 'if they are born here they are Scottish-Muslims.' (PK5-D)

Accepting a Scottish-Muslim identity was a duty:

'We must also have loyalty for the country we live in ... I hope that my children identify themselves as Scottish. They do prefer being called Scottish-Muslims ... of course they are Scottish.' (PK2-B)

But claiming a Scottish-Muslim identity was also regarded as good strategy:

'I hope my children are known as Scottish-Muslims, rather than Scottish-Pakistani or Scottish-Asian. We talk about our children being given equal opportunities, jobs, fair treatment, but by saying they are Pakistani or Indian we are making them feel different.' (PK4-B)

Like the English, ethnic Pakistanis report external pressures, *imposing* an identity from outside. Yet unlike the English, the imposed identity is often not a simple but a hyphenated identity—and Scottish, not British:

'You are not allowed to forget your identity.' (PK4-F); 'I would rather call myself "full Scottish" but ... I look like a Pakistani' (PK4-D)'; 'if I say to other people I am Scottish, a white person will not take it as a complete answer: Scottish what? [they ask]' (PK4-B); 'the young generation like thinking they are [simply] Scottish but it does not work ... a white person ... will say you are a Paki from Pakistan ... I think of myself as a Scottish Pakistani.' (PK4-G)

'I personally try my best to integrate with the Scottish community and I do get accepted but ... now and again you get reminded that you are different ... a newsflash ... something on TV ... you think: bloody hell I'm a Paki ... you get forced ... to think along those lines ... but most of the time I would see my identity as Scottish Muslim.' (IDI-2)

There was some functional value in being precise however:

'when you are identifying yourself, you owe it to yourself and others to be clear ... to curtail a long explanation you just say Scottish Pakistani ... Asian is not very clear ... if you need services you have to tell them who you are and what are your requirements.' (PK4-D)

The problem with official forms was not so much that they were intrusive as insufficiently precise:

'forms usually ask whether you are Scottish Asian or British Asian' (PK1-G); 'If you say Scottish Asian, they don't know if you are Muslim, Hindu, Bengali, or Arabian ... if you say you are Scottish Muslim [it is clear].' (PK4-D)

Few Pakistanis declare a simple non-hyphenated identity. But several report their children are adopting a simpler identity:

'We call ourselves Scottish Pakistani but [my children] say Glaswegian.' (PK4-C); 'the children ... prefer Scottish.' (PK3-E); 'I describe myself as Pakistani-Scottish but my children call themselves Scottish, not Pakistani.' (PK4-A); 'my children say: we are Scottish and you are the Pakistani, not us [laughs].' (PK2-C); '[my children] think they're pure Scottish and I am the one that is adding the Muslim word.' (PK2-B); 'my daughter ... was filling in a form about ethnic origin. She said: I want to write Scottish and I have a right to say that. Just because my father was born in Pakistan, it does not mean I must say Pakistani.' (PK4-B); 'my children are pure

Scottish, that is their nationality ... their identity ... this is their home, the only home they know.' (IDI-2)

8.1.3 *Flexible and Instrumental Identities*

We need to go beyond a focus on the existence of dual identities or even different elements within a non-nested multiple identity. We need to consider 'in what sense', 'when', and 'for what purpose' people use identities. It was a failure to recognize the variability of identity *according to purpose* that led Lord Tebbit to propose his notorious 'cricket test' of British identity (supporting the England team)—which almost all Scots, majority or minority, would fail.

Former Labour MP, later an SNP MP, and ultimately a defeated parliamentary candidate, Jim Sillars, got nearer to the truth when, in the bitterness of defeat, he accused Scots of being '90-minute patriots' (Jarvie and Walker 1994: 1). The nationalism of the sports field certainly does not translate in strength, and often not even in direction, to politics.

Pakistanis especially are self-consciously aware of the context dependence of their identities. In the survey we asked:

Does the way you think of yourself depend upon the circumstances? For example do you think of yourself in one way when watching sport and in another way when thinking about politics?

To be sure, that question only lists two possible scenarios out of the many we could cite. But it does expose significant differences between the identities of minorities and majorities and between the English and Pakistani minorities. Amongst the numerous Scots who 'lived with' English immigrants, only 33 per cent declared that they had context-dependent identities; but that rose to 43 per cent amongst English immigrants themselves; and to 56 per cent amongst ethnic Pakistanis.

A Pakistani shopkeeper in Glasgow, interviewed by *The Independent* in connection with the publication of some of our preliminary findings, began by declaring a set of *multiple* identities; then moved to the language of *priorities*, by asserting: 'we are Muslim first, Scottish second, Pakistani third'; and finally switched to the language of *context-dependent* identities, when he added that he supported 'Scotland in football but Pakistan in cricket' (*The Independent*, 30 October 2003).

Both English and Pakistani focus groups discussed the issue of 'which country to support' as considerable length. But English discussions centred exclusively on sport, and they spent more time expressing indignation at the Scottish tendency to support any team playing against the English than they did reflecting on their own support for different national teams. So their discussion, though lengthy, was not very revealing in terms of identities.

Ethnic Pakistanis, however, discussed support for other countries in terms of aid, politics and war, as well as sport. Their discussions centre on their own choices, not those of majority Scots. And they test to breaking point the conflicting claims of their Scottish and Muslim identities.

It was easiest to address the issue of conflicting identities in terms of sport:

'if the other nation was not Muslim then your support would automatically be Scottish ... If the team playing opposite Scotland was a Muslim team then 90% of the Muslim community would support the Muslim team.' (PK4-E)

They could avoid the issue:

'Pakistan in cricket ... Scotland in football ... but it's all quite light hearted, not terribly serious.' (IDI-5); 'Pakistan only plays cricket and Scotland only plays football.' (PK5-F); 'if the English cricket team is playing Pakistan we will clearly support Pakistan. Come on, we would support *any* team against England' [all laugh]. [But] if Scotland was playing we would need to think.' (PK4-E); 'then you would not know who to support.' (PK6-C); '[though] if there was a Scottish Muslim team against Pakistan, we would support the Scottish Muslim team.' (PK4-D, all agree)

Sometimes we can observe the tensions and flexing of identities within a single paragraph:

'if Scotland were playing Morocco, *I would want Morocco to win* ... but I have to admit over the last few years I have started to change my mind ... This is my homeland, my children are born and bred here and we are Scottish first ... [So now] if Scotland were playing against anybody, *I would want to see Scotland winning* ... If it's England its different ... I just have a problem with the English ... I wouldn't want England to win. I couldn't help it.' (IDI-9)

Any light-hearted banter disappears when the discussion moves away from sport:

'I would feel very uncomfortable if there was conflict between a Muslim and non-Muslim country' (PK5-D); 'If there was conflict between two countries like Scotland and Pakistan, I would be uncertain because I am Scottish-Pakistani. If there were conflict between Scotland and another nation, I would definitely have allegiance with Scotland.' (PK1-C); 'If any Muslim country were involved in conflict, we would support the Muslim nation.' (PK2-B); 'I would take the Muslim country's side because that is my identity.' (PK6-E); 'My heart goes out to Muslims in the world when it comes to politics.' (PK3-C)

And apart from their own flexibility about identity, there was some possibility of identity being flexible in the eyes of others. Both minorities spontaneously raised one criterion for becoming accepted by others as Scottish: accent. Though it is difficult to acquire a convincingly Scottish accent, it is not impossible. English immigrants find it difficult:

'after 40 years, somebody turned round to us and said how odd it was to hear an English accent on a Glasgow bus and I nearly exploded.' (E3-E)

But children pick up Scottish accents easily:

'a broad Scottish accent and nobody will ever know, they will always assume he's Scottish, but he's only five.' (E6-G); 'my daughter sounds Scottish.' (PK5-A); 'people will know you are Scottish once they have heard your voice.' (PK5-F)

Half the Pakistanis are native Scots, who have grown up speaking English with a Scottish accent. That makes it much easier to be accepted as, in some sense, Scottish.

8.2 The Limits of Flexibility: Primary and Secondary Identities

Our analysis of Moreno-scale identities amongst English immigrants and ethnic Pakistanis raises the question: why is it so difficult for the English to adopt a Scottish identity? And why is it so easy for the Pakistanis? Why are the (territorial) identities of the English so inflexible and those of the Pakistanis so flexible?

The short answer is that the identities of English immigrants are primarily territorial, the identities of ethnic Pakistanis primarily cultural; and while secondary identities are flexible, primary identities are not. So the primary identities of the English preclude a Scottish identity, but the primary identities of the Pakistanis are irrelevant to adopting a Scottish identity or even conducive to doing so.

Two thirds of majority Scots (64 per cent) say that to be 'truly Scottish' it is essential to be born in Scotland. Over two-fifths of English immigrants (42 per cent) agree, making it difficult for them to be 'truly Scottish' even in their own eyes. More surprisingly, although half the Pakistanis in Scotland would themselves meet the birthplace criterion, it is a criterion that they themselves consciously reject: only one fifth (20 per cent) feel that birthplace is a *necessary* condition, though most feel it is a *sufficient* condition. Paradoxically the minority that comes closer to meeting the birthplace criterion is the minority that rejects it more strongly (Table 8.2).

Birthplace tends to exclude English immigrants from being Scots—both from being accepted as Scots:

'we are still reminded of that.' (E4-A); 'My children certainly think they're Scottish but ... I'll never quite qualify.' (E3-A); 'ten years in the graveyard before you qualify.' (E3-G, all laugh)

But also, in many cases, from any wish to be Scots:

'I don't really want to ... I don't consider myself a Scot [just] because I live in Scotland ... I'm English ... I don't have any reason to consider myself a Scot.' (E1-A); 'I would never, ever say I was Scottish because I've not been born here.' (E5-A)

Although ethnic Pakistanis are less likely than English immigrants to view Scottish-birth as a necessary condition for being Scottish, some are keen to assert that it is a *sufficient* condition—so that despite Pakistani ancestry, brown skin, and Muslim faith, they have the right to be regarded as Scottish and to contribute to the evolving redefinition of Scottishness:

'if a person is born in Scotland he/she is automatically Scottish.' (PK4-C); 'those born in Scotland will naturally be Scottish.' (PK5-D, PK2-B similar); 'they have a right to be Scottish, whether it is accepted or not.' (PK4-F) ... 'if they want to be known as Scottish.' (PK4-B)

Table 8.2. Necessary criteria for being 'truly Scottish'

	Attitudes expressed by ...		
	Ethnic Pakistanis (%)	English immigrants (%)	Majority Scots (%)
To be truly Scottish it is necessary ...			
to be born in Scotland	20	42	64
to have Scottish parents	10	36	na
to be white	2	14	19
Someone should be regarded as a truly Scottish if they have lived in Scotland for a long time, but were not born in Scotland and do not have Scottish parents	83	65	na

Source: SSAS and Minorities Survey. Don't Knows etc. excluded from calculation of percentages.

8.2.1 *Non-Territorial Primary Identities*

The greater English emphasis on birthplace helps to explain why they are reluctant to identify themselves as Scottish. But birthplace alone cannot explain why Pakistanis are so willing to do so. Even those Pakistanis who were *born outside Scotland* are almost three times more likely to feel more Scottish (41 per cent) than more British (15 per cent). Instead, there is another explanation. The Moreno question's choice between British and Scottish misrepresents the way many people, including Scottish Pakistanis, feel (Table 8.3).

Surely, if given a wider choice, English immigrants would describe themselves as 'English' and the ethnic Pakistanis as 'Pakistani'? After all, they were only selected for interview because they themselves agreed that they were 'English-born' or 'ethnically Pakistani'. But surprisingly perhaps, these are *not* the predominant aspects of identity—not within either minority.

When given a wider choice, only 10 per cent of the Pakistanis describe themselves as 'primarily Pakistani' and only 22 per cent of English immigrants as 'primarily English'. For the English that may represent an instrumental 'coping strategy', trying to avoid confrontation with the majority by focusing on an aspect of their identity that, while not itself being 'Scottish', nonetheless does not in principle exclude Scotland or Scots. But for Pakistanis, all the focus-group comments suggest it should be taken at face value: as an indication of what, for them, is the most important aspect of their identity. We asked Pakistanis to say whether they felt primarily Pakistani, British, Scottish, or Muslim; and English immigrants to say whether they felt primarily English, British, Scottish, Episcopalian,

Table 8.3. 'Moreno scale' identities amongst ethnic Pakistanis born in Scotland and outside.

	Amongst Ethnic Pakistanis born *within* Scotland (%)	Amongst Ethnic Pakistanis born *outside* Scotland (%)
Exclusively British	1	7
More British than Scottish	3	8
Equally British and Scottish	34	37
More Scottish than British	45	30
Exclusively Scottish	15	11
None of these	2	7

Source: Minorities Survey. Don't Knows etc. excluded from calculation of percentages.

Catholic, or Protestant (recording any spontaneously volunteered combination of religious and territorial identities, though most feel able to choose a primary identity).

Almost two-thirds of Pakistanis (60 per cent) opt for 'primarily Muslim', followed a very long way behind by 'Pakistani' (10 per cent). Asking them to choose between British and Scottish—or even Pakistani—identities is, therefore, to focus on something of very secondary importance. Their primary identities are cultural, not territorial (Table 8.4). Everything else is secondary. They are explicit about this in focus groups:

'religion is more important than country' (PK2-A); 'Islam teaches that no matter where you live in this world, religion is most important . . . black or white or any origin, you are ultimately a Muslim.' (PK3-B); 'before anything we are Muslims first, and we should be proud of that, before Pakistani' (PK1-F, PK1-A agrees); 'we regard ourselves as Muslims and that's it . . . there is no difference between Pakistani Muslim, Scottish Muslim, Indian Muslim, Irish Muslim because we have something in common' (PK3-B, all agree); 'I identify myself [primarily] through my faith . . . a Muslim . . . a woman . . . Scottish.' (IDI-12)

The same view emerges in discussing children's identities:

'we are only Muslim . . . I just want my children to be good Muslims, wherever they live' (PK5-D); 'to be good Muslims, to be happy and to respect everybody.' (PK5-F); 'we want them to be known as Muslims' (PK3-C); 'most importantly they should be Muslim—and can then say if they are British or Scottish.' (PK1-E); 'I would hope first they are Muslims—and then leave it to them [to choose] British . . . or Scottish.' (PK1-C)

Table 8.4. Primary identities

	Amongst Ethnic Pakistanis (%)	Amongst English immigrants (%)	Amongst Scots 'living with' English immigrants (%)
Pakistani/English	10	22	0
British	7	53	31
Scottish	9	10	57
Muslim/Catholic + Protestant + Episcopalian	60	2	2
(VOL) P/E and British	4	3	1
(VOL) P/E and Scottish	3	3	0
(VOL) P/E and some religious identity	4	1	0
other	3	5	8

Source: Minorities Survey. Don't Knows etc. excluded from calculation of percentages.

(VOL): unprompted volunteered response. Categories with over 50% boxed.

'I would be upset if my children did not have a Muslim identity. Slightly upset if they did not think they were Scottish. It wouldn't be as big a thing if they did not think they were British.' (PK1-D)

Only 2 per cent of English immigrants opt for a religious identity as their primary identity. An absolute majority (53 per cent) opt for 'British', followed a long way behind by 'English' (22 per cent). So while identity is primarily cultural for Pakistanis in Scotland, it is primarily territorial for English immigrants.

But the fact that English immigrants' identities are primarily 'British' rather than 'English' is in sharp contrast to the identities of the English majority living in England who, on our BSAS 2003 data are twice as likely to feel English as feel British. Either English immigrants in Scotland have adjusted their identity, switching in large numbers to what they may regard as the more inclusive 'British' (or in some cases retained a British identity as the English in England have drifted away from it towards the more ethnic 'English' identity). Contemporary Scots fail to draw much distinction between 'British' and 'English' identities, however. So as an instrumental strategy to build bridges with Scots and Scotland, it fails externally with Scots—though it may still have some personal psychological value internally, making the holder of the identity feel less alien.

Religiosity provides some explanation for the differences of religious identity between Pakistanis and English immigrants. Almost all the Pakistanis in Scotland had been brought up as Muslims, 99 per cent are still Muslim and 89 per cent attend at least occasionally; over half (55 per cent) weekly. By contrast, although 76 per cent of English immigrants had been brought up as Christians, only 43 per cent still claim to be Christian, only 40 per cent ever attend; and only 15 per cent weekly.

Amongst English immigrants who do attend church regularly ('once a week'), 10 per cent opt for religion as their primary identification and 14 per cent as either their primary or joint identification. So the concept of religion as a primary identification is neither uniquely Muslim nor uniquely Pakistani; it is not unknown amongst the English; and it was probably much greater in Scotland's not-too-distant past, but it now applies to a relatively small minority even amongst practising Christians:

'religious, white, Episcopalian—the [Scottish] Episcopal Church, not the Church of England.' (E1-H); 'my nationality is British [though] I had a very strong emotional tie to Scotland because of my ancestry ... but my identity is first and foremost always a Christian ... and the nationality of being British has become less significant since I've been up here.' (E6-E)

Sectarian divisions might perhaps provide an example of continuing religious identifications amongst *majority Scots:*

'Catholic and Protestant, Celtic and Rangers ... people get murdered over it' (IDI-5); 'for far too many people on the Catholic/Protestant divide ... [these] are not religions ... not faiths [but] identities.' (IDI-17G)

But football apart, sectarian identities are weak. Only 2 per cent of 'majority Scots' in the 2003 SSAS survey listed Catholic or Protestant as their primary identity—and only 9 per cent put Catholic or Protestant amongst their top three self-identity descriptors.

8.3 Influences on Identity

There are sharp differences of identity within each minority. But as on attitudes towards culture, the factors that influence identity within the Muslim Pakistani minority are in some respects different from those that influence identity amongst English immigrants. Some factors are influential within both minorities—especially media sources and birthplace or length of time in Scotland. But others are more significant amongst English immigrants—contacts with England, the contrast between living in the capital and in rural areas, and religion.

8.3.1 *Ethnic Pakistani Identities*

Birthplace matters more in terms of purely spatial identities (which are secondary) than in terms of religious identities (which are primary). Compared to those who have lived for ten years or less in Scotland, ethnic Pakistanis born in Scotland are 20 per cent more likely to feel 'exclusively or more Scottish' and also 20 per cent more likely to prefer the description 'Scottish Muslim'—though they hardly differ at all on feeling 'primarily Muslim'.

The most religiously observant are around 18 per cent more likely to describe themselves as 'primarily Muslim'. Those who rely on a Pakistani paper are 25 per cent more likely to feel 'primarily Muslim or Pakistani'. Conversely, those who use English at home are 16 per cent less likely to feel 'primarily Muslim or Pakistani'.

Age and generation have only a relatively small impact, though the *direction* is significant. To a modest degree young Muslims feel more Muslim (13 per cent more).

The primary identity of ethnic Pakistanis, being Muslim, is *not* flexible but rigid. It is their secondary, spatial identities that are flexible. The fact that so many Pakistani immigrants of less than ten years standing (41 per cent) identify more strongly with Scotland than with Britain, yet only 2 per cent identify as 'primarily Scottish' shows how extremely quick they are to adopt a new territorial identity but also how secondary that territorial identity is. One consequence is that their identification with Scotland increases only by an insignificant few per cent amongst immigrant Pakistanis of longer standing.

8.3.2 *English Immigrant Identities*

By contrast English immigrants' identities vary sharply with the length of their stay in Scotland precisely because it takes them a long time to adjust what is, for them, a primary identity. They do not adopt a Scottish identity as instantly as Pakistanis. Paradoxically, the greater age variation of identity amongst English immigrants reflects the difficulty, not the ease, with which they are able to adjust territorial identities.

English immigrants are 17 per cent more likely to feel 'exclusively or more British rather than Scottish' if they visit England regularly, 16 per cent more if they are young (under 35 years), 33 per cent more if they have lived in Scotland for less than ten years, and also 33 per cent more if they rely on an English rather than a Scottish paper.

Compared to those of less than ten years standing, English immigrants who have spent 30 years in Scotland are 13 per cent less likely to feel primarily English and 14 per cent more likely to feel primarily Scottish.

The surprise is the extent to which English immigrant identities vary with religion. Episcopalians and Presbyterians have much in common but not identities. Episcopalians are 27 per cent more likely than Presbyterians to feel 'exclusively or more British'. And only 6 per cent of Presbyterians feel 'primarily English', compared to around 30 per cent of Episcopalians. Indeed a remarkable 24 per cent of Presbyterian English immigrants feel 'primarily Scottish'. (The figures are similar if based on religion of upbringing.)

In contrast to the Pakistanis whose primary identification is cultural and *reinforced* by observance because it brings them into closer contact with committed Muslims, English immigrant identities are primarily territorial and, thus, *eroded* by religious observance because it brings them into closer contact with Scots. One consequence is that the least observant are the most likely to feel 'primarily English'—even amongst Episcopalians. Amongst those who attend at least once a month, the Episcopalians (at

12 per cent) are twice as likely as Presbyterians (at 6 per cent) to identify as 'primarily English'. But non-observant Episcopalians are by far the most likely (at 37 per cent) to feel 'primarily English'.

8.3.3 *Partners*

The numerous Scottish partners of English immigrants have cultural attitudes and perceptions of Scottish Anglophobia that are broadly similar to those of English immigrants themselves. But their identities, unlike their attitudes and perceptions, are dramatically different both from English immigrants—and from majority Scots also. On the Scottish–British Moreno scale, the identities of those Scots who 'live with English immigrants' are not far from being halfway between the two extremes marked by majority Scots and English immigrants. And in terms of primary identities, while English immigrants appear to have switched from 'English' to 'British', their Scots partners have not fully reciprocated. Amongst the numerous Scots who live with English immigrants, 57 per cent opt for 'Scottish' as their primary identity and only 31 per cent for 'British'. The mixed household does *not* become primarily 'British'—only the English partner.

Similarly, although our sample is much smaller, those who 'live with' ethnic Pakistanis are 86 per cent Muslim by religion but only 39 per cent cite 'Muslim' as their primary identification, while 37 per cent cite 'Scottish' (22 per cent) or 'British' (15 per cent). territorial identities. In short, they adopt Islam as a faith more than as an identity. And they are nowhere near such observant Muslims as their Pakistani partners.

8.4 Political Consequences of Identity

The timing of attitudes towards constitutional and party preferences is critical—especially for opinion amongst ethnic Pakistanis. Our focus groups were held a year after 9/11 but before the invasion of Iraq. Our surveys took place after the invasion. Taken together, the evidence points to a sharp, possibly irreversible, change in the political attitudes of Scottish Muslims.

8.4.1 *Nationalism and Independence*

In the focus group discussions at the end of 2002, ethnic Pakistanis were divided in their opinion about Scottish independence. Some were in two minds: independence would be:

'good and bad' (PK5-B) ... 'roses also have thorns.' (PK5-E)

Some did accuse England of stealing Scottish resources:

'England took everything ... we now have nothing.' (PK4-C); 'Scotland should be separate.' (PK3-C); 'if we were free, we would have more resources.' (PK3-D); 'Denmark [is] just as small [but] successful ... [but] the UK will never allow Scotland to separate.' (PK6-E)

though the subtext is more interesting in what it reveals about identity:

'I am saying 'we' because we have lived in Scotland all our life ... the English are robbing our wealth.' (PK3-C)

On the other hand, some felt it would take too long before the benefits of independence could be enjoyed. It would:

'be like having to start a new business.' (PK5-A); 'take a lifetime ... our grandsons would reap the benefits, not ourselves.' (PK6-C)

And others felt the disadvantages outweighed the advantages:

'we lack certain resources that England has, and England lacks certain resources that we have ... best that we work together as a UK.' (PK1-F); 'we have relatives in Scotland and in England.' (PK2-B); 'I still want to feel close to ... our relatives ... and Britain is not very big to start with.' (PK2-A)

But for ethnic Pakistanis it was only a balance of interest:

'[in] the EU it would not matter whether Scotland was independent or a part of the UK. But it is not in our interest ... we would only be a small country in Europe.' (PK4-E)

And the Scottish Parliament was sufficient independence for some:

'your own Parliament ... that is independence.' (PK4-F)

In these late-2002 focus groups, Pakistani views were dispassionate, mixed, and balanced, though always from the perspective of 'us' Scots and 'our' national interest.

By contrast English immigrants were passionate, negative, and argued from a perspective of what might be good for 'them' Scots or 'their' national interest. There was not a single expression of support for Scottish independence. If some English participants felt it would be a good idea, they chose to keep such opinions to themselves. Independence would be:

'worse' (E6-G) ... 'much worse' (E6-E); 'not big enough' (E4-B); 'too small' (E1-G); 'far too small' (E4-F); 'too inward looking ... insular ... narrow minded.' (E6-E)

It would be an economic disaster. Scotland:

'couldn't afford it' (E1-H); 'not economically viable' (E4-F, E3-A); 'could not survive economically' (E2-F, E2-E); 'would not work financially [or on] defence' (E5-C); 'would have to re-apply to get into the EU' (E1-E)

Subsidies from England would end:

'they wouldn't get the money' (E3-E) ... 'Where does the money come from?' (E3-D) ... 'from England' (E3-H) ... 'from the taxes' (E3-D) ... 'from the UK' (E3-H); 'a disproportionate allocation.' (E3-B)

Scottish independence would cause social unrest and trigger conflict with England:

'getting the standard of living to drop—as it would have to do—would cause an enormous amount of social unrest and dissension ... a catastrophe' (E3-G); 'weaken Britain as a whole ... Yugoslavia has broken up' (E5-B); 'look at other European countries who have been torn apart' (E4-B); '[there would be an] enormous fight as to who owned the oil and you could bet that it would be England that would win.' (E6-G); 'The power supply to Scotland is weak' (E1-B); 'The gas fields are English.' (E1-H); 'English firms don't have to buy from Scotland.' (E1-E)

In the heat of discussion an SNP victory was equated with independence:

'if the SNP got in ... you would have to use a passport to get in and out across the Border ... cut themselves off from NATO' (E6-E); 'their mad cap spending schemes ... would just empty Scotland ... [SNP] proposals to raise income tax [would] make a lot of people leave Scotland' (E6-G); 'some businessmen in the town ... would actually shut up shop and go ... they said as much.' (E4-B)

'Jack McConnell [First Minister] was only saying recently that he wants to encourage more people to come to Scotland and particularly was aiming at educated asylum seekers' (E6-D) ... 'and then somebody wrote in the paper a lovely letter and said lets learn to live with the English before we start inviting anyone else in.' (E6-G)

Survey interviews took place after the invasion of Iraq and the subsequent the Scottish Parliament election. They confirm the huge difference between the attitudes of ethnic Pakistanis and English immigrants towards Scottish independence. But both English and Pakistani survey respondents were more favourable to independence in the 2003 survey than in the 2002 focus groups. In the survey, 68 per cent of English immigrants opposed independence and only 18 per cent supported it. But that 18 per cent contrasted with none at all in the focus groups who wished to speak up for independence (though some may have privately, but silently, approved). And in the 2003 survey, ethnic Pakistanis respondents were not so evenly divided as the participants in the earlier focus groups: a majority (49 per cent against 38 per cent) now favoured independence.

We do not attribute this difference between the focus groups and survey responses to a difference of method. It seems more likely to be due to the critical difference in timing: before and after the invasion. Patterns of voting support that interpretation.

8.4.2 Voting

Survey respondents were asked about voting in the 2001 British General election and the 2003 Scottish Parliament election. Both minorities vote differently from majority Scots. Compared to majority Scots, English immigrants are far more inclined to vote Conservative or Liberal-Democrat. Pakistanis also differ from the average Scot—but in other directions. In 2001, they voted 74 per cent Labour and 13 per cent SNP.

The Pakistanis' Scottish identities made it easy to vote SNP, and the SNP already had an affiliated organization 'Asians for Independence' (*The Times*, 29 April 2003) to welcome them. But until the Iraq invasion they had no great incentive to desert Labour. The SNP was anti-war in 2001 as in 2003. But in 2001 the invasion of Serbia was pictured (at the time) as a reluctant and tardy defence of oppressed Muslims in Kosovo, while in 2003 the invasion of Iraq was seen as a crusade by a belligerent, fundamentalist Christian, US President and was strongly opposed by Muslims. So for Muslims the consistently anti-war SNP was 'on their side' in international affairs in 2003—as it had not been in 2001. Various Muslim organisations, including the Lothian Muslim Voting Committee (*The Scotsman*, 25 April 2003) and the Muslim Association of Britain (*Evening Times*, 28 April 2003), called upon Muslims to switch to the SNP. And they did: only 28 per cent voted Labour, 47 per cent SNP. Pakistanis were now twice as likely as the average voter to back the SNP (Table 8.5).

In the concurrent (2003) local government elections:

'[Muslims] just went en masse to the SNP and the [kilt-wearing, Pakistani, SNP] councillor [newly elected in a relatively Muslim ward] . . . was shocked. He was not aware he was going to become a councillor.' (IDI-12)

'the biggest nail in the coffin for Labour after all these years has been the war on Iraq . . . they can say: this war on terror is not a war on the Muslim community. But that is how the resident Muslim community sees it.' (IDI-13)

Table 8.5. Voting—2001 British Parliament and 2003 Scottish Parliament

	Official Results			Amongst ethnic Pakistanis			Amongst English immigrants		
	2001 GE (%)	2003 FV (%)	change (%)	2001 GE (%)	2003 FV (%)	change (%)	2001 GE (%)	2003 FV (%)	change (%)
Labour	44	35	−9	74	28	−46	41	28	−13
SNP	20	24	+4	13	47	+34	4	12	+8
LibDem	16	15	−1	6	15	+9	26	27	+1
Conservative	16	17	+1	5	1	−4	27	25	−2
Other	4	9	+5	2	9	+7	2	9	+7

Sources: Minorities Survey. Official results for 2001 British General Election, and 2003 Scottish Parliament Election (First Vote).

But whatever the immediate incentive, the significant point for 'multicultural nationalism' is that a visible ethnic minority was *not alienated* from the party of Scottish nationalism but, under the stress of events in 2003, it had now became far *more favourable* to it than the average Scot. Setting aside the racist BNP (British National Party), which is far too easy a target, it is almost inconceivable that *any* English National Party, however moderate, could win twice as much support from Blacks and Asians as from the average voter in England.

8.4.3 *The Impact of 'Identities within Groups'*

Even within minorities, identities have an impact on participation, voting choice, and support for independence.

Amongst Pakistanis, participation in both British and Scottish elections was greatest amongst those whose primary identity was Scottish. Compared to those whose primary identity is Pakistani, those whose primary identity is Scottish were 20 per cent more likely to vote in the British election and 32 per cent more likely to vote in the Scottish election.

Amongst English immigrants, the pattern is slightly more complex. Participation in British elections was greatest amongst those whose primary identity is British, while participation in Scottish elections was greatest amongst those whose primary identity is Scottish. Compared to those whose primary identity is English, British identifiers were 11 per cent more likely to vote in the British election and Scottish identifiers 14 per cent more likely to vote in the Scottish election (Table 8.6).

Table 8.6. The impact of identities on voter participation

	Amongst ethnic Pakistanis, whose primary identity is ...				Amongst English immigrants, whose primary identity is ...		
	Pakistani (%)	Muslim (%)	British (%)	Scottish (%)	English (%)	British (%)	Scottish (%)
DNV at 2001 British General Election	37	38	27	17	26	15	21
DNV at 2003 Scottish Parliament Election	51	40	25	18	41	35	27
Difference	*+14*	*+2*	*−2*	*+1*	*+15*	*+20*	*+6*

Source: Minorities survey. DNV: did not vote. Columns arranged in order of increasing participation.

Turnout is lower for Scottish Parliament elections than for British Parliament elections amongst majority Scots, generally. And that was also true for English immigrants in 2003, most of whom identified with England or Britain. Indeed the 'drop-off' rate was greater amongst English immigrants than amongst majority Scots. But it was not true amongst Pakistanis, since so many of them identified primarily as Muslims and the turnout amongst them held up very well (dropping only 2 per cent on our figures)—not perhaps because it was a Scottish election so much as because it was a 'war election' (Table 8.7).

Table 8.7. The impact of identities on voters' changing choices

	Amongst ethnic Pakistanis, whose primary identity is ...				Amongst English immigrants, whose primary identity is ...		
	British (%)	Pakistani (%)	Scottish (%)	Muslim (%)	British (%)	Scottish (%)	English (%)
Labour at 2001 British GE	74	74	67	76	39	41	49
Labour at 2003 Scottish PE	49	32	20	26	30	27	30
Difference	*−25*	*−42*	*−47*	*−50*	*−9*	*−14*	*−19*
SNP at 2001 British GE	12	10	17	13	2	9	2
SNP at 2003 Scottish PE	30	57	41	49	8	21	10
Difference	*+18*	*+47*	*+24*	*+36*	*+6*	*+12*	*+8*

Source: Minorities survey. Entries are percentages of voters (excluding non-voters). Columns arranged in order of increasing defection rates from Labour.

Note that several pro-independence, anti-war parties including the Scottish Socialists as well as the SNP contested the Scottish elections. The Liberal-Democrats were anti-war though pro-federal rather than pro-independence. So intending Labour defectors had several options. Muslim identifiers in particular switched to Scottish Socialists as well as SNP.

Identities also affected voter choice and voter change. In 2003, the Labour vote declined amongst English immigrants and collapsed amongst ethnic Pakistanis. But it held up rather better amongst those who identified with Britain. Compared to Pakistanis who identified primarily with Britain, the Labour vote amongst those who identified primarily as Muslim dropped by twice as much (by 50 per cent instead of 25 per cent) while the SNP vote went up twice as much (by 36 per cent instead of 18 per cent).

Amongst English immigrants, those who identify with Scotland are the most pro-independence and those who identify with Britain the least. What is surprising however, is the high level of support for Scottish independence amongst those whose primary identity is England. The English identifiers appear to recognize sub-state claims to independence almost as much as the Scottish identifiers, and both Scottish and English identifiers have common perspectives that contrast with those of the more 'supra-national' British identifiers (Table 8.8).

Amongst ethnic Pakistanis there is another surprise. Identity makes little difference to their attitudes towards Scottish independence. But it is if anything the Muslim identifiers, not the Scottish identifiers, who most favour Scottish independence. At least independence might have kept Scottish troops out of Iraq. A difference of 2 per cent is not statistically significant. But what is politically (and statistically) significant is that primarily Muslim identifiers have no more reservations than Pakistanis with primarily Scottish identities about Scottish independence. And indeed their support for Scottish independence runs far ahead of that amongst majority Scots.

Table 8.8. The impact of identities on attitudes towards independence

	Amongst ethnic Pakistanis, whose primary identity is ...				Amongst English immigrants, whose primary identity is ...		
	British (%)	Pakistani (%)	Scottish (%)	Muslim (%)	British (%)	English (%)	Scottish (%)
It would it be better if Scotland was a completely *independent* *country*, separate from England	51	53	54	56	12	30	34

Source: Minorities survey. DKs and those with mixed views excluded from calculation of percentages. Columns arranged in order of increasing support for independence.

8.5 Conclusions: Bridges and Walls

English immigrants cannot identify with Scotland despite respecting its traditions, while Pakistanis can easily identify with Scotland despite wanting to change it. Pakistani identities are primarily cultural ('Muslim') rather than territorial, but insofar as they are territorial they are more Scottish than British. They were already sympathetic to devolution before 1997, but a majority now support complete independence, and by 2003 they had become twice as likely to vote SNP as the average Scot.

Identities also vary considerably and systematically within each minority. Because spatial identities are not the primary identities for a majority of Pakistanis, they find it particularly easy to adopt a Scottish identity irrespective of whether they have been born in Scotland or not. And for incomers it happens quickly. Only 9 per cent of English immigrants but 44 per cent of Pakistani *immigrants* identify more with Scotland than with Britain. Nonetheless, those ethnic Pakistanis who have been born in Scotland find it even easier: 61 per cent identify more with Scotland than with Britain. But being Muslim is at the heart of Pakistani identities, and although it varies somewhat with religious observance and language, it does not vary greatly.

The identities of English immigrants are primarily spatial, and because they put so much weight on birthplace, they find it exceedingly difficult to identify with Scotland. Insofar as they do adopt a Scottish identity they do so slowly—over decades. Mostly they remain sympathetic outsiders. Nonetheless their identities do vary, albeit by modest amounts. Those who have lived in Scotland for a long time or who are Presbyterian rather than Episcopalian are somewhat more likely to identify primarily with Scotland. But it is the non-observant Episcopalians that are least likely to identify with Scotland. The Scottish Episcopal Church may be in communion with the Church of England, but it has its own nationalist identity, often overlooked by majority Scots who (wrongly) call it the 'English Church'.

Culture and identity provide both 'bridges and walls' between Scots and these two minorities. But what is a bridge for one is a wall for the other. For English immigrants culture is the bridge and identity the wall. Their culture is close to that of majority Scots, and, more important, it is flexible. Many English immigrants explicitly advocate adapting and blending on principle; they show some interest in Scottish history and traditions; and they even adjust their religious affiliations. In the course of time they also come to identify a little more with Scotland—but only very slowly and in small numbers. But their identity is only really flexible to the point of switching to 'British' rather than 'English': they cannot easily or quickly adopt a 'Scottish' identity.

For ethnic Pakistanis, culture is the wall and identity is the bridge. They identify quickly, easily, and in large numbers with Scotland; but they want to change Scotland by adding to the variety of Scottish culture and traditions. The SNP's welcoming political stance over the years and especially its opposition to the invasion of Iraq has made it even easier for them to identify with Scotland, by establishing a theoretically contingent but in practice very positive (rather than merely neutral) connection between Scottish and Muslim identities.

9

After Devolution: Parliament and People

Devolution created new institutions: a Scottish Parliament and Executive—though the public draw little distinction between them, and the term 'Parliament' is used loosely to include both. In this chapter we review minority perceptions of and attitudes towards the new Parliament. But the Parliament's powers and performance may be less significant than the street-level changes that go with its creation. So as well as considering ratings of institutional performance we look at minorities' perceptions of the street-level changes that they associate with devolution: what they think devolution has done to the attitudes and behaviour of ordinary Scots. And in the peculiar circumstances of the time, we also look at how minorities distinguish the street-level changes that they attribute to devolution from the others that they attribute to concurrent events, notably 9/11.

9.1 The Parliament: Performance and Style

Throughout its full first term the new Parliament was much criticized—though more for extravagance and incompetence than for perversity.

The principle of devolution remained broadly acceptable. The Parliament's social policies also won broad acceptance. And its new, more open, and accessible style (compared to Westminster) was universally welcomed. But its performance was criticized for weakness, timidity, and incompetence. In the survey, English immigrants were evenly divided (47 per cent 'well' to 44 per cent 'not') on whether the Parliament had worked at least 'reasonably well in practice', though by a modest margin (50 per cent to 35 per cent) Pakistanis thought it had. Only 6 per cent of Pakistanis and 1 per cent of English immigrants thought it had worked 'very well'.

Political elites had lots to say about the Scottish Parliament. As its successes they cited its attention to Scottish affairs—so often neglected at Westminster:

'62 Acts in five and a half years . . . [without] a Scottish parliament . . . there might
have been five.' (IDI-21G; IDI-25G, IDI-13 similar)

There was more public access, and a specific committee to receive public
petitions:

'people are able to feed into the Parliament's committees in a way that simply
wasn't possible at Westminster.' (IDI-17G; IDI-15, IDI-18, IDI-20G, IDI-23G, IDI-
26G, IDI-27G similar)

Ministers as well as committees were far more accessible:

'a lot more contact' (IDI-11); 'easy to go to the Minister' (IDI-4, IDI-8G similar);
'I [met] the Social Justice Minister fairly regularly' (IDI-15) 'the Social Justice
Minister approached us directly . . . about increasing Islamophobic attacks.' (IDI-5)

And there was a broad consensus about some of the social policy successes:

'the pensioners package—free travel, central heating, personal care' (IDI-23G, cited
also by IDI-16, IDI-20G, IDI-21G, IDI-24G, IDI-25G, IDI-27G); '[deferred university]
tuition fees' (IDI-21G, IDI-24G, IDI-27G); 'a ban of smoking in public places'
(IDI-16, IDI-27G); 'land reform' (IDI-20G) and 'the first national park in Scotland'
(IDI-23G); and 'social inclusion' (IDI-12, IDI-23G)—'I had the chance [to address]
the Parliament . . . on behalf of Islamic Relief [as] part of the Time for Reflection
programme [which replaced prayers].' (IDI-2)

But there was also some consensus about its failures of competence:

'the [grossly expensive] building has got to be the biggest . . . awarding each other
gongs . . . pay packages' (IDI-23G); 'having built the building, we now have to
rebuild confidence' (IDI-21G); 'the biggest disappointment has been . . . ourselves'
(IDI-27G); 'you can count on one hand [MSPs] who . . . can debate.' (IDI-13)

And recurrent complaints that matters 'reserved' to Westminster left the
Parliament too weak:

'real decisions . . . still made in Westminster' (IDI-9); '[on] employment matters'
(IDI-21G); 'Iraq . . . nuclear weapons bases . . . immigration and asylum' (IDI-18);
'tax.' (IDI-12)

Even its powers, such as they were, remained underexploited by a timid
Parliament and Executive:

'They refer [decisions] to London' (IDI-2); 'it can drive you nuts, continually [being]
told: that is a reserved matter' (IDI-8G); 'Iraq . . . special branch operations . . . arrests
under the terrorism acts . . . Dungavel.' (IDI-13)

Dungavel, the Scottish 'detention centre' for asylum seekers, was operated by the UK Home Office, though the Scottish Parliament had control of all normal prisons. Dungavel staff:

'are very pleasant [to MSPs] but they are not that open ... because they work for Westminster' (IDI-20G); 'I do not particularly want a completely independent Scotland ... [but] the Scottish Parliament ... have no control over ... a detention centre on Scottish land.' (IDI-11)

Some, especially ministers, stressed that the Parliament had:

'been quite creative in using what powers they do have.' (IDI-5); 'there has never been an issue during my time as a Minister, where Westminster prevented me from doing anything ... constitutionalising issues is just a red herring.' (IDI-23G)

But others felt that, without 'constitutionalizing' issues, the Parliament could be less timid, more aggressive:

'the power to change the local tax system ... not used' (IDI-24G); 'Dungavel on the surface [is] a reserved issue, but [it involves] issues around families and children [which are devolved].' (IDI-26G)

At street level, minorities were less informed—and less positive. There was support for the principle of devolution. English immigrants recognized, sometimes with surprise, that Scotland was different:

'so many differences between Scotland and England ... in terms of government in particular.' (E3-C)

And devolution was not something peculiarly Scottish but a response to:

'the perception of ... not having a strong enough voice in London' (E1-G); 'the same sort of perception goes on in northern England' (E1-G) ... 'Cornwall' (E1-A); 'East Anglia' (E4-F); 'this wasn't just [for] Scotland.' (E5-A)

The only recurrent criticism of the devolution principle echoed the elites' irritation with 'reserved' powers. The Parliament lacked:

'sufficient autonomy ... to make it worthwhile' (E3-A); 'a puppet parliament' (PK6-E, E2-H similar) ... 'any major law has to get passed through Westminster' (PK6-C); 'the idea of the equality issue being a reserved issue is unreasonable.' (PK4-E)

But general support for the principle was combined with criticism of the performance—not however criticism of policy or style (which were broadly approved) but criticism of the location, bureaucracy, extravagance, and waste.

9.1.1 *Location*

Local identities are relatively strong in Scotland—significantly stronger than local identities in the Midlands or South of England (Miller, Dickson, and Stoker, 2000: 64). Essentially regional concerns about domination by the Glasgow/Edinburgh 'central belt', therefore, affect English immigrants (as well as many majority Scots) who live outside the central belt.

In the Borders, they had feared the Parliament:

'would be Glasgow City Council enlarged' (E4-C); 'local people . . . are more against . . . the central belt than against the English.' (E2-A , E2-D agrees, E3-H similar)

In Aberdeenshire they had feared Glasgow:

'would just spread [its control] over the rest of Scotland' (E3-G) . . . 'and take all the money.' (E3-E)

There is no end to 'nested' geographic identities and rivalries however. Within the central belt there is a longstanding rivalry between Glasgow and Edinburgh. So, while English immigrants mainly located *outside* the Glasgow area, adopted as their own the widespread local fears of domination by Glasgow, ethnic Pakistanis concentrated *within* Glasgow, adopted as their own the widespread local fears of domination by Edinburgh. Pakistanis could be Glaswegian nationalists as well as Scottish nationalists:

'the Parliament should be in Glasgow' (PK4-E, all laugh); 'Edinburgh was a bad idea' (PK4-F, PK4-B agrees); 'they could have used the [Glasgow] City Chambers. As a Glaswegian, I think it one of the most beautiful buildings in the world. Edinburgh is no use to us.' (PK5-G)

9.1.2 *Bureaucracy, Waste, and Extravagance*

Some English participants argued devolution was:

'bureaucracy' (E3-E); 'another layer of local government' (E1-H); 'always expensive' (E3-C); 'more and more bureaucrats and less and less done' (E5-C); 'just an extra expense.' (E1-F); 'a waste of time, waste of money' (E6-E); 'it takes up a tremendous amount of print . . . in Scottish newspapers.' (E3-C)

And more harshly, Pakistanis noted:

'the First Minister got sacked because [his expenses] money was misused.' (PK3-C); 'there are fat cats involved just making money out of [it].' (PK3-D)

But the best example of waste and extravagance was the new Parliament building. Amongst both minorities (as indeed amongst majority Scots), the cost of the building dominated spontaneous criticisms of devolution, more so than even their own more particular minority concerns:

'MSPs' salaries ... millions on the building.' (PK1-D); 'wasted' (E4-B); 'when you start having parliaments ... the cost ... is enormous ... a total waste of money on this new building—you could build a few hospitals for that, or schools' (E5-B); 'money... wasted on the parliament ... could be spent on the health service' (PK6-C); 'on health and education' (PK5-A); 'this ridiculous farce ... beggars belief' (E6-G); 'anybody that gets a job done on their home, the first question is ... how much will it cost?' (PK5-G); 'the true cost has not come through' (E4-C); 'the Taj Mahal of Scotland.' (PK5-F, all laugh)

Defenders of the building cited its iconic status, comparing it to Bilbao's Guggenheim if not the Taj Mahal.

Government insiders (elites coded G) were torn between their admiration for the architecture, their guilt at the cost, and their own collective incompetence:

'[visitors] are always delighted and amazed ... they get an incredible feeling of pride.' (IDI-24G)

—though the architecture was designed to distance the public from MSPs:

'three different entrances [for] MSPs ... workers ... public ... a step backwards.' (IDI-24G)

Devolution was:

'deeply marred by the fiasco over the building' (IDI-17G); 'people were proud when the Scottish Parliament was opened ... now sickened [by] the millions being spent.' (IDI-13); 'so much money' (IDI-16); 'valuable resources' (IDI-9); 'how could anybody close to the concerns of ordinary Scots spend that amount of dosh on a Parliament ... trying to impress people far away.' (IDI-10); 'you start building ... with the estimate of £40 million pounds and you end up with half a billion pounds.' (IDI-6G)

That phrase, 'half a billion' rather than '500 million', upset senior politicians when used by journalists. It seemed to elevate their incompetence into a higher league.

9.2 The Parliament: Both Inclusive and Exclusive

The new Parliament was at once inclusive and exclusive. It ran a high-profile campaign about including all cultures but failed to include them within its own membership. And it engaged so much with 'civic Scotland' that it was in danger of talking too much with 'the usual suspects'. Some English immigrants felt unrecognized, and Pakistanis had to compete with other more visible minorities and with 'gatekeepers' for the attention of the Parliament.

9.2.1 *'One Scotland, Many Cultures'*

Although equality legislation was reserved to Westminster, the Scottish Executive had responsibility for ensuring equality within—and possibly beyond (though not in conflict with)—the law. So, it undertook a major advertising campaign on the theme of 'One Scotland, Many Cultures'.

Elites criticized the cost of this campaign as they criticized the cost of the building:

'the purpose of it was good [but it] cost an awful lot of money [which] could have been used in different ways.' (IDI-5); 'any initiative to combat racism is welcome . . . [but] I would put more resources into anti-racist education.' (IDI-18); 'rather than spending huge amounts of money on posters' (IDI-12); 'a waste of money.' (IDI-9)

It was self-consciously aimed at majority Scots, not minorities themselves:

'the [anti-]domestic violence campaign . . . was aimed at women, not men . . . to get them to come forward . . . [but] the audience who we wanted to convince [with] the One Scotland, Many Cultures campaign [was] general Scots out there . . . saying . . . you guys are racist.' (IDI-23G)

But posters and mainstream TV advertising cannot be narrowly targeted: everyone can see them, interpret them, react to them. And, however critical they might be, ethnic minorities, and those sympathetic to them, could not ignore a campaign about racism. Some were, frankly puzzled:

'who are you targeting? . . . the Asian community or . . . the indigenous community? . . . I've never seen a translated leaflet of One Scotland, Many Cultures . . . [and] there is a lot of racism *within* the ethnic minority community.' (IDI-19)

Others criticized it for being:

'tokenistic, patronizing . . . a million pounds on advertising' (IDI-13); 'very good of them to try . . . [but] patronizing . . . offensive . . . a tokenist gesture.' (IDI-14)

Or ineffective:

'there is a limit to the power of those kinds of campaigns . . . the anti-smoking [campaign is] a different case . . . a long-term, consistent attempt to remove the

ability of manufacturers to advertise [as well as] increase anti-smoking advertising
... we are not doing anything [similar] about the way the media portrays diversity'
(IDI-17G); 'it takes a long, long time ... to change culture.' (IDI-23G); 'change the
language.' (IDI-26G)

But its defenders argued:

'people say [it] only scratches the surface ... [but] you keep scratching until you get
to where you want to be ... [it sent] a strong message [about racist] language that is
completely unacceptable ... [and presented] people from all ethnic backgrounds
talking with a Scottish accent ... that is important.' (IDI-21G)

And although IDI-14 dismissed 'tokenist gestures' as insignificant, others
appreciated the importance of symbolic action in politics:

'[equality is] not just about service provision ... unless we challenged the racism
that went on in Scotland, then everything that we were doing ... with equality was
just nonsense.' (IDI-25G); '[it said] here is where we stand ... against racism ... not
mumbled [in] a conference ... [but] broadcast from billboards.' (IDI-23G)

That stand was welcomed by those working with ethnic minorities:

'it has a crucial effect on the press and on the media' (IDI-16); 'money [was] spent
on an anti-racist advertising campaign in the way that we have not seen before
from any government in the UK. So whilst we might criticise ... we might also say
well done for trying.' (IDI-15); 'I do not know how ... effective [it will be] about
changing attitudes. [But] it is nice to have an official body like the government
being positive about people that are not white Scottish ... particularly because of
the very negative feedback there has been from England about minority groups,
from both the government and the press.' (IDI-11)

Fundamentally, it showed that:

'somebody cares, it always comes down to that.' (IDI-19)

So, although those who devised the campaign aimed to target and
reform the behaviour of majority Scots, probably the most significant—
and most immediately effective—impact was to convince minorities that
the Scottish Parliament and Executive really 'cared' about them. It was
indeed a 'gesture' but a very welcome and appreciated gesture, despite the
misgivings about its cost.

Unfortunately, the UK politicians sent a different message and forced
the Scottish Executive into actions—or more strictly 'inaction'—that sub-
verted the message of their own One Scotland, Many Cultures campaign:

'a good slogan' (IDI-6G); '[but] at the very same time they are ... carrying out the
policies of a [UK] government that are the most rancid and racist of recent years,
the policies of David Blunkett [on] Dungavel ... the Terrorism Act' (IDI-13); 'it was

very good that the Scottish Executive made such a clear stand ... devolution actually working ... making possible a different kind of agenda ... [but] Blunkett talking about asylum-seekers [gives] a green light to the worst kind of racist rubbish.' (IDI-16); 'if I was the Justice Minister, I would be saying to Westminster: we have got Guantanamo Bay in Dungavel.' (IDI-24G); 'it is one thing to put up a poster to say black and white people should live together. It is another ... for Blunkett at the same time—and a thousand times as loudly—to say that in some way immigrants, many of whom are Muslims ... are in some way connected with ... terrorism.' (IDI-10)

At street level too, Pakistanis were keenly aware of the One Scotland, Many Cultures campaign, though they also had mixed feelings about it. They were at once *pleased* by the intent, *doubtful* about the impact, and *critical* of the cost.

'There is more reality now with ... the anti-racism campaign.' (PK4-F); '[it] was necessary to prove good intentions [but] they need to ... take action.' (PK4-D); '[but] a million pounds was spent' (PK4-B); 'our money is for real services, affecting real people ... [it] could have been spent [more] wisely.' (PK4-E, PK4-B agrees)

Around half of both minorities in the survey (excluding DKs etc. 48 per cent of Pakistanis and 57 per cent of English immigrants) felt the Scottish Parliament was 'really committed' to fighting discrimination. But some English focus group participants felt it was not so committed to ensuring equal treatment for them:

'I can't see it, no.' (E1-H, all agree); 'They've thought about sectarianism and racism but ... not Englishness.' (E6-F) ... 'MSPs are as guilty as anybody else and they don't see it as an issue. Hating the English is part of being Scottish.' (E6-G) ... 'acceptable' (E6-F) ... 'the auld enemy' (E6-E, E6-D agrees); 'if the nationalists got [to] being the Executive, the situation would be even worse.' (E6-D, E6-G agrees)

One assumed, none too confidently, that the One Scotland, Many Cultures campaign might apply to the English:

'it would be interesting to see if social inclusion includes the English ... I just assume ... this whole business of social inclusion ... includes [us].' (E4-F)

But another felt excluded by it:

'its very easy to do these adverts where you have an Asian and a white face ... you can't do that with two white faces.' (E4-B)

Despite all the Scottish Executive's enthusiasm for its 'multicultural' advertising campaign and its focus on 'visible' minorities rather than the English however, Pakistanis are much more inclined than English immigrants to feel that the Parliament regards them as 'a problem' rather than 'making Scotland a better place'. The survey indicates that about half in both minorities feel the Parliament regards them as 'making Scotland a better place' (47 per cent of Pakistanis, 50 per cent of English immigrants). But 32 per cent of Pakistanis compared to only 12 per cent of English immigrants feel the Parliament regards them as 'a problem'. (No doubt these figures would be higher if the Parliament and Executive had not pushed a multicultural agenda however.)

9.2.2 Representation without Presence?

MSPs could, in principle, represent their constituents without being similar in gender, race, or religion. Indeed Edmund Burke famously argued that he could represent his constituents without even sharing their interests or opinions. But others look for some visible similarity between people and political representatives: representation not only by shared interests and opinions but by visible presence. Political elites were unconcerned about the representation of the English minority, but they were concerned about the representation of visible ethnic minorities, and they never argued that minorities could be adequately represented without themselves being present.

'One Country, Many Cultures ... That is not quite true in the parliament, is it?' (IDI-2); 'it is completely hypocritical [to] talk about equality and justice [in an] all-white parliament.' (IDI-13); 'you can have policies left, right and centre, but you still [need] equal representation on the board who are making these policies.' (IDI-2)

'after 300 years, an all white parliament again ... totally unacceptable ... promises made ... nothing materialized ... I cannot see any reason or any excuse why the same rules [that produced] more representation of women ... cannot be applied [to] ethnic minorities ... the will is not there.' (IDI-6G); 'I have become pessimistic ... disillusioned ... let down.' (IDI-4)

To white MSPs as well as to other elite interviewees, representation required visible ethnic faces in the Parliament:

'demands about representation [are] quite legitimate' (IDI-23G); 'we do not have a Muslim in Parliament ... so we do not represent the people of Scotland' (IDI-24G); 'we had to have positive discrimination to get some women up the ladder.' (IDI-20G); '[we need] mentoring schemes ... reserved places ... they pay lip service ... [but] don't try very hard.' (IDI-8G)

Chapter 7 discussed that the lack of Muslim MSPs in particular as an emotive symbolic issue. In the survey, 88 per cent of Pakistanis but only 41 per cent of English immigrants said there should be MSPs like them. But in an attempt to get away from the purely symbolic aspect of this issue however, we preceded the question about Muslim or English MSPs with a more diffuse, more Burkean, question about representation:

Do you feel the Scottish Parliament really *tries hard enough* to represent people *like you* in particular?

Confronted with this more diffuse question, both minorities criticize the Parliament for *not* 'trying hard enough to represent people like me'— English immigrants by only a small margin (42 per cent no; 36 per cent yes) but Pakistanis by a greater margin of 18 per cent (52 per cent no; 34 per cent yes).

Some English immigrants chose to interpret 'representation' in terms of competence and effort rather than in any ethnic sense, sometimes critically:

'very amateurish . . . like councillors . . . [with poor] debating skills.' (E1-A)

but more often favourably:

'more contact.' (PK-4G); 'I am being represented as a resident' (E4-G); 'the number of MSPs [provides] a much greater opportunity for them to get to know their localities better' (E5-A); 'MSPs have been higher profile than MPs' (E4-F); '[our MP] did what she could but she was working from Westminster. We are now meeting [MSPs] more often.' (PK-4D)

The sheer number of MSPs had ethnic implications, according to an English participant:

'If there are more MSP's then there is a chance that some of them will reflect minority interest.' (E2-D)

Irrespective of their symbolic exclusion, could a Parliament without a Pakistani or Muslim MSP adequately represent Muslim Pakistanis? In principle yes, but in practice:

'No' (all in PK6); 'No, there was supposed to be a new law . . . to do with religious discrimination in Scotland or Britain . . . but it did not go through.' (PK1-G) . . . 'The Scottish Parliament should be asking us for our help to make these laws that PK1-G is talking about. If we were [physically] represented in the Scottish Parliament these things would happen, but we are not.' (PK1-B); 'The political system at the moment does not represent us . . . We don't have a voice and nobody listens to us.' (PK3-D)

It is correct but irrelevant to note that the Scottish Parliament has no power to pass legislation on religious discrimination and that it was 're-served' to Westminster under the devolution settlement. Those partici-pants who criticized the representative role of the Scottish Parliament clearly held the 'all-white' Scottish Parliament, not the British Parliament, responsible for the lack of such legislation.

Other Pakistanis responded to the question about representation with the complaint that:

'we are not seen as a part of Scotland ... even today when you speak to someone from outside Scotland ... they are shocked that you are an Asian with a Scottish accent' (PK1-C, all agree); 'I have been up north and when you speak in a Scottish accent they are shocked and ask: where are you from?' (PK1-B)

Whatever the Scottish Parliament had done to include minorities within Scotland, these participants clearly felt that it had failed to define the image of modern Scotland in a sufficiently inclusive way—and that was as much the duty of a Parliament as rolling out a stream of legislation. And it might be achieved by having a non-white face to present to the world.

9.2.3 *Exclusion by Competition?*

Obviously, minorities can feel excluded if they feel the Parliament is paying *too little* attention to them. Less obviously, they might feel excluded if they feel the Parliament is paying *too much* attention to others.

Both minorities reject the general proposition that the Parliament is 'too concerned about the interests of people from ethnic minorities'—the English by a margin of 35 per cent and Pakistanis by a margin of 47 per cent. But while English immigrants also *reject* the proposition that the Parliament is 'too concerned about sectarian divisions between Protestants and Catholics' (27 per cent yes; 51 per cent no), ethnic Pakistanis *accept* it (46 per cent yes; 26 per cent no)—in both cases by large margins. Yet English immigrants tend to live in areas with less sectarian problems and Pakistanis in areas with greater sectarian problems. So, it is the minority that lives in the midst of sectarian problems, which is most inclined to criticize the Parliament for paying attention to sectar-ianism. This cannot be through lack of awareness: focus groups show that Pakistanis are all too aware of sectarian tensions. It must be because Muslim problems have to compete with sectarian divisions for Parlia-ment's attention.

In focus group discussions, we widened still further this concept of rivals for the attention of the Scottish Parliament. Did minorities feel that the Parliament:

'pays too much attention to some kinds of people or some kinds of groups? Too much attention to majorities, too much attention to minorities, too much attention to businessmen, or too much attention to whatever?' (moderator)

Given that wider choice, few participants in either English or Pakistani focus groups criticize the attention given by Parliament to the competing claims of sectarian divisions or ethnic minorities.

Instead, English participants criticize MSPs' attention to their own self-interest: 'as soon as they got in they went and raised their pay' (E5-C). Or criticize their focus on the 'central belt' (E5-C); their focus on social rather than economic affairs (E5-A, E5-B agrees); and their obsession with fringe issues:

'fox hunting' (E5-B); 'teaching homosexual practices in schools' (E3-G; E3-D and E3A agree) ... 'if you have been waiting for 300 years for a Parliament then ... I didn't think that was top of the agenda ... a lot of the initial agenda was generated by members of pressure groups who happened also to be MSPs.' (E3-G)

By contrast, Pakistani participants criticize the Parliament for paying too much attention to business, to gatekeepers or 'community leaders', and to wealthy Asians:

'I think they pay too much attention to community people such as YA and BM.' (PK5-F) ... 'these are the people that are very wealthy.' (PK5-D)

At best:

'The Scottish Parliament pays more attention to business people because they want to show Asian people as positive role models.' (PK6-E)

But:

'rich Asian businessmen don't know anything' (PK1-D); 'we hear about the same Asians all the time ... [even] if you are Asian don't expect me to vote for you, unless you can deliver the service and have the right personality.' (PK5-F); 'Asian people that are in prominent positions in politics don't let other people climb up the ladder.' (PK5-A)

And, more generally:

'The Scottish Parliament pays too much attention to those that don't have any knowledge about politics but do have the money.' (PK2-A); 'giving more preference to businessmen than young educated people.' (PK2-B); 'politicians always respect

181

money ... businessmen have all the influence, they will be invited to have dinner with politicians and we won't.' (PK1-D); 'money equals power' (PK1-G); 'they do like cheque-book politicians.' (PK4-D)

Elites also recognize the problem of competition:

'the Scottish Parliament's processes ... ensure that all views can be fed in and heard ... [but] some groups are uncomfortable because they feel that their stand is going to get lost in the big equality soup.' (IDI-17G)

Some complain about insufficient attention to their own groups:

'the Scottish Parliament and the British Parliament ignored the millions who marched against the [Iraq] war ... a demonstration of 10,000 people through Greenock to stop the closure of the hospital there ... might as well be whistling in the wind.' (IDI-14)

Or over-attention to rival groups:

'too much emphasis on LBGT—lesbian, bisexual, gay and transsexual ... you see massive amounts of funding going into that ... and we can't get a penny out of them.' (IDI-code withheld); '[the Parliament] talk [too much] about fishing and farming.' (IDI-1)

And competition between rivals so close that outsiders cannot distinguish the one from the other as they should:

'there is a difference between a faith group [and] a self defining ethnic group ... there is still a lot of prejudice out there ... saying: you have to be Pakistani ... that is not the way a lot of people want to define themselves ... there needs to be more recognition of Muslims [as Muslims].' (IDI-5)

But elites also articulate some less self-interested criticisms, echoing street-level criticism of the Parliament's overattention to the 'usual suspects', 'community leaders', or 'gate-keepers'—at the expense of ordinary citizens:

'we are in danger of talking to the same people [too often] ... we need to get beyond the usual suspects.' (IDI-23G); 'attention is paid to those ... who have political friends ... one or two Muslim groups [get] funded very heavily [because of] their links to councillors ... others do not get anything.' (IDI-9); 'within our own community there are a lot of gate-keepers.' (IDI-19)

9.2.4 Evaluating the Parliament

Across all our survey measures of minority attitudes towards the performance of the Scottish Parliament, ethnic Pakistanis are more critical than

English immigrants. Perceptions of the Parliament's performance vary within both minorities however.

Amongst Pakistanis in particular, some groups have clearer perceptions than others. Those who do not read a paper or who rely on Pakistani papers, have lived in Scotland for less than ten years, have no close Scottish friends, do not speak English at home, or have no job outside the home are *less critical* of the Scottish Parliament—and usually more positive about its performance, despite relatively high numbers who are unable to decide whether it has performed well or badly. Conversely, all the factors that bring Pakistanis more into contact with the mainstream not only clarify their views about the Parliament but increase their criticism of its performance. Amongst Pakistanis, *net positive evaluations* of the Parliament's performance (per cent 'very or reasonably well' minus per cent 'not very or not at all well') are 38 per cent lower amongst those who read a Scottish paper; 18 per cent lower amongst those who have close friendships with majority Scots; 29 per cent lower amongst those born in Scotland; 31 per cent lower amongst those who speak English at home; and 49 per cent lower amongst those who work in the private sector rather than within the home.

But amongst English immigrants, net positive evaluations are 32 per cent lower amongst those who rely on 'English' papers than those who read no paper at all. So, while relying on a paper they identify with their own minority *reduces* criticism of the Parliament amongst ethnic Pakistanis, it *increases* such criticism amongst English immigrants.

There is, however, one pattern that affects both minorities in a similar way: recent English immigrants, like recent Pakistani immigrants, are the least critical of the Scottish Parliament. English immigrants of less than 10 years standing have net positive perceptions of the Parliament that are 51 per cent higher than those who have spent more than 40 years in Scotland.

9.3 The Street-Level Consequences of Devolution

It is tempting to argue, as focus group participants did when discussing the new building (see Chapter 7), that what matters about a new national Parliament is 'what goes on inside' (E4-G) and whether it 'gets its job done' (PK4-B).

But that may be misleading. 'What goes on outside' may matter even more. The street-level consequences may be more important than the legislative and administrative achievements or failures. What do minorities and those who work with them think devolution has done to the attitudes and behaviour of ordinary Scots that they meet in everyday life?

9.3.1 More Pride, Less Xenophobia

Political elites have particularly clear views about the impact of devolution on Scottish pride and xenophobia. Some note an increasing emphasis on Scottishness:

'just having a Parliament makes that happen.' (IDI-15)

though more:

'in the media [than] in the culture ... Westminster has been marginalised ... the Scottish Parliament is much more reportable ... more relevant ... rather than increasing the Scottishness of Scotland or of Scots, we have increased the Scottishness of the political agenda.' (IDI-21G)

But *increasing* pride went with *decreasing* nationalism or xenophobia:

'one of the greatest achievements [of devolution] has been a kind of pride in Scotland, a pride that we moved up a step.' (IDI-8G); 'a feeling of we are our own country [but] nationalism is not the right word, because nationalism has other connotations' (IDI-15); 'the SNP ... lost seats ... we have not gone much more nationalist ... in terms of voting.' (IDI-26G); '[Scots are] less nationalist ... feeling they have got a bit more control at a Scottish level.' (IDI-5); 'the nationalistic drive is ... diminishing ... because we have got the Parliament ... people think: we have got what we wanted.' (IDI-9)

'Scottishness certainly has increased. People feel prouder being Scottish ... before devolution ... they felt they were being ignored [and] the movement for an independent Scotland was greater ... [now] people feel as though they have a form of independence.' (IDI-20G)

'The Scottish Parliament is definitely there to promote a sense of confidence and a renewed faith in being Scottish—but that is not so much [greater] Scottishness as [less] anti-Englishness.' (IDI-27G); 'Scottishness has increased [but] its less a conflict of identities now ... more an acceptance that Scotland is a strong identity ... conflict and aggressive bullying ... comes when identity is not strong in the first place ... people feel more positive about being Scottish now.' (IDI-17G); 'more proud ... more excited about being Scottish ... more control over their lives ... [whether] they really do or not almost doesn't matter ... but definitely *not* more parochial ... narrow focused ... racist ... [or] xenophobic.' (IDI-8G)

At street level, Pakistanis especially feel devolution has made Scots:

'even more proud.' (PK-2A); 'it is only natural for the Scottish people to feel proud and nationalistic.' (PK-3D) 'emphasis on Scottishness has increased ... gone to their heads a bit' (PK2-B); '[but] the desire for independence has declined.' (PK6-C)

And Pakistanis themselves feel proud:

'*We* are proud the Scottish Parliament has been set up.' (PK-3C); '*I have more identity now ... I am a part of Scotland* and I can make more decisions.' (PK-4F); 'Scottish people may feel even more Scottish—but *we* can now make requests to the Parliament ... when we could not before.' (PK-2B); 'Scots have done very well by creating this Parliament ... during my son's lifetime ... maybe Scotland might be free.' (PK-3C)

English immigrants also concede that devolution has lowered tensions between Scotland and England—at least on the Scottish side:

'Scots have always blamed the English for lots of things, now ... no one will be there to blame.' (E1-A); '[without] devolution we would have ended up with an Irish situation. [Devolution] released the steam in the kettle.' (E2-D)

though not perhaps on the English side:

'England has become much more aware of its identity.' (E3-A)

And some Pakistanis anticipate an English reaction:

'The English are not going to like the Scots, because the Scots have got their Parliament and have got their way.' (PK2-B); 'they are envious of us in England.' (PK4-E); '[but devolution] does not have a big profile down South.' (PK1-D, PK1-C agrees); 'problems between Scotland and England are historical—not promoted by the Parliament.' (PK5-G, PK5-D agrees)

9.3.2 *Not Drifting Apart*

Relatively few in either minority feel that Scotland and England have become more different since devolution. Many are unsure. But English immigrants are far more likely than Pakistanis to assert that the difference has not increased. In our survey the denial/acceptance ratio amongst Pakistanis is less than 3:1 (41:15 per cent), while amongst English immigrants it runs at almost 6:1 (59:10 per cent). English immigrants have stronger psychological reasons for wishing to claim that Scotland and England are not drifting apart of course: they cling to the unity of Britain.

9.3.3 *More Welcoming*

None of the elites we interviewed thought Scotland had become any less welcoming to minorities since devolution. Most take the positive view that devolution has made Scots more welcoming to minorities.

'people feel a bit more secure being Scottish with devolution ... more willing to accept anybody else is Scottish no matter what their colour—you hear examples of that all the time.' (IDI-15); 'probably more welcoming ... having a Parliament has given a little bit of self-confidence, national-confidence—whereas before ... English people would be seen much more as enemies.' (IDI-18); 'if anything people are looking away from England [now] ... it used to be the case that everything that went wrong in Scotland, we used to blame the English ... that excuse is no longer there ... [so] the incidence of anti-Englishness ... is less.' (IDI-27G)

But they tend quite self-consciously to project the visibly inclusive attitudes of the Parliament, Executive, and even the police onto their perceptions of the less visible public:

'more welcoming. *I don't know why I am saying that*, it's just a feeling that I have. It must be things that the [Scottish] government has been saying ... and the advertising thing.' (IDI-11); 'the Scottish Parliament [should be] a big plus to most Muslims' (IDI-27G); 'we had a few incidents ... with the BNP ... and we didn't have to respond ... Why? Because the Council and the politicians and the police all responded on our behalf—which was very welcoming. That's the beauty of Scottish people ... they respond on our behalf, and that is why I think it is welcoming for ethnic minorities.' (IDI-2)

At street level too, both minorities feel that since devolution Scotland has become, if anything, more welcoming 'to people who are not completely Scottish' rather than less. Over a quarter of the Pakistanis and over half the English immigrants feel the Parliament has made no difference. But amongst those who do detect a changing welcome, 55 per cent of Pakistanis and 61 per cent of English immigrants feel Scotland has become more welcoming. Given the large numbers who detect no change, these statistics do not indicate that minorities perceive any great improvement in Scottish hospitability. But they do show beyond statistical doubt that minorities feel devolution has *not* made Scots any less welcoming. Even small positive margins, and many with mixed views, indicate a very politically significant finding.

Consistent with the survey, focus group comments about whether Scotland had become more or less welcoming are fairly evenly balanced. Some only half-heartedly deny that Scotland had got less welcoming since devolution:

'not as much as I thought it would.' (E5-A)

Some are critical, but the criticisms are muted or more concerned fears for the future than problems in the present:

'The Scottish might start to see us differently.' (PK3-D); '[in] the Borders . . . they are beginning to be conscious of the fact that there are a lot more white settlers.' (E4-B)

But these views were balanced by more positive claims that devolution has made ordinary Scots more relaxed, calmed their resentments and prejudices:

'Scottish people who I know seem to have less of a chip than they used to . . . now they are a lot more comfortable.' (E4-G)

And English participants chose to move the discussion on from Scotland to England:

'Those living in England probably feel [Scotland] is less welcoming.' (E2-C); 'there's much more awareness of being English . . . it's a reaction against devolution.' (E2-E); 'they are very much more aware of themselves being English.' (E3-A); 'much more aware' (E3-G) . . . 'of the money flowing north.' (E3-A)

9.3.4 *Easier to Criticize*

Half the Pakistanis and two-thirds of English immigrants say devolution has had no impact on their ability to criticize Scotland when speaking to strangers. But amongst those who do detect some change, 58 per cent of Pakistanis and 72 per cent of English immigrants say it has got easier to voice criticisms of Scotland since devolution. Like survey respondents, many focus group participants also say devolution had had no impact at all on their ability to criticize Scotland. But none say devolution has made criticism more difficult. And many say it has become easier:

'you are freer to speak your mind. There are a lot more protests and demonstrations. You see more of them than you did ten years ago.' (PK1-G)

Pakistanis praised the Scottish Parliament for its accessibility and responsiveness which, they argued, made criticism so much more meaningful and effective.

'It has been easier for me to express criticism after the setting up of the Scottish Parliament.' (PK1-C); 'in the past you were always doubtful if any queries had actually reached Westminster but that has now changed [and] they will listen more' (PK2-B); 'you have more of a say.' (PK2-A)

English immigrants also felt the new Parliament facilitated criticism—but for a rather different reason. Criticism was:

'a lot easier' (E3-E) ... 'because ... our [Scottish] friends are equally critical.' (E3-C); 'so many real Scots are criticising their own parliament ... one can join in.' (E4-C)

9.3.5 *More at Ease*

Almost everyone in both minorities say they feel 'at ease' living in Scotland—after devolution as before. Two-thirds of Pakistanis and even more of the English feel no different after devolution than before. But amongst the relatively few who do feel different 55 per cent of Pakistanis and 62 per cent of English immigrants say they feel more at ease in Scotland after devolution. Most contributions to focus group discussions also suggest that participants do not feel any more or less at ease as a result of devolution. But the few who do, feel more at ease:

'I feel more at ease since the Scottish Parliament was set up.' (PK4-C); 'it's improved things ... 10 years back I was worried that we would end up with a Northern Ireland situation. I saw the pressures building up ... fortunately we've moved away from that.' (E2-D)

9.3.6 *But More Abuse and Insults*

Reports of changing personal experience of 'abuse and insults' since devolution do not fit the benign picture of a more relaxed, easier to criticize, more welcoming Scotland however. Only a sixth of English immigrants report any change, and they are evenly divided about whether it had increased or decreased. But over a third of Pakistanis report change and, amongst them, 59 per cent say 'abuse and insults' have increased since devolution. Given the nature of the times, we have no reason to doubt the accuracy of these reports. Later in the chapter we consider how reports of increasing 'abuse and insults' fit with perceptions that Scots have become 'more welcoming'.

9.3.7 *Assessing Street-Level Change*

Perceptions of street-level change vary within both minorities. Amongst Pakistanis, those with a good income, those that rely on a Pakistani paper, who have lived in Scotland for less than ten years, who do *not* speak English at home, who have no job outside the home or the family business are also the ones that are more positive about street-level trends—as they were about the performance of the Parliament itself. Apart from a good income (which increases net positive perceptions of a changing welcome by 27 per cent) the general pattern reflects contact with mainstream society.

And again the factors that bring Pakistanis more into contact with the mainstream make them *less* positive about street-level trends since devolution. Net positive perceptions of a changing welcome are 21 per cent less amongst those who read a Scottish paper (than amongst those who read none) and 23 per cent less amongst Scottish-born Pakistanis; but 24 per cent greater amongst those who work in their own family business; and 17 per cent greater amongst those who speak Urdu at home. Conversely, net perceptions of increasing levels of harassment and abuse are 28 per cent greater amongst those who read a Scottish paper and 25 per cent greater amongst Scottish-born Pakistanis; but 21 per cent less amongst those who work in their family business; and a few per cent less amongst those who speak Urdu at home.

Amongst English immigrants, perceptions of street-level trends in whether Scots are more or less welcoming are more uniform. There are slight differences between Presbyterians and Episcopalians and between English immigrants in rural/small-town Scotland and the capital. But these are trace-findings, hardly sufficient to overturn our basic finding that English immigrants' perceptions of street-level changes since devolution do not vary systematically to any great extent.

9.4 The Street-Level Impact of Concurrent Events

If only by small margins we have found that both minorities say post-devolution Scotland has become 'more welcoming', 'easier to criticize', and makes them feel even 'more at ease' than they were before devolution. But at the same time, Pakistanis detect an increase in the level of anti-Pakistani or anti-Muslim 'abuse and insults'—though English immigrants on balance detect almost no change.

9.4.1 '9/11'

Reactions to '9/11' undoubtedly increased the abuse of Muslims in Scotland as elsewhere. And it followed so closely after devolution that it is statistically impossible to disentangle the impact of devolution from that of 9/11. But focus groups provide a very clear distinction between concurrent causes. In focus groups, neither minority alleges that devolution was responsible for any increase in harassment and abuse.

At the outset, we hypothesized that rising Scottish self-consciousness, the long debate over devolution, and the eventual creation of a Scottish Parliament could have posed an added challenge to Muslims in Scotland. So in the focus-group discussions, we asked participants to compare the impact of Scottish nationalism, culminating in the creation of a Scottish Parliament, with the impact of 9/11 on Scottish attitudes towards Muslims. Both could have encouraged anti-Muslim feelings. But the response of focus-group participants was unequivocal—not only was the Scottish Parliament less of a problem, it was in their view, part of the solution. And some even found our question shocking:

'You cannot compare 9/11 and the Scottish Parliament in the same way [expressed in shocked manner]' (PK5-D, all agree); '9/11 was a lot worse . . . and I do *not* think the Scottish Parliament has been a negative thing.' (PK1-D)

'Obviously 9/11 shocked the world and affected Pakistanis, Muslims everywhere. But the creation of the Scottish Parliament has made no difference.' (PK2-A); 'There was a peace statement made in the [Glasgow] City Chambers from all the faiths wanting to work together and overcome the difficulties.' (PK4-E)

In this context, the only criticisms directed at the Scottish Parliament concerned its lack of power, authority, influence, or effectiveness:

'the Scottish Parliament is too weak' (PK6-C); 'I am glad to be in Scotland, but there is a question about what the Scottish Parliament can do' (PK1-D); 'Foreign policy is dealt with by [British] Central Government, the Scottish Parliament has got nothing to do with it.' (PK6-E)

Elites also attributed any adverse trends to 9/11 rather than devolution:

'the Scottish parliament are being proactive . . . pre-9/11 we were on a good track but post-9/11 it has just completely deteriorated . . . the media have played . . . a tremendous role in influencing people's opinions on Pakistani Muslims . . . devolution is trying to tackle some of the issues . . . but post-9/11 they have had a harder job.' (IDI-19)

A year after 9/11, Pakistani focus-group participants told us about 9/11 and its impact on their lives in the intervening year. It had been as traumatic for Muslims as for Americans, and a year later their memories of the time were still sharp. There was shock, disbelief, and shame:

'shock ... horrified ... numbness' (PK4-E); 'unbelievable' (PK6-G); 'ashamed that Muslims could be involved in this crime' (PK5-B), 'that my faith was being used.' (PK4-E)

But also resentment:

'They seem to associate terrorism only with Muslim countries' (PK2-A); 'look at what is happening in Ireland, Belfast' (PK2-B); 'if someone is going to carry out an act of terrorism, they don't need to be a Muslim ... there are all sorts of factions around the world representing different ideologies.' (PK4-E)

And fear. Fear of an anti-Muslim backlash:

'My mum and dad said don't walk outside the house with a headscarf ... It was scary ... very scary.' (PK1-G)

But also fear of terrorists:

'Terrorism can happen anywhere' (PK4-D); 'We saw the PanAm crashing in Scotland.' (PK4-E)

British people had become 'more unfriendly' towards Pakistanis and Muslims:

'it has made a difference ... people look at us with suspicion' (PK4-D); 'I heard of many physical attacks ... my husband warned me not to go to the Mosque.' (PK5-E)

But personal experience of the 9/11 aftermath was limited in scope and intensity:

'not really directly, but people can be cold' (PK5-A); 'racist looks' (PK2-B); 'cold stares' (PK2-A); 'I have been called Osama bin Laden a couple of times.' (PK3-E)

There was some disagreement about whether Scots (as distinct from other Britons) had become more unfriendly:

'It affected everybody in Scotland and in England.' (PK3-E)

but most thought the problem had not been so bad in Scotland as in England:

'not too many problems in Scotland' (PK5-G); 'it could have been much worse' (PK5-A); 'more trouble in England.' (PK4-A, PK2-D similar)

A few felt nowhere was safe after 9/11:

'after 9/11, no place in the world felt safe' (PK5-E); 'death ... finds you anywhere.' (PK5-A); 'in Bali and in Russia' (PK5-G); 'if this horrible thing had happened in Britain, I really don't know how people would react here ... no place is really safe.' (PK2-C)

But for a variety of reasons, including both fear of anti-Muslim reactions *and* fear of terrorism, most were glad to be living in Scotland rather than anywhere else:

'glad to be living in Scotland.' (PK6-G); 'much safer in Scotland.' (PK6-D, PK2-B); 'London is more likely to be bombed' (PK6-G) ... 'even when the IRA were bombing, they never came to Scotland.' (PK6-C); 'France would be bad ... Holland quite bad ... I wouldn't like to be in America at the time [of 9/11].' (PK1-C); 'most safe in Scotland ... In Pakistan or America, we might have been accused and attacked.' (PK3-C); 'safer in Scotland than in Pakistan.' (PK5-D)

It is quite a list. Participants felt safer in Scotland than in England, Europe, America—or Pakistan.

Interviews with Scottish political elites took place much later than the focus groups—three years after 9/11, by which time these elites had had time to reflect upon the consequences for minorities of 9/11, and subsequently the impacts of Afganistan and Iraq. They were in no doubt that Islamophobia had increased, throughout the world, after 9/11. But it had been moderated by the behaviour of the Scottish Parliament and Executive—and offset, in Scotland, by subsequent events in Afganistan and Iraq and the behavior of the UK government and its very English Home Secretary, David Blunkett.

First of all, they too reported a sharp increase in abuse immediately after 9/11:

'it got worse' (IDI-19); 'the root cause is the way the media ... and politicians used 9/11.' (IDI-18); 'post-9/11, the community was under a state of siege ... women wearing scarves, men with beards getting abuse.' (IDI-13); 'this guy ... puts his hands in the shape of a gun to my head and says you should all be shot.' (IDI-5); 'I had to move flats.' (IDI-13)

It frightened Muslims away from political action:

'there was a widespread feeling ... in the Muslim community ... that they would have to pay a higher price for associating with any radical groups: campaigns against the war, campaigns on behalf of Palestine ... We have seen this in the numbers who turn out.' (IDI-10); 'Prior to 9/11 ... Muslims turned out [at protest] meetings. After that ... young, militant Muslim campaigners [still] turn up but other [Muslims are] scared to be seen.' (IDI-13)

It changed the terminology of abuse:

'before 9/11 it was just the fact that you were black ... post-9/11 the hijab' (IDI-19); 'before you were called a Paki or a black bastard, now Taliban ... bin Laden ... it is [now] OK to kick a Muslim because it's *not* being racist: "we are not racist but [your] culture is wrong, uncivilised'' ... nobody said that to all Christians when bombs went off in Birmingham, Manchester, Liverpool, London ... nobody said: lets go and bomb Boston because they supply money to the IRA.' (IDI-13)

But the reaction to 9/11 was perhaps less in Britain than elsewhere, and especially so in Scotland:

'not the degree of backlash that many feared.' (IDI-25G); 'since 9/11 ... many people see young Muslim men as terrorists ... but it has not been as pernicious in Scotland in terms of the use of stop and search ... terrorist laws [whose implementation] down south has had a huge impact on young Muslim men ... an impact in Scotland but not ... to the same extent ... an unnecessary nervousness in the majority community [in Scotland] but not ... to the same extent.' (IDI-8G); '[In England you see] the "BNP in blazers"—quite happy to exploit the rise in intolerant feelings and perceptions ... policies which pander to [racism] which isn't any more defensible than believing in it ... It is encouraging that that is not happening so much in Scotland.' (IDI-17G)

Devolution was absolved from all blame: indeed it was *not part of the problem* but, insofar as it had any influence, *part of the solution*:

'things have got worse ... that has got nothing to do with the Scottish Parliament [but with] 9/11.' (IDI-7); '9/11 made a difference, not anything else.' (IDI-15); 'we are persecuted a lot more now ... that is what the Scottish Executive has to deal with.' (IDI-19)

Post-devolution, Scots got:

'more friendly ... less xenophobic—but I would qualify that because there has been a serious rise in Islamophobia right across Britain, right across Europe—not because of devolution.' (IDI-18); 'less friendly ... not because of the Scottish Parliament [but] because of ... the war on terrorism ... negative reporting ... 9/11 allowed racists to vocalise their feelings.' (IDI-12); 'xenophobia, racism are stoked by other processes [than devolution].' (IDI-10); 'things have got worse [but] there is no link to the Scottish Parliament ... the [UK] anti terrorist law, the war on Iraq ... have made it more difficult for Muslims.' (IDI-9); 'not devolution [but] 9/11 and the war on terror' (IDI-1); 'the events of 2001 ... [by contrast] devolution aims to say we want to involve people of all communities.' (IDI-25G)

'a great increase in racism ... some of it because of 9/11 [but] possibly not all of it ... the media ... just leap from one scapegoat to another ... immigration ... asylum-seekers ... gypsies ... politicians could stop it [but] are allowing it.' (IDI-16);

'Scots are probably less friendly towards minorities in Scotland ... people have become more friendly [because of devolution]. But the increase in Islamaphobia, resulting from ... 9/11, the war on terrorism, war on Iraq has had a very negative impact.' (IDI-5)

9.4.2 *The 3-step causal chain*

More surprisingly, Scottish elites articulated a 3-step causal chain theory:

1. 9/11 caused increasing abuse of Muslims, but
2. that increased public sympathy for Muslims, and thereby
3. increased their integration with the rest of Scottish society.

They argued that things got worse—and better—for Scottish Muslims, at the same time:

'On one level ... things are bad, [but] on another ... hundreds of thousands ... have come out over the last two or three years ... Muslims, ethnic minorities, whites, Christians, Atheists, marching alongside each other under the same banner of unity against racism ... against the war ... for peace. That is something positive ... On one level ... things have got bad and on another ... *things are actually getting better* ... not [just] in the Parliament but actually on the streets and in the communities ... Speaking as a Muslim who works for asylum-seekers ... [we got] no help from ... the Mosque ... [but] Churches have provided accommodation for bail addresses for mothers and children.' (IDI-13)

'[Scotland is] less welcoming—but it is not to do with the Scottish parliament, it is to do with all those other things, like 9/11 and war on Iraq ... a lot of abuse and some physical attacks ... though the other side of that was that people who were very horrified by the way 9/11 was being interpreted ... [and] a lot of non-Muslim white people were going out of their way [to support us]. I got cards, phone calls from [white] friends to say that was terrible and *our hearts with you as a Muslim* ... I actually think it may have helped to get [Executive] funding as well, because Islamaphobia has been around a long time but nobody recognised it [before] ... 3½ years ago ... a conference on Islamaphobia ... had to be abandoned because there was not enough interest ... people just did not recognise that it existed ... the post-9/11 backlash against Muslims was awful, but *the good side* was that it made people much more aware of what was going on and therefore its provided support ... for Muslims.' (IDI-5)

'From a Muslim perspective, it has got worse [post-9/11] but *it has got better* as well ... The media is attacking Muslims left, right and centre ... that is the worst side. But *the good side* is people have shown a lot of interest in Islam ... getting closer to Muslims and becoming more friendly to Islam.' (IDI-2)

'9/11 polarised views which may already have been there ... people who genuinely want to challenge racism and to oppose war have been far more vocal ... other individuals who have a different attitude have also become more vocal . . . [9/11 has not] shifted the balance but it may have polarised things [in Scotland] . . . In the south east of England attitudes have shifted markedly in a less tolerant direction [but not here].' (IDI-17G)

Even the central Mosque put a good interpretation on the abuse:

'We had problems initially after September 11ᵗʰ but then that was dealt with nicely. Stones were thrown, glass broken . . . then we had good co-operation, I must say . . . police as well as politicians, all of them came . . . CCTV cameras were installed . . . we *appreciated that*.' (IDI-code withheld)

And Iraq proved a further means of integration within Scotland:

'the first couple of months [after 9/11] . . . were very difficult . . . people were being abused . . . attacked . . . in the street and in the shops . . . [but after] America attacked Afghanistan and . . . Iraq . . . the situation [changed] dramatically . . . people on the street [were] expressing their anger against this unjustified war rather than attacking Muslims . . . They were annoyed at first because they thought Muslims had killed so many people. But when they see innocent people dying every day in Iraq . . . Palestine . . . Afghanistan [there is] *a great deal of sympathy for the Muslims now* rather than tension or anger or frustration. They are more angry with the [UK] government than with Muslims.' (IDI-6G)

'If you looked at the march that took place . . . against . . . the plan to invade Iraq . . . Muslims . . . were a small proportion. [Majority] *Scots were standing up for Iraq*.' (IDI-21G)

These quotations should be read for what they are: opinion, perception, not necessarily fact. Perhaps the speakers were trying desperately to see the bright side. But that is irrelevant to our argument. We are not arguing that Scots *were* wonderfully hospitable to Muslims after 9/11 (though they may have been surprisingly so) but that Scotland was *perceived*, by Muslims and those who worked with them, to be some shelter from the storm.

9.4.3 *Asylum-Seeker Dispersal*

The new post-1999 UK policy of dispersing asylum seekers from the south of England to central Scotland also polarized Scottish opinion. Islamophobia was boosted by:

'asylum-seekers, not the asylum-seekers themselves [but] media scaremongers and . . . at [UK] level . . . David Blunkett . . . things he said have . . . led a lot of racists to feel its fine to be racist. [UK-mandated dispersal] of asylum-seekers to Glasgow has also led people . . . to get more racist as well . . . [By contrast] the Scottish Executive have actually been quite constructive in trying to combat that . . . it would be *a lot worse if we did not have the Scottish Executive* doing what it has done.' (IDI-5)

'In my constituency . . . asylum-seekers . . . have been very well received . . . no offences [against them] . . . partly [because it] has got a very large Irish ethnic population . . . [Their] grandparents . . . got a lot of abuse for being Irish . . . There was a welcome committee arranged . . . no "reportable" incidents—whereas in other parts of Glasgow . . . some pretty serious incidents . . . at least one death.' (IDI-21G)

'The Scottish character has *not* changed [for the] worse. But the situation has . . . Increasing numbers . . . badly handled . . . Scots as a whole are not . . . any less at ease with diversity. [But] there is more diversity around—so those few people . . . who are not comfortable with that, have more to kick against . . . but I do *not* believe the number of people who have prejudices, or the strength of those prejudices, is increasing in itself.' (IDI-17G); '[Though] perhaps it has simply highlighted problems with racism that we have always had.' (IDI-14)

9.5 A Future in Scotland

Both minorities remain 'at ease' in post-devolution Scotland. But would they be even more at ease somewhere else? Quite a number—almost entirely English—feel they could be more at ease *outside* Scotland, in:

'areas where you would feel less conscious of your nationality. I've been made more welcome in France.' (E6-G); 'I am uncomfortable . . . living in a narrow-minded society.' (E2-F); 'I would prefer to be in England.' (E2-G); 'if we'd had prior knowledge of what it was like, moving into Scotland, we would never have done it—not in a million years.' (E6-E); 'I would give anything to move back down to England.' (E2-F)

Conversely, many felt more at ease living *in* Scotland. But only a few of them were English:

'I am at ease here.' (E2-H); 'very comfortable here' (E2-G); 'we've had the opportunity to go back to England and we've stayed here.' (E6-B, E6-D agrees)

Most were Pakistanis:

'less at ease . . . outside Scotland.' (PK1-D, PK1-B agrees); 'we all like living in Scotland.' (PK6-E, all agree); 'love Scotland.' (PK3-C); 'would not change it for the world.' (PK5-A); 'no other place is worth living in' (PK3-D, all agree); 'happy here.' (PK1-F); 'the best place to be.' (PK3-E, all agree); 'fine in Scotland' (PK4-F, all agree); 'nice.' (PK5-D)

'Thank God we are Scottish ... English people are very rude and bad mannered. There is no peace in England and you can find that peace here.' (PK2-C); 'more problems in other parts of Britain.' (PK2-A, others agree); 'I don't like living in England at all.' (PK2-B)

In other places, including Ireland or, more recently, the former soviet Republics, the establishment of national parliaments has been swiftly followed by an exodus of minorities. Excluding a very few who are uncertain about their future, 84 per cent of Pakistanis and 88 per cent of the English see their long-term future in Scotland. Only 6 per cent of English immigrants look forward to a future in England and the same number of Pakistanis to a future in Pakistan (4 per cent of Pakistanis see their future in England). We do not have figures for the numbers of majority Scots who see their future in Scotland but, given the high emigration rate amongst majority Scots, the minorities look as settled as the majority.

9.6 Conclusion: Multicultural Nationalism within a Multinational State

We began by outlining the potential problems of multiculturalism within a multinational state, especially when multiculturalism intersected with growing sub-state nationalism. Those who wished to advance the claims of historic, territorial nationalism were unlikely friends for incomers of any kind, especially if those incomers would not or could not assimilate. We argued that 'multicultural nationalism' comes very close to being a contradiction in terms, an oxymoron. In particular, we argued that rising Scottish self-consciousness, the long debate over devolution, and the eventual creation of a Scottish Parliament could have posed a challenge both to English immigrants and to Muslims in Scotland. Problems and challenges can be overcome, but it would be a greater achievement for sub-state nationalism than for state or imperial nationalism to cope with ethnic and cultural diversity. Sub-state nationalism has more ethnic overtones than state nationalism even when it claims to be 'civic', and 'multicultural Scottish-nationalism' is, therefore, more problematic than 'multicultural British-nationalism'. For Muslims, 9/11, the 'war on terror' or, in Huntington's phrase, 'the clash of civilisations' added to the problems of multiculturalism everywhere, including Scotland.

But the viability of multicultural nationalism in practice is an empirical rather than a theoretical question. In practice, some of the potential problems have proved to be solutions. Amongst majority Scots, England has a key role in defining and encouraging Scottish nationalism. So, while Scottish nationalism does stimulate phobias, it stimulates Anglophobia but not Islamophobia. And conversely, Muslims in Scotland adopt Scottish identities, Scottish attitudes, Scottish nationalism, and even some degree of Anglophobia—consciously or unconsciously using these as tools of integration.

Scottish elites, like Scottish football fans, have been determined to present to the world a better image than their English counterparts. It is part of their national pride. Nationalist elites, as well as the devolutionists who designed the new political system, have, therefore, been deliberately inclusive. Street-level nationalists (not quite the same as SNP voters) have not been so inclusive. But their exclusive tendencies have been restrained, except in regard to the English. So their position as sub-state nationalists, focused on the English 'other' has proved something of a solution rather than a problem for other minorities within Scotland.

Culture and identity have also provided bridges as well as walls. For English immigrants, identity is the wall: they cannot easily or quickly adopt a Scottish identity, even if Scots would accept them as Scottish. But their culture is similar to that of Scots, and they are willing to adapt and blend culturally, even in matters of religion. Ethnic Pakistanis are not willing to change their religion: they offer to enrich the cultural diversity of Scotland, not assimilate. But because religion is their primary identity, their territorial identities are easily changed. They adopt a Scottish identity easily and quickly. And (territorial) identity, therefore, becomes a bridge rather than a wall.

Harassment, ethnic jokes, and insults alienate both minorities—and English immigrants are at least as sensitive to it as ethnic Pakistanis, though they are more angered than hurt by it. The Pakistanis suffer more than the English immigrants, especially since 9/11, and are more hurt and frightened by the abuse. But even harassment and abuse proves—for Muslim Pakistanis at least—something that binds them closer to Scotland. Whatever the conflicts between Muslims and non-Muslims in Scotland, they feel conflict is worse in England and very much worse across the world. And after the invasion of Iraq, which was strongly opposed by the SNP, they sense a broad wave of sympathy in Scotland, which offsets or even outweighs their experience a greater street-level harassment that they blame on 'atypical' Scots. In 2003, Muslim Pakistanis, therefore, switched en masse from Labour to the SNP, and a majority backed complete independence for Scotland. Indeed their support for the SNP and independence now greatly exceeds that amongst majority Scots.

Finally, although both minorities (like most majority Scots) criticize the performance of the new Scottish Parliament, both feel that its impact at street level has been more positive than negative. Even English immigrants feel devolution has defused tensions, calmed frustrations, and forced Scots to blame themselves rather than others for their problems. Both minorities already felt 'at ease' in Scotland before devolution, but they feel even more so after devolution. And Muslims self-consciously distinguish between the positive impact of devolution and the concurrent, negative impact of world events and the UK government responses.

So, for the moment, and against the theoretical odds, multiculturalism and sub-state nationalism have not merely coexisted but actually interacted positively within Scotland. But this is multiculturalism as Jenkins and Joppke define it: integration without complete assimilation, pursued in an *un*principled, pragmatic, flexible, and reasonable manner. In Scotland, it has not so far been separate development.

References

Abizadeh, A. (2002). 'Does Liberal Democracy Presuppose a Cultural Nation? Four Arguments', *American Political Science Review*, 96(3): 495–509.

Adams, J. Clemens, E. S., and Orloff, A. S. (eds.) (2005). *Remaking Modernity*. Durham, NC: Duke University Press.

Aleinikoff, T. A. (1998). 'A Multicultural Nationalism?', *The American Prospect*, 9(36): 80–6.

Allen, C. and Nielsen, J. S. (2002). *Summary Report on Islamophobia in the EU after 11 September 2001*. Vienna: EUMC European Monitoring Centre on Racism and Xenophobia.

Almond, G. and Verba, S. (1963). *The Civic Culture*. Boston, MA: Little Brown.

Anderson, B. R. (1991). *Imagined Communities: Reflections on the Origin and Spread of Nationalism*. London: Verso.

Ashley, J. and White, M. (2005). 'Be Proud of Being English, says Blunkett', *The Guardian*, 14 March.

Bailey, N., Bowes, A., and Sim, D. (1997). 'The Demography of Minority Ethnic Groups in Scotland', in A. Bowes and D. Sim (eds.), *Perspectives on Welfare: The Experience of Minority Ethnic Groups in Scotland*. Aldershot: Ashgate, pp. 16–34.

Bairner, A. (1994). 'Football and the Idea of Scotland', in G. Jarvie and G. Walker (eds.), *Scottish Sport in the Making of the Nation: Ninety-Minute Patriots*. Leicester: Leicester University Press, pp. 9–26.

Banton, M. (1985). *Promoting Racial Harmony*. Cambridge: Cambridge University Press.

Barry, B. (2001). *Culture and Equality: An Egalitarian Critique of Multiculturalism*. Cambridge: Polity Press.

Barth, F. (1969). *Ethnic Groups and Boundaries*. London: Allen & Unwin.

Bauman, Z. (2001). *The Individualized Society*. Cambridge: Polity Press.

Blunkett, D. (2005). *A New England: An English Identity Within Britain*, IPPR, 14 March, 2005 accessible at: www.ippr.org

Bond, R. and M., Rosie. (2002). 'National Identities in Post-Devolution Scotland', *Scottish Affairs*, 40: 34–53, table 5.

—— —— (2004). 'Becoming Scotland—What Does it Take?', Paper presented at Scottish Social Attitudes Conference, *The New Scotland Four Years On*, Edinburgh, 6 February 2004.

References

Bowes, A. M., McClusky, J., and Sim, D. F. (1990). 'Racism and Harassment of Asians in Glasgow', *Ethnic and Racial Studies*, 13(1): 71–91.

—— Sim, D. (eds.). *Perspectives on Welfare: The Experience of Minority Ethnic Groups in Scotland*. Aldershot: Ashgate.

Boyle, R. and Lynch, P. (eds.) (1998). *Out of the Ghetto? The Catholic Community in Modern Scotland*. Edinburgh: John Donald.

Bradley, J. M. (1994). 'Ethnicity: The Irish in Scotland—Football Politics and Identity', *Innovation* 7(4).

—— (1995) *Ethnic and Religious Identity in Modern Scotland*. London: Avebury.

—— (1998) 'Image, Perceptions and the Ghetto', in R. Boyle and P. Lynch (eds.), *Out of the Ghetto? The Catholic Community in Modern Scotland*. Edinburgh: John Donald.

Brand, J. and Miller, W. L. (1979). *ESRC Scottish Election Study, 1997*. Data-set available from the ESRC Data-Archive, University of Essex.

Breuilly, J. (1993). *Nationalism and the State 2nd* edition. Manchester: Manchester University Press.

Brown, A., McCrone, D., and L. Paterson, (1998). *Politics and Society in Scotland*. London: Macmillan.

—— —— —— Surridge, P. (1999). *The Scottish Electorate: The 1997 General Election and Beyond*. Basingstoke: Macmillan.

Brown, D. (2000). *Contemporary Nationalism: Civic, Ethnocultural and Multicultural Politics*. London: Routledge.

Brown, M. (2000). 'Seeking Equality in a Diverse World', *CRE Connections*, Spring: 7–14.

Brubaker, R. (1992). *Citizenship and Nationhood in France and Germany*. Cambridge, MA: Harvard University Press.

—— (1996). *Nationalism Reframed: Nationhood and the National Question in the New Europe*. Cambridge, MA: Cambridge University Press.

—— (2004). *Ethnicity without Groups*. Cambridge, MA: Harvard University Press.

—— (2005). 'Ethnicity without Groups', in J. Adams, E. S. Clemens, and A. S. Orloff (eds.), *Remaking Modernity*. Durham, NC: Duke University Press, pp. 470–92.

Bruce, S. Glendinning, T., Paterson, I., and Rosie, M. (2004). *Sectarianism in Scotland*. Edinburgh: Edinburgh University Press.

Cant, B. and Kelly, E. (1995). 'Why is There a Need for Racial Equality Activity in Scotland', *Scottish Affairs*, 12: 9–26 esp. at p. 19.

Cantle, T. (Chair) (2001). *Community Cohesion: A Report of the Independent Review Team*. London: Home Office.

Chatterjee, P. (1993). *The Nation and its Fragments: Colonial and Postcolonial Histories*. Princeton, NJ: Princeton University Press.

CHE/Centre for Human Ecology (2000). *Who's a Real Scot? Embracing Multicultural Scotland*. Edinburgh: Centre for Human Ecology.

Church of Scotland Committee on Church and Nation (1923). *The Menace of the Irish Race to our Scottish Nationality*. Report to General Assembly, Edinburgh.

—— (2002). *The Demon in our Society: Sectarianism in Scotland*. Report to General Assembly, Edinburgh.

Colley, L. (1992*a*). 'Britishness and Otherness: An Argument', *Journal of British Studies*, 31 (4): 309–29.

Colley, L. (1992*b*). *Britons: Forging the Nation*. London: Yale University Press.

—— (1999). *Downing Street Millennium Lecture: Britishness in the 21st Century*. Accessible at www.number-10.gov.uk

CRE Commision for Racial Equality (1999). *Racial Attacks and Harassment*. Accessible at: www.cre.gov.uk

—— (2004/5). 'What now for Multiculturalism?', *CRE Connections*, Winter. Accessible at www.cre.gov.uk/publs/connections

CRE-Scotland (2000). *1999/2000 Report*. Edinburgh: CRE Scotland.

CSG (1998). *Consultative Steering Group on the Scottish Parliament. ('McLeish Committee') Report*, esp. Key Principles; and Annex H: Mainstreaming Equal Opportunities. Accessible at: www.scotland.gov.uk/library

Curtice, J. (1999). 'Is Scotland a Nation and Wales not?', in B. Taylor and K. Thomson (eds.), *Scotland and Wales: Nations Again?* Cardiff: University of Wales Press, pp.119–47.

—— Heath, A. (2000). 'Is the English Lion About to Roar? National Identity after Devolution', in R. Jowell, J. Curtice, A. Park, K. Thomson, L. Jarvis, C. Bromley, and N. Stratford (eds.), *British Social Attitudes 17th Report: Focusing on Diversity*. London: Sage, pp.155–74.

—— (2005). 'Brought Together or Driven Apart?', in W. L. Miller (ed.), *Anglo-Scottish Relations from 1900 to Devolution and Beyond*. Oxford: Oxford University Press, 2005, pp.153–70.

Devine, T. M. (2000). *Scotland's Shame?: Bigotry and Sectarianism in Modern Scotland*. Edinburgh: Mainstream.

Edensor, T. (1997). 'Reading Braveheart: Representing and Contesting Scottish Identity', *Scottish Affairs*, 21: 135–58.

—— (2002). *National Identity, Popular Culture and Everyday Life*. Oxford: Berg.

Evening Times (28 April 2003). 'Shock as Glasgow Muslims are Told: Don't Vote Labour', p. 1; and 'SNP Wins Backing as Iraq Backlash Campaign Targets Politicians. Anti-war Muslims told to vote out Labour', p. 4.

Ewing, K. D. and Gearty, C. A. (1990). *Freedom Under Thatcher: Civil Liberties in Modern Britain*. Oxford: Oxford University Press.

Favell, A. (1998). 'Multicultural Race Relations in Britain: Problems of Interpretation and Explanation', in J. Christian (ed.), *Challenge to the Nation-State: Immigration in Western Europe and the United States*. Oxford: Oxford University Press, pp.319–49.

Fedorowich, K. (1999). 'Reconstruction and Resettlement: The Politicization of Irish Migration to Australia and Canada 1919–29', *English Historical Review*, 114(459): 1143–78.

References

References

References

References

References

References

References

Fekete, L. (2004). 'Anti-Muslim Racism and the European Security State', *Race and Class*, 46(1): 3–29.

Findlay, A. M., Hoy, C. and Stockdale, A. (2004). 'In What Sense English? An Exploration of English Migrant Identities and Identification', *Journal of Ethnic and Migration Studies*, 30(1): 59–79.

Finn, G. P. T. (1994). 'Faith, Hope and Bigotry: Case Studies in Anti-Catholic Prejudice in Scottish Soccer Society', in G. Jarvie and G. Walker (eds.), *Scottish Sport in the Making of the Nation: Ninety-Minute Patriots*. Leicester: Leicester University Press.

Foweraker, J. and Landman, T. (2002). 'Constitutional Design and Democratic Performance', *Democratization*, 9(2): 43–66.

Gallagher, T. (1987). *Glasgow: The Uneasy Peace—Religious Tension in Modern Scotland*. Manchester: Manchester University Press.

Gellner, Ernest. (1983, 1994). *Nations and Nationalism*. Oxford: Blackwell.

—— (1992). *Postmodernism, Reason and Religion*. London: Routledge.

Gerholm, T. and Ithman, Y. G. (eds.) (1988). *The New Islamic Presence in Western Europe*. London: Mansell.

GHS General Household Survey (2002). By ONS (Office of National Statistics). Accessible at: www.statistics.gov.uk

Goldmann, K. Hannerz, U., and Westin, C. (2000). 'Introduction', in K. Goldmann, U. Hannerz, and C. Westin (eds.), *Nationalism and Internationalism in the Post-Cold War Era*. London: Routledge.

—— —— —— (eds.) (2000). *Nationalism and Internationalism in the Post-Cold War Era*. London: Routledge.

Greenfeld, L. (2000). 'Democracy, Ethnic Diversity and Nationalism', in K. Goldmann, U. Hannerz, and C. Westin (eds.), *Nationalism and Internationalism in the Post-Cold War Era*. London: Routledge, pp. 23–36.

GRO (2004). Special table supplied to authors by GRO Scotland. Edinburgh: General Register Office for Scotland.

Grodeland, A., Miller, W. L., and Koshechkina, T. Y. (2000). 'The Ethnic Dimension to Bureaucratic Encounters in Postcommunist Europe: Perceptions and Experience', *Nations and Nationalism*, 6: 43–66.

Guardian, The (2002). John Carvel, 'Sense of Britishness More Prevalent Among Ethnic Minorities, Survey Shows', 18 December, p. 7.

Hardie, A. (1998). 'Minority of Scots Dislike English, ICM Survey Reveals', *The Scotsman*, November 30.

Hearn, J. (2000). *Claiming Scotland: National Identity and Liberal Culture*. Edinburgh: Polygon.

Heath, A. and Smith, S. (2005). 'Varieties of Nationalism in Scotland and England', in W. L. Miller (ed.), *Anglo-Scottish Relations from 1900 to Devolution and Beyond*. Oxford: Oxford University Press, 2005, pp. 133–52.

Henderson, A. (1999). 'Political Constructions of National Identity in Scotland and Quebec', *Scottish Affairs* 29: 121–38.

Herald, The (2003). 'First Asian Provost Takes up Office', 17 May, p. 6.

—— (2003). 'Swinney Attacks "racist" Labour Policies', 8 September.

—— (2003). 'SNP Fails to Split Coalition Over Asylum Seekers Stuck in [detention] Regime', 12 September, p. 7.

—— (2003). 'Evicted Asylum Seekers Denied Final Appeal: Lack of Access a Disgrace, SNP Claims', October 10, p. 10.

—— (2004). 'Dungavel to Continue Holding Asylum-seeker Children', 6 September, p. 6.

Hogwood, B. W. (2001). 'Regulatory Reform in a Multinational State: The Emergence of Multilevel Regulation in the United Kingdom', Paper presented at the ECPR Joint Sessions, Grenoble, April 2001.

Hopkins, P. E. (2004). 'Young Muslim Men in Scotland: Inclusions and Exclusions', *Children's Geographies*, 2(2): 257–72.

Horne, J. (1995). 'Racism, Sectarianism and Football in Scotland', *Scottish Affairs*, 12: 27–51.

Houston, R. A. and Knox, W. (2001). *History of Scotland*. London: Allen Lane.

Hussain, A. and Miller, W. L. (2004*a*). 'Anglophobia & Islamophobia in Scotland', Paper presented at the Scottish Social Attitudes Conference, Royal Museum of Scotland, Edinburgh, 6 February 2004.

Hussain, A. and Miller, W. L. (2004*b*). 'Comparative Islamophobia—in Scotland and England', Paper presented at the 32nd Annual Conference of the National Association for Ethnic Studies, Philadelphia PA, 1–3 April, 2004.

Ignatieff, M. (1993). *Blood and Belonging*. London: Vintage.

Independent, The (2003). Paul Kelbie 'Pakistanis Living in Scotland Feel More at Home North of the Border than the 400,000 English who Live There', 30 October, p. 10.

Inglis, C. (ed.) (1996). *Multiculturalism: New Policy Responses to Diversity*. MOST Policy Papers, No.4. Paris: UNESCO.

Jackson, P. (ed.) (1987). *Race and Racism*. London: Unwin Hyman.

Jarvie, G. and Walker, G. (1994). 'Ninety-Minute Patriots? Scottish Sport in the Making of the Nation', in G. Jarvie and G. Walker (eds.), *Scottish Sport in the Making of the Nation: Ninety-Minute Patriots*. Leicester: Leicester University Press, pp.1–8.

Jedrej, C. and Nuttall, M. (1996). *White Settlers: The Impact of Rural Re-population in Scotland*. Luxembourg: Harwood.

Jeffery, C. (2005). 'Devolution, Social Citizenship, and Territorial Culture', in W. L. Miller (ed.), *Anglo-Scottish Relations from 1900 to Devolution and Beyond*. Oxford: Oxford University Press, pp.113–29.

Joppke, C. (1998). 'Immigration Challenges the Nation-State', in C. Joppke (ed.), *Challenge to the Nation-State: Immigration in Western Europe and the United States*. Oxford: Oxford University Press, pp.5–46.

—— (ed.) (1998). *Challenge to the Nation-State: Immigration in Western Europe and the United States*. Oxford: Oxford University Press.

—— (1999). *Immigration and the Nation-State: The United States, Germany, and Great Britain*. Oxford: Oxford University Press.

References

Joppke, C. and Lukes, S. (eds.) (1999). *Multicultural Questions*. Oxford: Oxford University Press.

Jowell, R., Curtice, J., Park, A., Thomson, K., Jarvis, L., Bromley, C., and Stratford, N. (eds.), *British Social Attitudes 17th Report: Focusing on Diversity*. London: Sage.

Kellas, J. (1998). *The Politics of Nationalism and Ethnicity*, 2nd edn. Basingstoke: Macmillan.

Kelly, E. (1999). 'Stands Scotland Where it did? An Essay in Ethnicity and Internationalism', *Scottish Affairs* 26: 83–99.

—— (2000). 'Racism and the Scottish Parliament', in G. Hassan and C. Warhurst (eds.), *The New Scottish Politics*. Norwich: The Stationery Office.

Kepel, G. (1994). *A l'ouest d'Allah*. Paris: Éditions du Seuil.

Kidd, C. (2003*a*). 'Unenlightened Days when Racism was Thought to be Trendy', *The Scotsman*, 13 January, p. 13.

—— (2003*b*). 'Race and the Scottish Nation, 1750–1900.' *Royal Society of Edinburgh Lecture*. 13 January 2003.

Kiely, R., McCrone, D., and Bechhofer, F. (2005). 'Whither Britishness? English and Scottish people in Scotland', *Nations and Nationalism*, 11(1): 65–82.

Kohn, H. (1944, 1967). *The Idea of Nationalism: A Study of its Origins and Background*. Toronto: Collier Books.

Kumar, K. (2003). *The Making of English National Identity*. Cambridge: Cambridge University Press.

Kundnani, A. (2002). 'The Death of Multiculturalism', *Race and Class*, 44(4): 67–72.

Kymlicka, W. (1995). *Multicultural Citizenship*. Oxford: Oxford University Press.

—— (2001). *Politics in the Vernacular: Nationalism, Multiculturalism and Citizenship*. Oxford: Oxford University Press.

Laborde, C. (2001). 'The Culture(s) of the Republic: Nationalism and Multiculturalism in French Republican Thought', *Political Theory*, 29: 716–35.

Levine, H. B. (1999). 'Reconstructing Ethnicity', *Journal of the Royal Anthropological Institute* (New Series), 5: 165–80.

Maddens, B. and Berghe, K. V. (2003). 'The Identity Politics of Multicultural Nationalism', *European Journal of Political Research*, 42(5): 601–27.

Markova, I. (ed.) (2004). *Trust and Democratic Transition in Post Communist Europe*. Oxford: Oxford University Press/British Academy.

Mason, A. (2000). *Community Solidarity and Belonging*. Cambridge: Cambridge University Press, ch. 5, esp. pp. 127–29.

Mason, D. (2000). *Race and Ethnicity in Modern Britain*, 2nd edn. Oxford: Oxford University Press.

—— (2003). 'Changing Ethnic Disadvantage: An Overview', in David Mason (ed.), *Explaining Ethnic Differences: Changing Patterns of Disadvantage in Britain*. Bristol: Policy Press, pp. 9–19.

McCarthy, A. (2005). 'National Identities and Twentieth-century Scottish Migrants in England', in W. L. Miller (ed.), *Anglo-Scottish Relations from 1900 to Devolution and Beyond*. Oxford: Oxford University Press, 2005, pp. 171–82.

McConnell, J. (2003). Speaking at the City Challenge Conference, Edinburgh, 25 February 2003. Reported at length in *The Scotsman*, 26 February 2003, p. 9: 'McConnell Bids to Attract more Refugees to Scotland' and supplement, pp. 2–3: "Your Country Needs You" above a picture of visible ethnic minorities'; *The Independent* 26 Feb 2003, p. 7: 'Scots Seek Immigrants to Reverse Brain Drain'; *The Guardian*, 26 February 2003, p. 6: 'Scotland Launches Drive to Draw in Foreign Workers'; *The Herald* 26 February 2003, p. 2: 'Immigration is McConnell's Solution to Population Fall'.

McCrone, D., Stewart, R., Kiely, R., and Bechhofer, F. (1998). 'Who Are We? Problematising National Identity', *Sociological Review*, 46: 629–52.

—— (2002). 'Who Do You Say You Are? Making Sense of National Identities in Modern Britain', *Ethnicities*, 2(3): 301–20.

McIntosh, I., Smith, D., and Robertson, D. (2004*a*). 'We Hate the English, Except for You, cos You're Our Pal: Identification of the English in Scotland', *Sociology*, 38 (1): 43–60.

—— —— —— (2004*b*). 'It's as if you're some alien . . . . Exploring anti-English Attitudes in Scotland', *Sociological Research Online*, 9 (2). Accessible at: http://www.socresonline.org.uk/9/2/mcintosh.html

Miles, R. and Dunlop, A. (1987). 'Racism in Britain: The Scottish Dimension', in P. Jackson (ed.), *Race and Racism*. London: Unwin Hyman, pp. 119–41.

Mill, J. S. (1991). *Considerations on Representative Government*. Buffalo, NY: Prometheus Books.

Miller, D. (1989*a*). 'In what Sense must Socialism be Communitarian?', *Social Philosophy and Policy*, 6(2): 51–73.

—— (1989*b*). *Market, State and Community: Theoretical Foundations of Market Socialism*. Oxford: Oxford University Press.

—— (1995). *On Nationality*. Oxford: Oxford University Press.

—— (1998). 'The Left, the Nation-State, and European Citizenship', *Dissent*, Summer: 47–51.

—— (2000). *Citizenship and National Identity*. Oxford: Polity Press.

Miller, W. L. (1985). 'Politics in the Scottish City, 1832–1982', in George Gordon (ed.), *Perspectives of the Scottish City*. Aberdeen: Aberdeen University Press, pp.180–211.

—— (2005). 'From last Empress to First Minister', in W. L. Miller (ed.), *Anglo-Scottish Relations from 1900 to Devolution and Beyond*. Oxford: Oxford University Press, pp. 1–15.

—— (ed.) (2005). *Anglo-Scottish Relations from 1900 to Devolution and Beyond*. Oxford: Oxford University Press.

Miller, W. L., Timpson, A. M., and Lessnoff, M. (1996). *Political Culture in Contemporary Britain: People and Politicians, Principles and Practice*. Oxford: Oxford University Press, 1996.

—— White, S., and Heywood, P. (1998). *Values and Political Change in Postcommunist Europe*. Basingstoke: Macmillan.

References

Miller, W. L., Dickson, M., and Stoker, G. (2000). *Models of Local Governance: Public Opinion and Political Theory in Britain*. Basingstoke: Palgrave.

—— Grødeland, Å., and Koshechkina, T. (2001). *A Culture of Corruption? Coping with Government in Postcommunist Europe*. Budapest: Central European University Press, ch. 6.

Modood, T. (2004). 'Multiculturalism or Britishness: A false debate?', *CRE Connections*. London: Commission for Racial Equality, Summer. Accessible at: www.cre.gov.uk/publs/connections

—— Werbner, P. (eds.) (1997). *The Politics of Multiculturalism in the New Europe: Racism, Identity and Community*. London: Zed.

—— Berthoud, R., Lakey, J., Nazroo, J., Smith, P., Virdee, S., and Beishon, S. (1997). *Ethnic Minorities in Britain: Diversity and Disadvantage: 4th PSI Survey*. London: Policy Studies Institute, esp. ch. 9: 'Culture and Identity'.

Moreno, L. (1986). 'Decentralisation in Britain and Spain: The Cases of Scotland and Catalonia'. Ph.D. thesis, Edinburgh University, Edinburgh.

—— (1988). 'Scotland and Catalonia: The path to home rule', in D. McCrone and A. Brown (eds.), *The Scottish Government Yearbook*. Edinburgh: Edinburgh University Unit for the Study of Government in Scotland, pp. 166–81.

Murray, W. J. (2000). *The Old Firm: Sectarianism, Sport and Society in Scotland*. London: John Donald.

Neolle-Neuman, E. (1984, 1993). *Schweigespirale: The Spiral of Silence*. Chicago: University of Chicago Press.

Parekh, B. (1991). 'British Citizenship and Cultural Difference', in G. Andrews (ed.), *The Making of English National Identity*. Cambridge: Cambridge University Press, pp. 183–204.

—— (2000a). *Rethinking Multiculturalism: Cultural Diversity and Political Theory*. Basingstoke: Macmillan.

—— (2000b). *The Future of Multi-ethnic Britain. Runnymede Report*. London: Profile Books.

Paterson, L., Brown, A., Curtice, J., Hinds, K., McCrone, D., Park, A., Sproston, K., Surridge, P. (2001). *New Scotland, New Politics?* Edinburgh: Polygon.

Plamenatz, J. (1973). 'Two Types of Nationalism', in E. Kamenka (ed.), *Nationalism: The Nature and Evolution of an Idea*. Canberra: Australian National University Press, pp. 22–37.

Porter, B. (2000). *When Nationalism Began to Hate: Imagining Modern Politics in Nineteenth-Century Poland*. New York: Oxford University Press.

Pulzer, P. (revd. edn. 1988). *The Rise of Political Anti-Semitism in Germany And Austria*. London: Peter Halban; Cambridge, MA: Harvard University Press.

Rafferty, J. (1998). 'Scotch Wrath', *Sunday Times Magazine*, 4 October, pp. 16–22.

Richardson, R. (ed.) (2004). *Islamophobia: Issues, Challenges and Action—The Commission on British Muslims and Islamophobia*. Stoke-on Trent: Trentham Books. Accessible at: Runnymedetrust.org/projects/CommissionOnBritishMuslims.html

Runnymede Trust (1997). *Islamophobia: A Challenge for us All*. London: Runnymede Trust.

Saeed, A., Blane, N., and Forbes, D. (1999). 'New Ethnic and National Questions in Scotland: Post-British Identities Amongst Glasgow Pakistani Teenagers', *Ethnic and Racial Studies*. 22(5): 821–44.

—— (Sept./Oct. 2002). 'A Community Under Suspicion: Riots and British Asians', *Scottish Left Review*, 12.

—— (2004). '9/11 and British Muslims', in J. Carter and D. Morland (eds.), *Anti-Capitalist Britain*. London: New Clarion Press.

Saggar, S. and Heath, A. (1999). 'Race: Towards a Multicultural Electorate?', in Geoffrey Evans and Pippa Norris (eds.), *Critical Elections*. London: Sage.

Said, E. (1978). *Orientalism*. New York: Pantheon.

Salmond, A. (2005). 'Natural State of a Nation is to Govern Itself', *The Herald*, 21 April 2005, p. 9.

SCC/ Scottish Constitutional Convention (1995). *Final Document: Scotland's Parliament*. Accessible at: www.almac.co.uk/business_park/scc/scc-rep.htm

Schnapper, D. (1992). *L'Europe des immigrés*. Paris: Bonnin.

Scotsman, The (2002). Signed article by John Swinney, SNP leader, 'Patron Saint Should Promote Scotland', 19 November, p. 8.

—— (2003). 'Scottish Muslims Urged to Boycott Labour', 25 April, p. 13.

Scottish Executive (2000). *Researching Ethnic Minorities in Scotland*. Edinburgh: Scottish Executive, Central Research Unit.

—— (2005). *Analysis of Religion in the 2001 Census: Summary Report*. Edinburgh: Scottish Executive, Office of the Chief Statistician.

Sendich, M. and Payin, E. (1994). *The New Russian Diaspora: Russian Minorities in the Former Soviet Republics*. Armonk, NY: Sharpe.

Short, D. and Stockdale, A. (1999). 'English Migrants in the Scottish Countryside', *Scottish Geographical Journal*, 115(3): 177–92.

Smith, A. D. (1971, 1983). *Theories of Nationalism*. London: Duckworth.

—— (1986). *The Ethnic Origins of Nations*. Oxford: Blackwell.

—— (1991). *National Identity*. London: Penguin.

Smith, P. (1991). *Ethnic Minorities in Scotland*. Edinburgh: Scottish Office.

SNP/Scottish National Party (1997). *Manifesto*.

SP. Scottish Parliament *Debate* (9/6/99). This is the Scottish equivalent of *Hansard*.

Spicer, M. (ed.) (2002). *The Scotsman Guide to Scottish Politics*. Edinburgh, Scotsman Publications.

SSAS (2003). *Scottish Social Attitudes Survey*. Data-set available from ESRC Data Archive, University of Essex.

Sweeney, S. (2005). *Europe, the State and Globalisation*. Harlow: Pearson Longman.

Tajfel, H. and Turner, J. (1986). 'The Social Identity Theory of Intergroup Behaviour', in S. Worchhhhel and W. G. Austin (eds.), *Psychology in Intergroup Relations*. Chicago: Nelson-Hall.

Tamir, Y. (1993). *Liberal Nationalism*. Princeton, NJ: Princeton University Press.

References

Taylor, B. and Thomson, K. (eds.) (1999). *Scotland and Wales: Nations Again?* Cardiff: University of Wales Press.

Times, The (2003). 'Muslims Urged to Vote Against Pro-war Labour', 29 April, p. 8.

Todd, E. (1994). *Le destin des immigrés*. Paris: Éditions du Seuil.

Van den Berge, P. L. (2002). 'Multicultural Democracy: Can it work?', *Nations and Nationalism* 8(4): 433–49.

Vincent, A. (1997). 'Liberal Nationalism: An Irresponsible Compound?', *Political Studies*, 45(2): 275–95.

Virdee, S. (2003). 'The Asian Experience in Scotland', in J. Crowther, I. M., and M. Shaw (eds.), *Renewing Democracy in Scotland*. Edinburgh: NIACE National Institute of Adult and Continuing Education, pp. 93–5.

Watson, M. (2003). *Being English in Scotland*. Edinburgh: Edinburgh University Press.

Worsley, P. (1984). *The Three Worlds: Culture and World Development*. London: Weidenfield & Nicolson.

WP (Hansard) Westminster Parliament *Debate* (11/11/98).

Wright, K. (convenor) (1999). *People and Parliament: Reshaping Scotland, Part 1: Identities*. Edinburgh: People and Parliament Trust. Accessible at: www.alastairmcintosh.com/articles/1999_p&p/summary.htm

Index

Lightning Source UK Ltd.
Milton Keynes UK
UKHW020416151118
332380UK00009B/240/P